EMERGENT URBANISM

Emergent Urbanism
Urban Planning & Design in Times of Structural and Systemic Change

Edited by

TIGRAN HAAS
Royal Institute of Technology, Stockholm, Sweden

KRISTER OLSSON
University of Gothenburg, Sweden

ASHGATE

Published by
Ashgate Publishing Limited
Wey Court East
Union Road
Farnham
Surrey, GU9 7PT
England

Ashgate Publishing Company
110 Cherry Street
Suite 3-1
Burlington, VT 05401-4405
USA

www.ashgate.com

British Library Cataloguing in Publication Data
A catalogue record for this book is available from the British Library.

Library of Congress Cataloging-in-Publication Data
Emergent urbanism : urban planning & design in times of structural and systemic change / [edited] by Tigran Haas and Krister Olsson.
      pages cm. -- (Design and the built environment)
   Includes bibliographical references and index.
   ISBN 978-1-4094-5727-5 (hardback) -- ISBN 978-1-4094-5728-2 (ebook) -- ISBN 978-1-4724-0746-7 (epub) 1. City planning. 2. Urban policy. 3. Urbanization. I. Haas, Tigran. II. Olsson, Krister.
   HT166.E47 2014
   307.1'216--dc23

                                                                                                    2014006617

ISBN 9781409457275 (hbk)
ISBN 9781409457282 (ebk – PDF)
ISBN 9781472407467 (ebk – ePUB)

Printed in the United Kingdom by Henry Ling Limited,
at the Dorset Press, Dorchester, DT1 1HD

Contents

List of Figures

List of Tables

Notes on Contributors

Dr. Gregory Ashworth holds the position of Professor of Heritage Management and Urban Tourism in the Department of Planning, Rijksuniversiteit Groningen, the Netherlands. His main academic interests revolve around heritage management, a topic on which he has published extensively. His main publications include *The European City: Western Perspectives* (1991), *A Geography of Heritage* (2001), *Senses of Time: Senses of Place* (2005), and many others.

Dr. Andrew Ballantyne is the Professor of Architecture School of Architecture, Planning and Landscape at Newcastle University. Professor Ballantyne is author and editor of several books. He has held research and teaching posts at the universities of Sheffield, Bath, and Newcastle. He has written on architectural history and theory, and his latest book is *Key Buildings from Prehistory to the Present* (2012).

Dr. Timothy Beatley is the Teresa Heinz Professor of Sustainable Communities, and the Chair of the Department of Urban and Environmental Planning, School of Architecture at the University of Virginia, Charlottesville, United States. He is the author or co-author of more than 15 books on the wider subject of sustainable and resilient cities, urban and environmental planning. His latest book is *Biophilic Cities: Integrating Nature into Urban Design and Planning* (2010).

Mark C. Childs is the Professor of Architecture and Director of the Design and Planning Assistance Center, School of Architecture and Planning, University of New Mexico. Childs is also the author of *Parking Spaces: A Design, Implementation, and Use Manual for Architects, Planners, and Engineers* (1999) and *Squares: A Public Place Design Guide for Urbanists* (2006). His latest book is *Urban Composition: Developing Community through Design* (2013).

Dr. Andrea Colantonio is the Senior Research Fellow at the Centre for Analysis of Social Exclusion (CASE), LSE Cities, London School of Economics and Political Science. His main research interests are in the areas of economic and social development, institutional governance and urban growth, with special emphasis on sustainability policy, planning and assessment methods. He has been widely published and has participated in many international research projects.

Dr. Alexander R. Cuthbert is Emeritus Professor of Planning and Urban Development in the Faculty of the Built Environment at the University of New South Wales, Sydney, Australia. He is the author of three volumes: *Designing Cities: Critical Readings in Urban Design* (2003) (as editor), *The Form of Cities, Political Economy and Urban Design* (2006), and *Understanding Cities: Method in Urban Design* (2009).

Dr. Kim Dovey is Professor of Architecture and Urban Design in the faculty of Architecture, Building and Planning, University of Melbourne. His research on social issues in architecture and urban design has included investigations of housing, shopping malls, corporate towers, urban waterfronts and the politics of public space. Books include *Framing Places: Mediating Power in Built Form* (1999, 2008), *Fluid City* (2005), and *Becoming Places* (2009).

Dr. Nan Ellin is Chair of the Department of City and Metropolitan Planning at the University of Utah, where she also holds the post of Professor of Urbanism. Dr. Ellin was previously a Professor at the School of Geographical Sciences and Urban Planning, Arizona State University. Nan Ellin is the author of *Good Urbanism* (2012), *Postmodern Urbanism* (1999), and *Integral Urbanism* (1996), co-author of *Phoenix: 21st Century City* (2006), and editor of *Architecture of Fear* (1997).

Dr. Tigran Haas is the Associate Professor of Urban Planning and Design and the Director of the Civitas Athenaeum Laboratory CAL (Applied Social Science Lab) at the School of Architecture and the Built Environment at KTH – Royal Institute of Technology, Stockholm, Sweden. His key works are *New Urbanism and Beyond: Designing Cities for the Future* (2008) (as editor), and *Sustainable Urbanism and Beyond: Rethinking Cities for the Future* (2012) (as editor).

Dr. Mihalis Kavaratzis is a Lecturer in Marketing School of Management, University of Leicester, and was the Associate Professor of Marketing and Tourism, International Business School in Budapest, Hungary. He has published a significant number of articles on the theory and practice of place marketing and place branding. His latest book is with Gregory Ashworth (as editors), *Towards Effective Place Brand Management: Branding European Cities and Regions* (2010).

Dr. Douglas Kelbaugh is the Professor of Architecture and Urban Planning and former Dean of Taubman College of Architecture and Urban Planning at the University of Michigan. With Peter Calthorpe he edited and co-authored *The Pedestrian Pocket Book* (1989). Kelbaugh authored *Common Place: Toward Neighborhood and Regional Design* (1997). Its sequel, *Repairing the American Metropolis: Beyond Common Place*, was published in 2002.

Dr. Ali Madanipour is the Professor of Urban Design, Director of Global Urban Research Unit at the School of Architecture, Planning and Landscape, Newcastle University. He is the author, co-author and editor of more than 12 books. His forthcoming works include *Public Space and the Challenges of Urban Transformation in Europe* (2014, as co-editor), *Democratic Urbanism: Rethinking Urban Design* (2014), and *Critical Concepts in Built Environment: Planning Theory* (2015).

Dr. Jonathan Metzger is the Assistant Professor at the School of Architecture and the Built Environment at KTH – Royal Institute of Technology, Stockholm Sweden. He has edited (with Amy Rader Olsson) *Sustainable Stockholm: Exploring Urban Sustainable Development in Europe's Greenest City* (2013), and his forthcoming book is (as editor with P. Allmendinger and S. Oosterlynck) *Displacing the Political: Democratic Deficits in Contemporary European Territorial Governance* (2014).

Dr. Peter Newman is an environmental scientist, author and educator. He is currently John Curtin Distinguished Professor of Sustainability at Curtin University (formerly Curtin University of Technology), Perth, Australia. Author of more than 10 books, his latest publications include *Cities as Sustainable Ecosystems: Principles and Practices*, with Isabella Jennings (2008), and *Resilient Cities*, with Timothy Beatley and Heather Boyer (2009).

Dr. Krister Olsson is Senior Lecturer at the Department of Conservation, Gothenburg University, Sweden. He holds a doctoral degree in regional planning from KTH – Royal Institute of Technology, Stockholm, Sweden. His research has included both theoretical and empirical studies of urban and regional development strategies and planning. It has in particular been directed toward heritage management, urban planning and design and place marketing. Between 2011 and 2014 he has been working at the National Heritage Board in Sweden.

Dr. Saskia Sassen is the Robert S. Lynd Professor of Sociology and Co-Chair of the Committee on Global Thought, Columbia University. Her recent books are *Territory, Authority, Rights: From Medieval to Global Assemblages* (2008), *A Sociology of Globalization* (2007), and the 4th, fully updated, edition of *Cities in a World Economy* (2011). *The Global City* came out in a new fully updated edition in 2001. Her books have been translated into 21 languages.

Dr. Emily Talen is the Professor of Urban Planning at the School of Sustainability, Arizona State University, Adjunct Faculty, University of Illinois at Urbana-Champaign, and Visiting Professor at Massachusetts Institute of Technology, School of Architecture. Her key works are *City Rules: How Regulations Affect Urban*

Form (2011), *Urban Design Reclaimed* (2009), *Landscape Urbanism and Its Discontents: Dissimulating the Sustainable City* (2013, with Andres Duany), and *New Urbanism and American Planning: The Conflict of Cultures* (2005).

Dr. William Uricchio is Professor of Comparative Media Studies and Principle Investigator of the MIT Open Documentary Lab and the MIT Game Lab at the Massachusetts Institute of Technology. He is also Professor of Comparative Media History at Utrecht University and a Fellow of the Institute for Advanced Study (Lichtenberg-Kolleg) at Georg-August-Universität Göttingen. Publications include *Reframing Culture, We Europeans? Media, Representations, Identities* (2008), and *Media Cultures* (2006).

Dr. Hans Westlund is Professor in Regional Planning at KTH – Royal Institute of Technology, Stockholm, Sweden and Professor in Entrepreneurship, Jönköping International Business School, Sweden. He is the author of *Social Capital and Rural Development in the Knowledge Society* (2013, with Kiyoshi Kobayashi), *Innovation in Socio-Cultural Context* (2013, with Frane Adam), *Social Capital in the Knowledge Economy* (2006), and *Regional Development in Russia* (2000).

Dr. Sarah Williams is currently an Assistant Professor of Urban Planning and the Director of the Civic Data Design Project at Massachusetts Institute of Technology's (MIT) School of Architecture and Planning School in Boston, United States. She is the Director of the Spatial Information Design Lab Columbia University. Sarah has won numerous awards, including being named in the top 25 planners in the technology and 2012 Game Changer by *Metropolis* magazine.

Acknowledgments

Tigran Haas and Krister Olsson want to thank KTH – Royal Institute of Technology, School of Architecture and Built Environment, for providing the intellectual base for this project. Tigran Haas would like to thank The Axel and Margaret Ax:son Johnson Foundation, especially Peter Elmlund and Kurt Almqvist for continuous support. Much appreciation goes to Valerie Rose, publisher for the Ashgate geography, architecture, planning and landscape lists. This project would have never happened without her. Immense gratitude goes to Professor Douglas Kelbaugh, Professor Saskia Sassen, Professor Emily Talen and Professor Gregory Ashworth for inspiration and support in our work and for wonderful support with this publication. We would also like to thank Helene Littke for the great editing work she has done, Dr. Charlotta Fredriksson for the heat of the moment brainstorming conversation in Strindberg Cafe, Helsinki, some few years ago, that brought about the seeds for this project and to all the researchers that we discussed and debated the concept of "Emergent Urbanism" with in the last few years. We are grateful for the description of urban planning and design as the amalgamation of *context*, *process* and *product*, which has been developed from an original idea by Associate Professor Emeritus Reza Kazemian, Urban and Regional Studies, KTH. Finally our special thanks go to all the authors for their kind contributions, time, patience and willingness to participate in this extraordinary project. We are really grateful for all the wonderful work they have contributed for this book.

Tigran Haas and Krister Olsson,
Stockholm

Chapter 1

Introduction: Emergent Urbanism and Beyond

Krister Olsson and Tigran Haas[1]

Urban Structural and Systemic Change

In the last few decades, many European and American cities and towns experienced economic, social and spatial structural change. Globalization of culture and economy, increased mobility, de-industrialization and the growing importance of service sectors have transformed urban and regional economies into post-industrial knowledge-based economies. Corresponding to these structural changes, the construction of place is a characteristic of urban transformation, as cities shift from being centers of production to centers of consumption (Pacione 2005). Moreover, urban development also faces challenges from processes of global warming and climate change, and the local implications that follow.

Structural change is evident in motivating initiatives to develop new infrastructures for production (e.g. investments in the education system and re-location of public institutions), transportation and communication (e.g. investments in roads, railroads and mobile telephone systems), and consumption (e.g. development of internet-based shopping and external shopping centers). It is, in particular, investments in transportation infrastructures which have explicitly aimed for urban regeneration and regional integration, by linking cities together and thereby integrating local labor markets.

The alteration of infrastructure can produce positive and/or negative impacts from the perspective of local places (Graham and Marvin 2001). It can strengthen the regional connections of some places, but it can also degrade local urban environments and sense of place. Advances in technology have influenced urban activities in a way that has led to a fragmentation of urban space (Madanipour 2008). In fact, transformation in many cities and towns has resulted in deteriorated urban environments that have lost their use and function, evidence of which can be found in housing areas, industrial structures and public institutions. These cases demonstrate the way in which the transformation of urban form is most probably followed by a change in direct and indirect use, as well as by broader shifts in the perception and understanding of the urban landscape.

To address transformations of this type, as well as issues of climate change, ecological and landscape transmutations and other issues of sustainable development, a number of theories and ideals have directly or indirectly influenced the practice of urban planning and design, where specific strategies for urban regeneration have also included place marketing and city branding efforts (Carmona et al. 2010). It can be noted that urban planning and design, in adopting international trends, has led to the creation of architectural and commercial uniformity in many cities. A move toward sameness of places is further stressed by a strong conjunction between development planning and real estate development, which increasingly exists in the hands of international developers rather than as a local initiative. In this sense, localities and identity in a given urban context are put under scrutiny in terms of their potential for change, rather than forming a prerequisite for urban planning and design in themselves.

A stimulating theoretical and practical conundrum lies in the possibility of using urban planning and design measures to revive cities, communities and neighborhoods and achieve associated prosperity, status and financial gains. Can urban planning and design be viewed as an effective measure for the reinvention of cities and towns that experience structural change? Or are the current planning and design proposals exacerbating the problems that such change poses for local communities?

---

1 Unless otherwise specified, all figures in this chapter are the authors' own.

What is Urban Planning and Design?

Urban design is not a straightforward concept, and there is no commonly accepted definition of urban design in academia or in practice. In its simplest interpretation, urban design can be described as architecture on a larger scale and within a broader context, or as a bridge between architectural design and urban planning (Haas 2008, Krieger and Saunders 2009). Urban design connects many disciplines: architecture, planning, landscape architecture and engineering. "The process of urban design is to resolve the political, economic, and social vectors with the goal of arriving at urban forms that works" (McCullough 2008: 4), and as such urban design can be understood as a deliberate action to shape urban form, upon the basis of political, economic and social considerations (Cuthbert 2006).

Urban planning is defined here as a political, economic and social "framework" that has direct and indirect consequences for technical and political processes. It is primarily concerned with the welfare of the citizens; with water and land use management; with shaping and composing—designing—the urban environment, including transportation, (tele)communication networks; and with ecology, through the protection and enhancement of the natural environment (Levy 2000, Hall and Tewdwr-Jones 2009).

Planning can be distinguished as a process-oriented activity and design as a product oriented activity. Therefore, urban planning and design is a cross-border field specializing in static and dynamic urban conditions. Dynamic processes are characterized by flows of people and their interactions, as well as the infrastructure arteries that give kinetic energy to the environment. The dynamic defines the way we look at our spatial landscapes and the manner in which we experience a particular urban condition and context. Static processes are defined by their permanence of assemblage, i.e. the creation of stable built forms and shapes—the streets, buildings, squares and open spaces that define the environment in order to provide a stable reference system and a structure of performance. One cannot exist without the other and both permeate space, place and time. Thus, following this reasoning urban planning and design is here understood as an amalgamation of Context—the specific urban setting and its development characteristics, Process—processes of structural change and of planning and design, and Product—the urban landscape that derives from these processes in the specific context, see Figure 1.1.

Throughout the last three decades, a number of theories, approaches, models and ideologies—ideals—have influenced the practice of urban planning and design. The effects of these ideals can be seen in the form of our urban environments. Dominant ideals within today's urban planning and design discourse have been examined

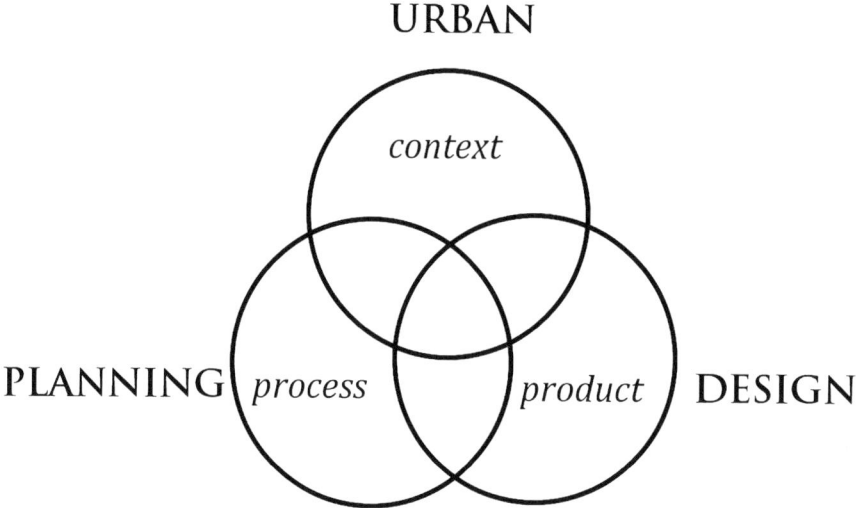

Figure 1.1   Urban planning and design—the relation between context, process and product

and defined in various ways, often resulting in differing categorizations and definitions: territories of urban design (Krieger 2006), images of perfection (Madanipour 1996), the four movements (Schwarzer 2000), urban design force fields (Fraker 2007), integrated paradigms in urbanism (Kelbaugh 2008a, 2008b), urbanist cultures and approaches to city making (Talen 2005), new directions in planning theory (Fainstein 2000), models of good design practice (Lang 2005), and typologies of urban design (Cuthbert 2006).

The Content and Scope of the Book

In this book we discuss and examine—with the help of an impressive list of authors with different fields of expertise in urban planning and design—the specific ideals and trends dominating today's urban planning and design discourse in a comprehensive and problematizing way, including in particular analysis of how forces of structural change contribute to shape the urban landscape. Hence, the book contributes to a discussion about various urban planning and design ideals, approaches and investigations in the light of urban transformation happening in cities in the larger sense of economic, social and/or spatial structural change. One central objective is to contribute to a conceptual framework for discussion and analysis of contemporary theory and practice in the field of urban planning and design.

The chapters in the book are tentatively structured according to the interdependency of the urban context, processes of planning and urban change and the urban design product. The chapters are written by some of the leading urban minds of today covering *state-of-the-art* and on-the-edge topics in urban planning and design. The authors argue, from different perspectives, that urban planning and design is a result not only from deliberate planning and design measures, but a complex product of those measures and infrastructure planning, as well as derive from economic, social, cultural and spatial processes of structural change, including also the impacts that are the product of massive transformation of our societies in the wake of climate, energy and costs. In a world faced with the increasing scarcity of energy and natural resources, especially water resources, the loss of environmentally rich land reserves, and an increased population, discussion and analysis of the urban planning and design field from different angles in this book, serves as a call to rethinking, a compendium of new information, and a possible intellectual road map for moving forward. In the book, we call this complexity of interactions and ideas—"Emergent Urbanism."

The New Urban Context

The first six chapters in particular put an emphasis on the new urban context and the prerequisites it bring about for contemporary and future urban planning and design. Alexander R. Cuthbert takes as one starting point Jean Luc Godard's classic dystopian movie *Alphaville*, and as another Sir Norman Foster's utopian construction of Masdar city in Abu Dhabi, and from that discusses the future of urban space and form. In the following chapter Timothy Beatley argues for what he calls biophilic urbanism, that is a city that puts nature first in its design, planning and management, and, thus, recognizes the human need of daily contact with nature, as well as the environmental and economic values that nature provides. Next Andrew Ballantyne also takes a starting point in a film—*Koyaanisqatsi* from 1982—and argues that if we in planning and design would scale time instead of space, we would apprehend new aspects of things around us. Ali Madanipour outlines the significance of innovation in the knowledge economy, and examines the role of diversity and dialogue for innovation, as well as discusses urban implications, including development of production sites such as science and technology parks and cultural districts. Thereafter Kim Dovey reminds us that we are in the midst of greatest transformation of our urban landscapes, especially when it comes to informality which is on the greatest emerging facts and challenges. In an emergent system, Dovey sees the form and identity of the outcome that will remain provisional and contingent—an urbanism in a "state of becoming", a new shift away from the any kind of fixed outcome, design product or master plan. Coherence, evocation and simulation are the hallmarks of the closing chapter by William Uricchio where his premise centers round our ideas of the city, a city and urban space bound by new proliferating technologies of seeing coupled with rapid transformations of the city, providing an opportunity to reflect on the larger processes of mediation between the city and its image, as he sees it—of the urban as a space, process and condition, that are bound up in our everyday modes of representation.

Processes of Planning and Urban Change

Chapter 7 through Chapter 12 focuses primarily on various processes of planning and urban change. Hans Westlund discusses the role of social capital in spatially concentrated growth processes of the knowledge economy in megacities. Gregory Ashworth and Mihalis Kavaratzis look into the role of another form of capital in urban development, namely the use of culture in city branding, including for example cultural experiences and cultural industries. In his chapter Mark C. Childs propose the term Urban Composition to assemble various disciplines of urban planning and design to promote cross-disciplinary thinking and practices in order to accomplish vital settlements. In the following chapter Jonathan Metzger examines in depth the subject of place, and, thus, in that sense asks the question what constitutes vital settlements understood as place, rather than as space. Nan Ellin asks the comprehensive question what good urbanism is, and concludes among other things that just like complementary medicine looks at the whole person including the physical environment, complementary urbanism looks at the whole environment, including people. In the next chapter Andrea Colantonio discusses the challenge of defining and measuring social sustainability in urban contexts, and argues for emerging themes and indicators, such as identity, sense of place and culture, in parallel to traditional pillars of social sustainability, such as equity and poverty.

The Urban Design Product

The urban design product is the main focus in the last five chapters. Peter Newman draws our attention to the most urgent problem at hand—one of the "summit" of fossil fuel age and the adaptation that awaits us. He shows that a completely new kind of city is emerging, one that represents a combination of old proven techniques in creating walkable and transit-oriented urban fabric along with new green technologies. This is also paralleled by new emerging tools to help accelerate this phenomenon. Saskia Sassen points to the fact that it is important to recognize the fact of urban capabilities and the possibility that this might be a mode of speech as it mixes the material and social physics of a city. As she asserts, these capabilities are systemic properties that aim at securing "cityness"—complex space that thrives on diversities and tends to triage conflict into a "strengthened civicness." In her chapter Emily Talen provides a historical overview of the relation between regulation, flexibility and structural forces that transform cities, and argues for planning codes that are flexible enough to be responsive to local needs and expectations. In her contribution to this volume Sara Williams writes about the responsive city, in which we as citizens are provided with and in different ways share and contribute with all kinds of information almost everywhere. She concludes that the development of bottom-up technology can empower citizens to create more efficient, adaptable and responsive communities. In the final chapter Douglas Kelbaugh performs a critical comparison of Landscape Urbanism and New Urbanism, and argues that there is not enough urbanism in Landscape Urbanism, and not enough ecology in New Urbanism. Nevertheless, he concludes that the world needs an urban design product that is denser, more equitable and less carbon-based than what these two ideals currently advocate.

In the end, what we need to see and understand, in the context of our short introduction, is that as urban planners and designers we must be cognizant of the way that the urban landscapes and structures that we provide, and the built objects that we design, affect people and spaces directly and indirectly. However, we must equally recognize how forces of economic, social and spatial structural change contribute to shaping the urban landscape. The resulting Emergent Urbanism affects people's urban experience, either stimulating or limiting how people live their everyday lives.

References

Carmona, M., T. Heath, T. Oc, and S. Tiesdell. 2010. *Public Places—Urban Spaces: The Dimensions of Urban Design*. 2nd edn. Amsterdam: Architectural Press.

Cuthbert, A. 2006. *The Form of Cities: Political Economy and Urban Design*. Oxford: Blackwell Publishing.

Fainstein, S.S. 2000. New directions in planning theory. *Urban Affairs Review*, 35(4), 451–78.

Fraker, H. 2007. Where is the urban design discourse? *Places Journal*, 19(3), 61–3.

Graham, S. and S. Marvin. 2001. *Splintering Urbanism*. London: Routledge.

Haas, T. (ed.) 2008. *New Urbanism and Beyond: Designing Cities for the Future*. New York: Rizzoli.

Hall, P. and M. Tewdwr-Jones. 2009. *Urban and Regional Planning*. London: Routledge.

Kelbaugh, D. 2008a. Three Urbanisms: New, Everyday, and Post. In *New Urbanism and Beyond: Designing Cities for the Future*, edited by T. Haas. New York: Rizzoli.

Kelbaugh, D. 2008b. Introduction. Further Thoughts on the Three Urbanisms. In *Writing Urbanism*, edited by D. Kelbaugh and K.K. McCullough. New York: Routledge.

Krieger, A. 2006. Territories of Urban Design. In *Urban Design Futures*, edited by J. Rowland and M. Malcolm. London: Routledge.

Krieger, A. and W. Saunders. 2009. *Urban Design*. Minneapolis, MN: University of Minnesota Press.

Lang, J. 2005. *Urban Design: A Typology of Procedures and Products*. Burlington, MA: Elsevier/Architectural Press.

Levy, J. 2000. *Contemporary Urban Planning*. Saddle River, NJ: Prentice Hall.

McCullough, K.K. 2008. Introduction. In *Writing Urbanism*, edited by D. Kelbaugh and K.K. McCullough. New York: Routledge.

Madanipour, A. 1996. *Design of Urban Space*. New York: Wiley.

Madanipour, A. 2008. Urbanism and the Articulation of the Boundary. In *New Urbanism and Beyond: Designing Cities for the Future*, edited by T. Haas. New York: Rizzoli.

Pacione, M. 2005. *Urban Geography: A Global Perspective*. London: Routledge.

Schwarzer, M. 2000. The contemporary city in four movements. *Journal of Urban Design*, 5, 127–44.

Talen, E. 2005. *New Urbanism and American Planning: The Conflict of Cultures*. New York: Routledge.

PART I
The New Urban Context

Chapter 2
Alphaville and Masdar:
The Future of Urban Space and Form?

Alexander R. Cuthbert[1]

> Soon spectacles will no longer be a prosthesis, but the hereditary attribute of a species which no longer possesses the faculty of sight.
>
> Jean Baudrillard, *Cool Memories*

Introduction

A central objective of this book is to contribute to a conceptual framework for discussion and analysis of contemporary theory and practice in the fields of urban planning and design. I have spent much of the last 10 years on this task, outlining a unified field theory which I refer to as *The New Urban Design*. Possessing the same structure, the three books can be read in series or in parallel, and may best be described as a matrix of possibilities (Cuthbert 2003, 2006, 2011). I mention this *en passant* for two reasons. First, I wish to liberate myself here from the constraints of prior logic in order to more freely explore certain ideas. These are potentially outrageous, possibly illogical, perhaps bordering on fantasy; all qualities on which the creative process depends. Second, I am likely the only contributor to this volume who lives in a developing country. I cannot in good faith pretend that the problems of urban development in the *Global North* are not intimately linked to those of the *Global South*. I begin with two short yet relevant vignettes.

Take 1: In 1965 Jean Luc Godard made a *film noir* called *Alphaville*, a dystopian science fiction movie about a technocratic dictatorship. Alphaville is controlled by a sentient computer system called Alpha 60, and the hero, Lemmy Caution is charged with the assassination of its creator. Significantly, the film set relied on the prevailing environment of Paris for its execution. So tomorrow's built form was not envisioned as being much different to the present. The changes are psychological. Emotion is banned, surveillance is ubiquitous and the prevailing ideology is that of George Orwell's *1984*. As in Fritz Lang's *Metropolis*, it is a Marxian nightmare of alienation and oppression. Individualism is a capital offence, and scientific rationalism prevails over imagination and feeling.

Take 2: In 2013 a new city of 50,000 persons called Masdar is being constructed. It is designed by one of the world's iconic architects, Sir Norman Foster, in conjunction with a Feudal Islamic Autocracy in Abu Dhabi. Masdar is located about 17 km south of the city and close to the airport. More people will commute inwards on a daily basis (60,000) than are resident (40–50,000). The city places its entire faith in the idea that only in technology lays the solution to the problems of sustainable urban development. The model assumes a universal mandate in the design of cities; the only hedge against the destructive impact of consuming fossil fuels. Only renewable energy resources will be used. As the world's first zero-carbon city, Masdar will be free of cars. Energy production will rely on natural sources such as solar power, wind farms and geothermal energy, with the addition of the world's largest hydrogen power plant.

Between these two social technologies, one dystopian, the other utopian, to which I will return, lie a myriad other potential mutations, demanded by the forces of global capitalism. Whose interests and ideologies will dictate the requisite variety of urban form? I will begin by addressing the disciplinary dilemma that has permeated the environmental professions over the last 50 years (Cuthbert 2007). Next, issues issues stemming from the global political economy need discussed, concentrating on the principle that social structures create spatial structures, not the reverse. Two significant ideological paradigms are then interrogated. First, that of

---

1   Unless otherwise specified, all figures in this chapter are the author's own.

sustainability. Second, that of an evolving and benign capitalism. Finally, implications and speculations for urban space and form are drawn from this necessarily short, contingent and speculative analysis.

The Disciplinary Dilemma

Even after 35 years, Scott and Roweis' wrenching analysis of *Urban Planning in Theory and Practice* remains the gold standard, equally applicable to mainstream urban design:

> Mainstream planning theory engages in a form of generalisation that we might designate as indeterminate abstraction, immunising itself against refutability. Mainstream theory tends to impede critical scrutiny of the real world of urban planning, and consequently to license false consciousness and cognitive myopia. (Scott and Roweis, 1977: 1011–113)

In other words, without an appropriate theorisation of globalisation, of capital formation, of the emergent state and hence of the forces driving development, only the most superficial interpretations of urban planning and design can arise. Currently there are two major explanations of *urban* design, one primarily material, the other economic and political. In 1953 the architect Jose Louis Sert, defined urban design as *project design* pure and simple (Cuthbert 2009). There is much to commend this position. It offers a direct and comprehensible approach to building the city. A multitude of case studies exist from which we can learn. Models can be built of differing design strategies which can be understood, evaluated and applied. This approach has widespread support within the environmental professions, despite some clear paradoxes. For example if urban design came into existence in 1953, what exactly happened in the preceding ten thousand years of urban history? Or how do we account for the remaining 90% of all construction that is not anyone's project?

The second approach is a more arduous proposition. It demands an altogether different level of engagement with urban form, one originating in political economy (Cuthbert 2003, see Figure 2.1).

This paradigm is not without its own flaws, but it is of an undeniably higher intellectual pedigree. Of interest to us is *spatial* political economy which draws on 250 years of tradition beginning with Adam Smith and Marx, surfacing today in the *oeuvre* of Manuel Castells, David Harvey, Allen Scott, Ed Soja and others. In this context professional disciplines simply vanish since their links to private capital, monopolistic practices and self interest distort urban analysis. So within *the New Urban Design*, projects represent only one form of spatial organization in the political economy of cities. Urban form may then be interpreted as fixed capital within the overall reproduction of capital from space (see Figure 2.2).

The Global Economy

Cities have formed the crucibles of civilisations for some 10,000 years. Today we exist in an era best described as informational capitalism, where the production of information now surpasses the production of the material world in value. Currently the state of the world's economy and the ravages of the capitalist system blanket the production of urban form with apocalyptic possibilities. Clearly, cities cannot evolve humanely and sustainably without structural change to global capitalism. Urban Planning and design will be driven by the resulting conflicts.

Also axiomatic is that the current crises of this system are bonded with neo liberal ideology that drives the neocorporate state. Thus the so-called 'issues' of capitalist imperialism are obscured ('problems' having been been abolished). In the Global South, food aid is its lowest in 20 years, with the U.N. trying to feed one billion hungry people on $1.40USD a day. Of the $5 billion USD promised to the U.N. by the wealthy nations, only half was delivered in 2009. So we can cut that figure to seventy cents. Consequently *the dispossessed* experience such violence as 'nothing short of savagery' (Amin 1997). Putting it mildly, the world capitalist system is chronically unstable, self-serving, racist and potentially fatal for the world's ecosystems. But poverty is no longer limited to the Global South. As of September 2010, the U.S. Census bureau reported that 15.1%

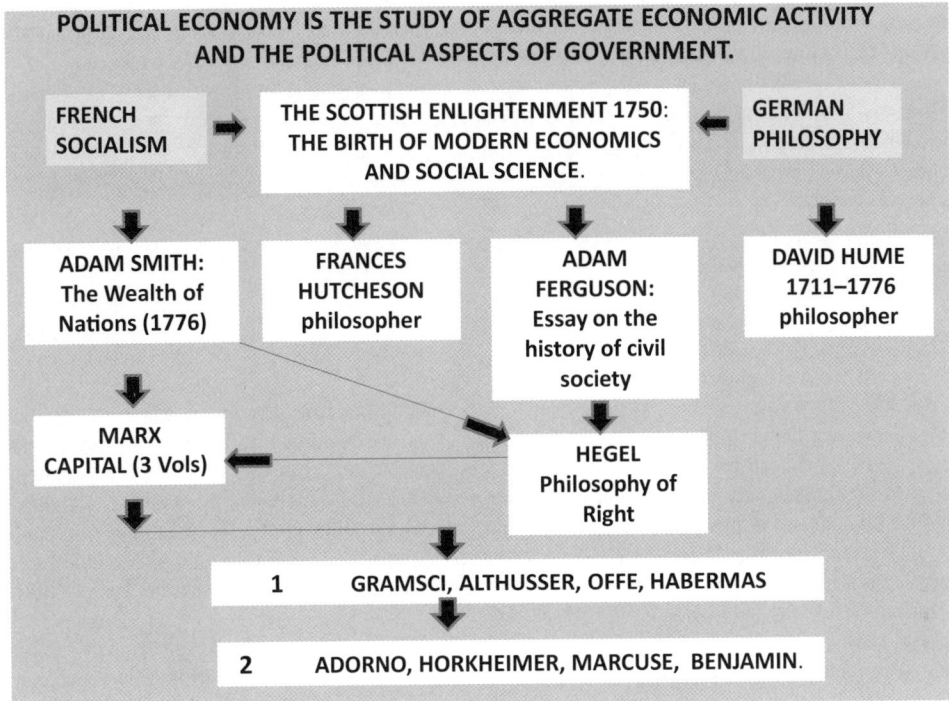

Figure 2.1　　Political economy

THE PRODUCTION OF SPACE

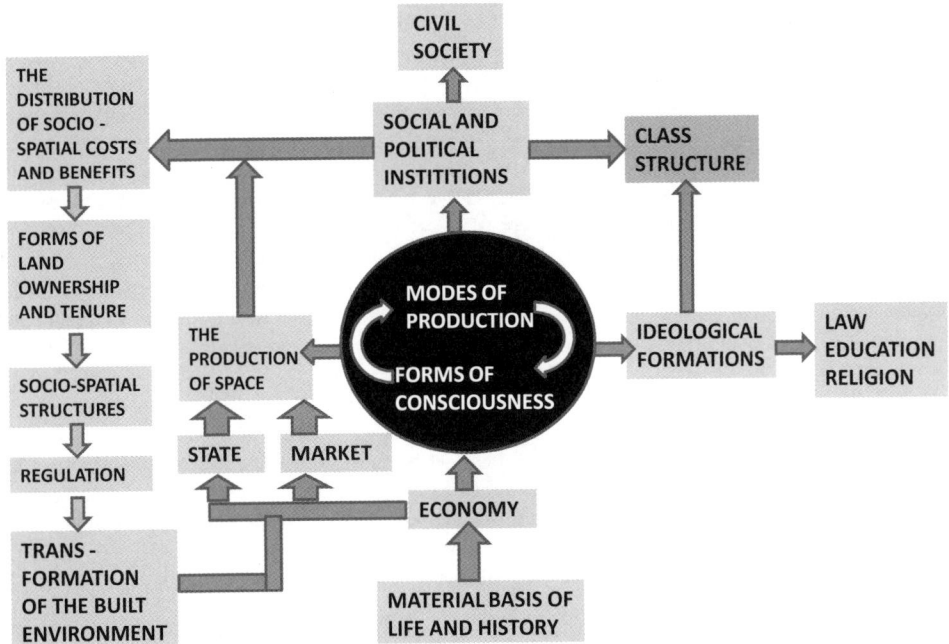

Figure 2.2　　The production of space

or 46.2 million Americans were living below the poverty line, placing it in the company of Azerbaijan (15.5%), and Chile, (15.1%) and just behind Romania (13.8%), Croatia (11.1%) and Vietnam (14.5%).

The most recent effect of such instability was the Sub Prime Mortgage Scandal, originating between 1996 and 1998. At a stroke, the poor in the U.S. lost between USD$ 70 and USD$ 90 billion in assets. Even this toxic debt was marketed as a profit making venture by Wall Street investment banks. Consequently in September 2008 as Lehman Brothers and other Wall Street banks crashed and burned with the freezing of credit markets worldwide;

> Wall St bonuses added up to US$ 32 billion, just a fraction of the total in 2007. This was a remarkable reward for crashing the world's financial system. The losses of those at the bottom of the social pyramid matched the extraordinary gains of the people at the top. (Harvey 2010.)

The perfidy of the Wall Street Bank's with their voodoo economics did not stop there. Led by Lehman Brothers, the Wall Street Cartel then demanded USD$ 700 billion from the public purse to replace the losses of their own financial Armageddon and the blitz of the world economy. The sum was duly paid by the Bush Government, on the principle that private loss = public debt. But this was only the beginning of a crisis that continues today. The rout spread rapidly across the globe, affecting all economies, industries, urban development and property markets, social programs and aid to the Global South. It hit the little PIGS (Portugal, Ireland, Greece and Spain) with a financial tsunami, leaving 25% of the adult population of Greece and Spain and 25% of the youth in the UK unemployed. Britain is now facing an unprecedented triple dip recession and across the Euro zone real wages are down 40 to 50%.

> By the spring of 2009, the IMF estimated that over US$ 50 trillion in asset values worldwide (roughly equal to one year's total global output of goods and services) had been destroyed as two billion people struggled to survive on less than $US 2 per day. (Milmo 2012).

Futures markets, derivatives and the trading debt meant that capital accumulation could occur artificially. The financial and corporate worlds created fictitious capital from betting among and between its own 'products' with individual bonuses up to USD$ 3 billion paid in money capital to the lead players despite failing in their jobs. In reality 'The credit system and finance capital became, as Lenin, Hilferding, and Luxemburg all remarked at the beginning of the twentieth century, major levers of predation, fraud and corruption' or what Harvey refers to as *accumulation by dispossession* (Harvey 2003: 137–82).

This continuing carnage takes place under the ideological flag of neoliberalism, whose belief in self-regulation, non-interventionism, entrepreneurialism, primitive accumulation, open markets, and private property were sold as being in everyone's best interest. However, 'Neoliberalism is not the root of the problem: it is the ideology used, often retrospectively, to justify a global grab of power, public assets and natural resources by an unrestrained elite' (Monbiot 2012: 18). The consequence is that private sector influence penetrates governments at all levels of structure and function – in their administrative, legal, and financial operations, and in the production of symbolic and cultural capital. But its transport mechanism remains the neocorporate state, including urban planning, through which its economic policy is liberated in regard to the built environment.

Since the fiscal crises of the late 1970s, an enforced partnership between governments and the state became necessary. This opened up the possibility that the state's regulatory role (e.g. in welfare, finance and urban planning) – became aligned with private capital. Those who were meant to be regulated then participated in writing up their own mandate, to be rubber stamped by supine and submissive state governments. But in addition to state neocorporatism, private enterprise adopted another ideological cloak to mask its real strategies, that of sustainability. In the process it subverted or otherwise poisoned a valuable movement, swallowing it whole and undermining seventy years of dedication that began with Rachel Carson in 1962.

Ideology Lures: The Problematic Of Sustainability

To date, attempts to solve climate change at Kyoto, Cancun, Brussels, Bali, and Copenhagen have all failed disastrously. Meanwhile, the combined environmental damage of the 3000 largest global companies has been conservatively estimated at $2.2 trillion USD. This sum equals one third of their profits, which if paid as fines could bankrupt the global financial system. But even this is trivial to American debt as a whole (personal, institutional and national) of around $50 trillion USD. This sum can never be repaid by the world's largest borrower which continues to print monopoly money as the solution to its debt crisis. Driving this wrecking ball is the neoliberal agenda. Here, two ideological formations are prime. Firstly the nebulous term *sustainable* envelopes business, commerce and government like a religious mantra as its principles are perniciously undermined. Second is the false consciousness that capitalism will recant and become sustainable with improved politics and equality for all.

Problematically the term *sustainable* has been elevated to sublime uselessness, having been devoured whole by the ideological structure of transnational neocorporatism, and perverted in its interests. With its absorption by the market, the term *sustainable* camouflages the fact that *scarcity is not a problem of nature* but of politics. *Sustainable* has now become both semantically impotent and subversive, given its support for the world's largest polluters and their ongoing destruction of nature. *Sustainability* now has anodyne qualities. Paradoxically, it is these very qualities that are invaluable to the reproduction of capital. So populations in the West now support an ideologically based *sustainability* that undermines their own best interests, extends the destruction and commodification of nature and its 'services', increases levels of pollution, and imposes yet another layer of imperialism on the developing world of the global south.

The latest example of cost cutting by a *single* company, British Petroleum, resulted in the Deepwater Horizon disaster at a potential social cost of USD$ 100 billion, the decimation of a local economy and the ruining of thousands of lives. Needlessly, the search goes on for new sources of fossil fuels as we cannot afford to burn 80% of what we already know about. Even the minimalist attempt at global carbon trading has already been corrupted by big capital, and carbon piracy is now in full swing in the Peruvian Amazon. Consequently economic growth measured as GDP (Gross Development Product) will likely exhaust the biosphere before it sinks and only the rich will afford to live sustainably (Monbiot 2012).

So we now have green/sustainable Formula 1 race cars, oil companies, banks, corporations, NGOs etc. Corporate power hides behind the mask of benevolence, philanthropy and patriotism, ignoring that their primary obligation is to shareholders' interests. Instead, using Manichaean politics, they advertise themselves as 'building communities', 'creating jobs', 'helping people help themselves', 'developing sustainable growth' etc., and chanting *e pluribus unum*. Clearly the underlying problem will not be solved by insulation bats in roofs, solar panels, bio-fuelled buses, wind farms in Denmark, a Toyota Prius in the garage or even a thousand Masdars. These are cosmetic fixes for the wealthy, with the structural problems of the capitalist system remaining undiminished.

Ideology Rules – Natural Capitalism Forever!

The perfect neo-corporate response to this collective tragedy is the idea of *natural capitalism* (Hawken, Lovins and Lovins 1999). This is indeed a masterful deception. The idea that somehow capitalism will, after 300 years or so of expansion, morph into a more benign form is the perfect political response. While capitalism might indeed find new ways for its armature of banks and multinational corporations to make profits out of sustainable developments, its practices of exploitation and domination will remain intact. Class structure, the extraction of surplus value, private ownership of the means of production, a legal system that supports the entire apparatus and a vice like grip on government polices everywhere, will guarantee that business will proceed as usual. What is unsustainable is the belief in endless growth, and that technology can replace the need for a new moral economy and massive sacrifices on the part of the developed world. As Kendall suggests, 'The spirit of capitalism invoked in natural capitalism marks the ignorant disregard for, and injury to, human and natural capital as an ethical transgression' (2008: 61). So in the uncritical adoption of neo liberal ideology, and acceptance of the concrete nature of pre-existing capitalist enterprise, urban design has moved forward by moving backwards.

> The central occupation of urban design has shifted to the construction of sophisticated, high-profile, branded advertisement campaigns used to leverage popular, "democratic" support for large-scale real-estate development .... and in the light of this, architects and planners have adopted a rhetoric of sustainability that wholly embraces a humanitarian ethics in regard to ecological catastrophe. (Adams 2010: 2–3).

Irrefutably, no corporation will ever voluntarily sacrifice market share to sustainable practices. All corporations are involved in two wars: First in their own wars of mutual destruction among and between the various capitals – finance, industrial commercial, property etc.; second in an ongoing ambiguous conflict with the state whose presence is simultaneously demanded (in service provision and legal sanction) and undermined (as a regulator). As state neocorporatism flourishes, the coincidence of interests may reduce or even eliminate this conflict. But currently, in order to defray the social wage, the state demands a share of profits that no corporation wants to pay, and which they appear to think is voluntary. So the scale of major corporate tax fraud is immense. In a single country, Britain, 'the overall picture is now familiar: Google, Amazon, Starbucks, and many other multinationals are using different jurisdictions and complex accounting rules to avoid paying tax' (Ashley 2012: 21). The tax gap, the difference between what should be collected and what actually is paid is an astounding USD\$ 50 billion per annum. This is almost equal to the entire defence budget of the UK, a sum that could rebuild all welfare systems, health and education on an annual basis. In its turn, no nation will willingly sacrifice gross development product for the greater good. And no politician will sacrifice votes to their moral conscience. As Nicolas Sarkozy recently said 'we know what to do, we just don't know how to get re-elected if we do it'.

Problems of Space and Form

Undeniably, space is being transformed to accommodate new forms of imperialism and a new political, social, and moral order (Hardt and Negri 2000, Harvey 2003). What this will mean in terms of urban design and urban space can only be speculated, but it seems more realistic to focus on changing spatial qualities, characteristics and relationships, than on actual project types. Here the economic differences signified in the *Society of the Spectacle* will become magnified in a global world of decreasing resources and increasing competition and inequality (Debord 1967). In this process, urban planning and design have been seriously compromised in support of the neocorporate state, one where the mega-project, mega-spectacle and mega-brand will likely dominate (Orueta and Fanstein 2008). Reflecting this culture of commodity fetishism, the concept of branding will become magnified, with the effect that:

> Generic spaces are deterritorialised, disembedded, and lifted out from their context. Brands as generic spaces do not refer to any particular place (Casey 1997), or context. For Lash (2002), generic spaces can be seen as prototypes of natural, physical spaces that are context-less and identity-less. (Yakhlef 2004: 239)

At the largest compass, the overall spatial matrix will likely be one of increasing alienation between traditional ethnicities, religions, cultures and classes, overlaid by new cyberclasses on the basis of access to and mastery of information. Urban form will necessarily adapt to accommodate the polarising of existing community, increasingly held together by a shared ideology of consumerism and the mindless pursuit of the spectacle. David Harvey has outlined in principle the overall spatial framework in *A Matrix of Spatialities* (Harvey 2006 Figure 2.4).

This does not carry over into form however, but some other clues exist. Soja outlines six discourses on urban form transformation in the Postmetropolis (Soja 2000). Appadurai concentrates on the division of space by global cultural flows, e.g. ethnoscapes, mediascapes, technoscapes, financescapes and ideoscapes (Appadurai 2000). In addition, many other urban forms are emerging that might not fit standard concepts such

Table 2.1   A matrix of spatialities for Marxian Theory

	Material space (experienced space)	Representations of space (conceptualised space)	Spaces of representation (lived space)
Absolute space	private property; built environments	use values and concrete labour	alienation versus creative satisfaction
Relative space	market exchange; trade; circulation	exchange values	money and commodity fetishism
Relational space	abstract labour process; fictitious capital	money value	capitalist hegemony

Source: Simplified from Harvey (2006), Figure 2.

as; plasticulture urbanism, massive residential cruise ships, squatter and migrant settlements, new forms of industrial park etc. (Easterling 2005).

Hence we can speculate two possible architectures, one of profusion and one of despair. In the architecture of profusion, corporate power will strive to fulfil *desires*, to build more sophisticated target markets, on which basis Castells suggests that new communities are being formed, unanticipated in any planning literature. Electronic communication is rapidly transforming historic spaces of *meaning* into new tribal communities, microterritories that constitute ever new forms of consumption, with the effect that:

> Because the spatial manifestations of dominant interests take place around the world, and across cultures, the uprooting of experience, history and specific culture as the background of meaning is leading to generalisation of ahistorical, acultural architecture. (Castells 1996: 418)

Cities which attempt to project a unique image and opportunities, either real or symbolic, will be 'brand based' on their capacity to commodify history, simulate authenticity, provide sites for spectacles, or conserve exotic natural settings. Burgeoning centres for spectacle and commodity fetishism are already nascent in Abu Dhabi, Winnipeg, Los Angeles and Las Vegas. Reflecting the uneven development implicit to capitalism, these will not constitute discrete geographic entities, iconically represented by Masdar. They will instead crystalise what it represents, a new global phenomenon-

> The growing division of the world into refined, high-end enclaves and vast formless ghettos where issues like sustainability have little immediate relevance. (Ouroussoff 2010)

In contrast, the architecture of despair will be predominantly located in the global south will struggle to fulfil needs. But it will likely expand in the north as financial markets increasingly self destruct and migrations become unmanageable. Mike Davis notes that by the late 1990s, one billion workers or *one third of the world's labour force* were either unemployed or underemployed, most in the South. In contrast to traditional society where a reserve army of labour was required as insurance against market exigencies, his fear is that this 'reserve' is becoming stigmatised as a 'permanently redundant mass'. This mass does of course require space, and its settlements that have no prior historical reference point are likely to become permanent entities. Neither do they fall into any 'project type' that we know about. As if endemic poverty was insufficient, Pentagon brains:

> assert that the "feral failed cities" of the third world is where Pentagon doctrine is being reshaped accordingly to support a low intensity war of unlimited duration against criminalised elements of the urban poor. (Davis 2006a: 199–205)

Conclusion

Clearly there will be no standard *tomorrow* to urban form and urban space. Masdar lays claims to a certain universality, and the intentions appear laudable. But they are also seriously unhinged, given the state of urbanisation today. In fact we only have to look a few metres beyond its boundary to expose the real design problem, and ignoring the idea that a single architect should have the right to design *any* city.

The truth of the matter is that a squeaky clean and sanitised Masdar is being constructed by a feudal dictatorship called Abu Dhabi, whose wealth reflects a geopolitical monopoly over oil by Arab states. Its sole interest is in maintaining such power through oils sales hence polluting what remains of our atmosphere. The society is class, gender and racially divided, and divided absolutely. Rather than reforming their society and economy, feudal relations are maintained and technology marketed as a panacea. Ninety percent of the population (1.26 million) are immigrant workers living in appalling conditions, supporting the excesses of the remaining 10% (Elsheshtawy 2008). Migrant workers average around USD$ 200 per month for up to 84-hour weeks, labour unions and citizenship are denied, debt bondage is rife and a culture of repression, imprisonment and forced deportation is characteristic across the UAE. Masdar sends the wrong message, and therefore represents a clear and present danger as a model for urban development anywhere on the planet.

More likely is the world of Lemmy Caution, one where electronic communication rules and surveillance is ubiquitous, along with violence and crime. As in *Aphaville*, all new power structures will likely be multivalent and hidden. There will be no symbolic expression of an organised state or even of the controlling and faceless expression of transnational corporate authority. New global empires will express no visible symbols of the new political order, making its presence felt within neo-Benthamite structures of surveillance and control. Given that the UK now has one CCTV camera for every 10 people, surveillance society is already with us. As in *Alphaville*, massive *bidonvilles* and slums will still exist, but so will a stripped down administrative apparatus necessary to the success of the neocorporate state and the 'creative class'. Alienation will likely rule as a method of subverting social unrest.

So the real answers to the problem of sustainability lie in the transformation of capitalism, for few sustainable solutions begin to attack the fundamental issue of environmental justice – the moral economy that lies at the heart of a sustainable planet. With such an economy place, then perhaps we might avoid what Madeleine Bunting predicts as the real story of the next few years – potentially 'the savage dismantling of social democracy' and its symbolic manifestation in the built environment.

References

Adams, R. 2010. *Longing for a Greener Present: Neoliberalism and the Eco-city.* Available at: http://www. radicalphilosophy.com/commentary/longing-for-a-greener-present [accessed 28 February 2013].

Amin, S. 1997. *Capitalism in the Age of Globalisation.* London: Zed Books.

Appadurai, A. 2000. Disjuncture and Difference in the Global Cultural Economy. In Benyon, J. and Dunkerley, D. (eds). *Globalisation: The Reader.* Part B1 93–100.

Ashley, J. 2012. War looms over fair tax share. *Guardian Weekly.* 7 October 2012: 21

Carson, R. 1962. *The Silent Spring.* London: Hamish Hamilton.

Castells, M. 1996. *The Rise of the Network Society.* Oxford: Blackwell.

Cuthbert, A.R. (ed.) 2003. *Designing Cities – Critical Readings in Urban Design.* Oxford: Blackwell.

Cuthbert, A.R. 2006. *The Form of Cities – Political Economy and Urban Design.* Oxford: Blackwell.

Cuthbert, A.R. 2007. Urban Design: Requiem for an era – review and critique of the last 50 years. *Urban Design International.* 12 (4), 177–223.

Cuthbert, A.R. 2009. *Review article – Urban design*, Alex Krieger and William S. Saunders (eds), Minneapolis, MN: University of Minnesota Press.

Cuthbert, A.R. 2011. *Understanding Cities: Method in Urban Design.* Oxford: Routledge.

Davis, M. 2006. *Planet of Slums.* London: Verso.

Debord, G. 1967. *The Society of the Spectacle.* Practical Paradise Publications.

Easterling, K. 2005. *Enduring Innocence: Global Architecture and its Political Masquerades*. Cambridge, MA: MIT Press.

Elsheshtawy, Y. 2008. Transitory Sites: mapping Dubai's 'forgotten' spaces. *International Journal of Urban and Regional Research*. 32 (4), 968–88.

Hardt, M. and Negri, A. 2000. *Empire*. Cambridge, MA: Harvard University Press.

Harvey, D. 2003. *The New Imperialism*. Oxford: Oxford University Press.

Harvey, D. 2006. *Spaces of Global Capitalism: Towards a Theory of Uneven Geographical Development*. London: Verso.

Hawken, P., Lovins, A. and Lovins, H. 1999. *Natural Capitalism*. London: Little Brown.

Kendall, B.E. 2008. Personae and natural capitalism: negotiating politics and constituencies in a rhetoric of sustainability. *Environmental Communication*. 2 (1), 59–77.

Milmo, D. 2012. We need an Olympic approach to economy. *The Guardian Weekly* 14 September 2012: 16.

Monbiot, G. 2012. *The Guardian Weekly*. 14 February 2012: 18.

Orueta, F.D. and Fainstein, S. 2008. The new mega-projects; genesis and impacts. *International Journal of Urban and Regional Research*. 32 (4), 759–67.

Ouroussoff, N. 2010. In Arabian Desert, a Sustainable City Rises. *The New York Times*. Available at: http://www.nytimes.com/2010/09/26/arts/design/26masdar.html [accessed 2 January 2013].

Scott, A.J. and Roweis, S.T. 1977. Urban planning in theory and practice-a reappraisal, *Environment and Planning D: Society and Space*. 9(4), 1097–119.

Soja, E. 2000. *Postmetropolis*. Oxford: Blackwell.

Yakhlef, A. 2004. Global brands as embodied "generic spaces": the example of branded chain hotels. *Space & Culture*. 7 (2), 237–48.

Chapter 3
Imagining Biophilic Cities

Timothy Beatley[1]

That we need daily contact with nature to be healthy, productive individuals, and indeed have co-evolved with nature, is a critical insight of Harvard myrmecologist and conservationist E.O. Wilson. Wilson popularized the term *biophilia* two decades ago to describe the extent to which humans need connection with nature and other forms of life. More specifically, Wilson describes it this way: "Biophilia ... is the innately emotional affiliation of human beings to other living organisms. Innate means hereditary and hence part of ultimate human nature" (Wilson 1993).

To Wilson, biophilia is really a "complex of learning rules" developed over thousands of years of evolution and human-environment interaction:

> For more than 99 percent of human history people have lived in hunter-gatherer bands totally and intimately involved with other organisms. During this period of deep history, and still further back they depended on an exact learned knowledge of crucial aspects of natural history ... In short, the brain evolved in a biocentric world, not a machine-regulated world. It would be therefore quite extraordinary to find that all learning rules related to that world have been erased in a few thousand years, even in the tiny minority of peoples who have existed for more than one or two generations in wholly urban environments. (Wilson 1993: 32)

Stephen Kellert of Yale University reminds us that this natural inclination to affiliate with nature and the biological world constitutes a "'weak' genetic tendency whose full and functional development depends on sufficient experience, learning, and cultural support" (Kellert 2006: 4). Biophilic sensibilities can atrophy and society plays an important role in recognizing and nurturing them.

The Nature of Cities

While we are already designing biophilic *buildings* and the immediate spaces around them, we must increasingly imagine biophilic *cities*, and should support a new kind of biophilic *urbanism*. As the planet barrels rapidly down the path of urbanization the need for green and *nature-full* cities is an ever more urgent need.

There is already much nature in cities, of course, more than we realize. It is both big and small, visible and hidden. It is intricate, yet sweeping. It is amazing in its biological functioning, ever-present yet highly dynamic, and vastly underappreciated for its ubiquity in cities. In understanding the nature of cities it is necessary to think beyond our usual approach to visualizing or imagining space and place, and to understand that nature is everywhere in cities if we look: it is above us, flying or floating by, it is below our feet in cracks in the pavement, or in the diverse micro-organic life of soil and leaf litter. Nature reaches our senses, well beyond sight, in the sounds, smells, textures and feelings of wind and sun. Understanding the natural history of a city helps us to see cities as ever-changing, ever-evolving palettes of life.

In the higher reaches of our cities, the rooftops and facades also harbor nature, sometimes by design, and sometimes by accident and natural volunteerism. New forms of nature are being created in cities all over the nation in the form of ecological rooftops and rooftop gardens, hosting grasses and sedum, and increasingly found (over time and with the right design elements) to harbor great diversity in terms of invertebrates, bird and plant life. We know, for instance, that butterfly species will visit rooftops on high-rise structures, and food, for humans and nature alike, can be grown here as well.

---

1   Unless otherwise specified, all figures in this chapter are the author's own.

This nature in cities is the raw ingredient for a new global urban society organized around wonder. Few have made a more compelling and eloquent plea for the importance of wonder in the natural world than Rachel Carson more than half a century ago. In a 1956 essay entitled "Help Your Child to Wonder," she describes the value and pleasures of exposing her young nephew to the nature found along the Maine coast:

> If I had influence with the good fairy who is supposed to preside over the christening of all children I should ask that her gift to each child in the world be a sense of wonder so indestructible that it would last throughout life, as an unfailing antidote against the boredom and disenchantments of later years, the sterile preoccupation with things that are artificial, the alienation from the sources of our strength. (Carson 1956: 46)

Carson counsels looking at the sky, taking walks and uncovering and experiencing nature, even if (as parents) we are not able ourselves to identify a species or a constellation. It is about cultivating an awareness of the sights, sounds, natural rhythms around us, paying attention and learning to see the mystery and beauty in everything around us.

We need wonder and awe in our lives, and nature has the potential to amaze us, stimulate us, propel us forward to want to learn more about our world. The qualities of wonder and fascination, the ability to nurture deep personal connection and involvement, visceral engagement in something larger than and outside ourselves, offers the potential for meaning in life few other things can provide.

My landscape architecture colleague Beth Meyer argues that with matters of environment and sustainability we need also to emphasize the beauty and pleasure and enjoyment we derive. We often forget about the aesthetics, or try to reduce them to monetary values. At the end of the day, watching that circling hawk or turkey vulture, walking or bicycling through an urban woods, harvesting and eating produce from one's garden, listening to the sounds of katydids and tree frogs on a humid August evening, are deeply pleasurable; they are the building blocks of a life enjoyed. We climb trees as kids because this is a fun and enjoyable thing to do, and as adults unfortunately we often forget these pleasures (and of course rarely climb trees!).

In our recent documentary film *Nature of Cities* we spent a stimulating several days in Austin, Texas, filming the 1.5 million Mexican free-tailed bats that have inhabited the underside of the city's Congress Avenue bridge during the summer months. People line-up hours before nightfall to get a good look at the wondrous columns of bats emerging from the bridge. Merlin Tuttle, founder of Bat Conservation International (BCI), dutifully recites the many environmental (and economic) benefits provided the city by these bats. And they are considerable, including the millions of mosquitoes they eat each day. But ultimately the sight of thousands of bats flying off, in distinct columns that can be seen for several miles, is an immense and beautiful thing. It is the raw emotion and beauty of the natural world, a primordial spectacle unfolding against a backdrop of high-rise buildings and a human-dominated (at least we think) urban environment.

In many American cities the biodiversity is aquatic and sometimes offshore, as in Seattle, which has abundant and wondrous life in the not-far depths of the bay and sound. Much of the biodiversity of King County, in which the city of Seattle lies, is found in the "deep subtidal habitat" of Puget Sound, in some places almost 900 feet below the surface, and including "over 500 benthic and 50 pelagic invertebrates" (King County 2008: 57). And while some are known and recognizable to residents, such as the king crab, many are not. That the Seattle metro region is also home to such unique marine critters as the giant Pacific octopus and giant acorn barnacle suggests a wildness and mystery very close at hand.

And new forms of nature can be fostered in the many leftover spaces of the city. A visit to the Green Roofs Research Center, in Malmö, Sweden, shows the extent of possibilities—here they have planted and monitor hundreds of green roof test plots, testing different plant and soil combinations. Some of these plots are for so-called brown rooftops—places in the urban environments (there are many) where plants can be used to restore and even take up pollutants in highly contaminated and degraded settings (phytoremediation). And the Malmö center's immense research rooftop also shows the potential of different, sometimes surprising delivery methods—their standard green roof, as Trevor Graham who runs many of the center's green city efforts explains, is made from recycled polyurethane car seats, and in several places there are small mounted frames, with sedum growing vertically, showing the potential for a kind of natural artwork suitable for hanging in one's living room!

Figure 3.1   **Biophilic cities are places where there is abundant nature nearby and where connections with flora, fauna and fungi (as pictured here) are fostered**

Figure 3.2   **A bicyclist along the Akerselva River in Oslo. This is an important natural and recreational asset for Oslo residents, and the city has embarked on a long-term plan to uncover and restore the major rivers that run through the city**

These new forms of nature are catching on, and are now encouraged and in some places mandated by codes, and we will see more of this happening in every city around the world. And new creative developments in cities—such as *Via Verde* (the green way), a 200-unit complex of affordable housing planned for a 1.5 acre site in the South Bronx of New York—will find many ways to insert and grow nature. In this case, the nature takes the form of a connected multi-functional garden "that begins at street-level as a courtyard and plaza, and spirals upward through a series of programmed, south facing roof gardens that end in a sky terrace" (New Housing, New York Legacy Project 2007). Increasingly biophilic cities will understand rooftops, courtyards, and facades as places to cultivate nature.

What is a Biophilic City?

Exactly what is a biophilic city, and what are its key features and qualities? Perhaps the simplest answer is that it is a city that puts nature first in its design, planning and management: it recognizes the essential need for daily human contact with nature as well as the many environmental and economic values provided by nature and natural systems.

A biophilic city is at its heart a *biodiverse* city, a city full of nature, a place where in the normal course of work and play and life residents feel, see, and experience rich nature—plants, trees, animals. The nature is both large and small—from tree-top lichens, invertebrates, even microorganisms, to larger natural features and ecosystems that define a city and give it its character and feel. Biophilic cities cherish what already exists in and near cities (and there is much, as we have already seen) but also work hard to restore and repair what has been lost or degraded, and to integrate new forms of nature into the design of every new structure or built project. We need contact with nature, and that nature can also take the form of shapes and images, integrated into building designs, as we will see.

A biophilic city ought to be judged by the existence of nature and natural features, but also in some way its biophilic sensibilities or *spirit*; how important is nature and how central to the lives and *modis operandi* of the city, its leaders and its populace? A bit harder to quantify, this *biophilic spirit* or sensibility suggests a value dimension, the sense that residents and public officials alike recognize the importance and centrality of nature to a rich and sustainable urban life. This quality could easily fit as both an activity and an approach to governance.

Every city will have its natural spectacles—some large, others more nuanced—but a biophilic city is one that pays attention, a city that sees and conveys this sense of beauty and wonder and caring. It may be the running of the Steelhead trout in Niagara River, or the appearance of Orcas in Prince William Sound, or the migratory return of robins along the east coast of the U.S. A biophilic city celebrates this wonder and sees in these events the opportunity to connect, to strengthen bonds, to mark the cycles of life and seasonality. This celebrating often involves the direct experience of that biodiversity and nature, such as watching migratory birds, or visiting a park or green area, or it might be a more referential form of biophilic expression.

As the accompanying Table 3.1 suggests, how actively citizens enjoy the nature around them and actively participate in this nature is also an important measure of a biophilic city. Participation is an interesting word to use here because it implies a level active engagement beyond just passively observing something; it suggests a keen and active interest in the subject. Citizens of a biophilic city, and their leaders, are not removed from the nature around them, but are highly aware of it and present in its midst. A biophilic city is a city in which a large percentage of its population is actively enjoying nature. This enjoyment and engagement can take many different forms, of course, from walking and hiking in natural areas, to bird-watching and plant- and tree-identification, to organized nature events and activities, from fungi forays to nature festivals.

Biophilic cities help to make it easier to enjoy nature and reflect an understanding that exposure to and enjoyment of nature are key aspects of a pleasurable and meaningful life.

There are many potential outlets and venues for our need to connect with nature, and most are also intensely social. Facilitating contact with nature has the great potential to help create new friendships and build social networks, in turn helping to make urbanites healthier and happier. In San Diego, the activities of a number of "friends" of the canyons groups help to conserve and protect the canyon as a neighborhood and community resource, but also provide opportunities for neighbors to interact and socialize, in a way and to

Figure 3.3   Jane Martin, shown here, is a landscape architect in San Francisco, working to make it easier to replace hard surfaces in the city with sidewalk gardens, like this one in the Mission District

an extent that would otherwise not occur. In the Rose Canyon, for instance, residents from different sides of the canyon have places and opportunities to converse and come together, something that would have been difficult without the pull of nearby nature.

Cities must also begin to see the value and importance of facilitating such connections with nature, and perhaps offering help and support in the Australian Bushcare model. Here local groups of citizens and community volunteers organize around a specific urban ecosystem—a patch of green space, a stream, a park—and with the help of a municipal staff person ("bushcare officer" usually), spend weekends and spare hours cleaning up, repairing, and tending over these spaces. The result is not only ecological repair, but also making friends and the re-building of community, as well as becoming more embedded in place and environment.

Creatively involving citizens in the conducting of science is another way to intimately engage people with the nature around them. In San Diego, citizens have been trained to become "parabotanists" (like paralegals), helping to collect plant specimens in this highly biodiverse county. There are now 200 citizens serving as *parabotanists*, working to collect plant data for the San Diego County Plant Atlas Project (begun in 2002). The project records plants on a 3-square-mile grid. Parabotanists are now steered to collecting on grid square where less plant data exists. Once they sign up for a square they are mailed maps and permits from the museum.

Table 3.1   Some important dimensions of biophilic cities (and some possible indicators thereof)

Biophilic conditions and infrastructure	• Percentage of population within a few hundred feet or meters of a park or green space; • Percentage of city land area covered by trees or other vegetation; • Number of green design features (e.g. green rooftops, green walls, rain gardens); • Extent of natural images, shapes, forms employed in architecture, and seen in the city; • Extent of flora and fauna (e.g. species) found within the city;
Biophilic behaviors, patterns, practices, lifestyles	• Average portion of the day spent outside; • Visitation rates for city parks; • Percent of trips made by walking; • Extent of membership and participation in local nature clubs and organizations;
Biophilic attitudes and knowledge	• Percent of residents who express care and concern for nature; • Percent of residents who can identify common species of flora and fauna;
Biophilic institutions and governance	• Priority given to nature conservation by local government; percent of municipal budget dedicated to biophilic programs; • Existence of design and planning regulations that promote biophilic conditions (e.g. mandatory green rooftop requirement, bird-friendly building design guidelines); • Presence and importance of institutions, from aquaria to natural history museums, that promote education and awareness of nature; • Number/extent of educational programs in local schools aimed at teaching about nature; • Number of nature organizations and clubs of various sorts in the city, from advocacy to social groups.

Source: Beatley 2010.

Figure 3.4   **A beautiful green wall, designed by Patrick Blanc, graces the front of the BHV department store in Paris, France. This vertical garden provides many benefits, including cooling and shading, conserving energy, retaining and slowing storm water and providing habitat for birds, among others**

A biodiversity "hotspot" and the most floristically biodiverse county in the U.S., recording and protecting this biodiversity takes on special importance. The plant atlas will eventually result in an "internet-accessible, databased plant atlas based upon vouchered specimens." There are more than 1,500 native species of plants in San Diego County and so there is much to document and record, and citizens here plant an important role. Volunteers go through training by San Diego Natural History Museum, and once trained, collect and press the plants and record data about the plant's location. A museum botanist verifies the plant's identification.

A biophilic city then is a city with an extensive and robust *social capital*, to extend Robert Putnam's concept (Putnam 2001). Evidence is compelling that we need extensive friendships and social contact to be healthy and happy, as well as our contact with nature, so finding creative ways to combine these needs becomes an important goal in the biophilic city. I have been calling this *natural* social capital, acknowledging that there are many ways that learning about and experiencing nature can also help to nurture friendships and help to overcome the increasing levels of social isolation felt at least by Americans. How many social organizations or clubs, or community events or activities, explicitly focus around the unique nature of cities? The extent of creative social possibilities is almost limitless: weekend fungi forays, wildlife tracking clubs, *bioblitzes* and nature festivals, wild flower and birding clubs, among many others.

Nudging that happens is often a function of the range of organizations, some public some private, that exist in a city and that can help in supporting the educating and engagement of citizens. One measure of a biophilic city is the extent of the organizational support, the quality and reach of the biophilic organizations that exist in a city that can actively work to nudge us towards nature. Bird-watching, and nature hikes through the city might be one option, but there should be many: swimming, canoeing and kayaking in urban waters, visiting parks near and far, experiencing nature on a sidewalk or rooftop or building façade as one walks to work or to the subway, among many others.

Many cities around the world are located on or near water bodies and a measure of their biophilic tendencies is how easy it is for residents to enjoy these aquatic environments. In some cities, such as Boston, non-profit organizations have worked to make it economic and easy to learn how to sail. In that city a junior sailing program run by the non-profit Community Boating Inc., offers children the chance to learn how to sail for only $1 for the entire June–August season. Many American cities, moreover, have worked hard to reestablish direct physical contact and connection with rivers, creeks, harbors, though waterfront parks and trails and opportunities to get out on a kayak or canoe.

Biophilic cities are cities that work to expand the opportunities to spend time outside and in close proximity to nature. Partly this means rethinking the ways parks and green spaces are used. New York City has been a leader in creating opportunities for urbanites to camp on weekends in city parks. The program occurs in the summer months and is quite popular. In 2009, family camping took place in every borough of the city. These camping evening are especially from the perspective of kids quite enjoyable and exciting. The city's Parks and Recreation Department provides the tents and sleeping bags, and there typically barbeques, night hikes, skywatching and even S'mores!

Biophilic cities are to be identified not just by the presence or absence of nature, of green spaces, and green infrastructure, but other forms of investment also that facilitates a biophilic life. A biophilic city invests in a robust network of public (and private) institutions that will educate about, restore and protect, and nudge residents toward enjoying nature. These include traditional environmental education and natural science institutions such as local botanical gardens, zoological parks, and natural history museums, among others. Environmental education centers have been very effective in some cities, in some cases based in urban neighborhoods.

And biophilic cities are also concerned about and work to protect nature beyond their borders. Each city has opportunities to express care about the environment and other life in the world. Large cities exert a tremendous pressure on global biodiversity through their material flows and consumption patterns, and one measure of a biophilic city is the extent to which it seeks to moderate or reduce those impacts.

New York City, for instance, has recently acknowledged that it purchases a large amount of tropical hardwoods, an estimated $1 million worth each year. The city uses this wood—South American species such as *Ipe* and *Garapa*—for such things as benches, boardwalks, and ferry landings. The 10-mile-long Brooklyn Bridge Promenade is constructed of *Greenheart*, another South American hardwood. In recognition of the destructive impact of such purchases Mayor Bloomberg announced a plan in 2008 to significantly reduce the city's purchasing of such wood—a 20 percent reduction immediately and larger reductions later as the city researches and pilots alternative wood sources and alternative materials that could be used (NYC.gov 2009). Describing tropical deforestation as an "ecological calamity," and noting that it may be responsible for as much as 20 percent greenhouse gas emissions, Mayor Bloomberg has made an eloquent plea for cities to become better stewards of the global environment. "New Yorkers don't live in the rain forest. But we do live in a world that we all share. And we're committed to doing everything we can to protect it for all of our children" (*The Nature of Cities* 2010). City purchasing policies and decisions is an important opportunity for biophilic values to gain expression.

Biophilic Cities in Our Future?

What constitutes a biophilic city is still very much a matter of discussion and debate. Less a definitive list or set of principles, the categories described about are meant to identify at least some of the potential building blocks of a biophilic city. It is unlikely that a singular coherent vision of a biophilic city will emerge. Rather, perhaps there are many different *kinds* of biophilic cities, many different expressions of urban biophilia. And they might be expressed by different combinations and emphases of the qualities and conditions described here. At the simplest level, though, a biophilic city is a city that seeks to foster a closeness to nature—it protects and nurtures what it has (understands that that abundant wild nature is usually a lot), actively restores and repairs the nature that exists, while at the same time finding new and creative ways to insert and inject nature into the streets, buildings, and urban living environments. And a biophilic city is an outdoor city, a city that makes walking and strolling and daily exposure to the outside elements and weather possible and a priority.

But as the above discussion also indicates, a biophilic city is not just about it physical conditions or natural setting, and it is not just about green design and ecological interventions—it is just as much about a city's underlying biophilic spirit and sensibilities, about its funding priorities, and about the importance places on support for programs that entice urbanites to learn more about the nature around them, for instance. A biophilic city might be measured and assessed more by how curious its citizens are about the nature around them, and the extent to which they are engaged in daily activities to enjoy and care for nature, than more the physical qualities or conditions, or for instance the number or acres of parks and green spaces per capita that exist in a city.

There are a variety of important research questions about designing and planning biophilic cities in the future. We still have, for instance, relatively little knowledge of the *cumulative* recuperative and healing powers of urban nature. How do the many smaller green features in a city or urban neighborhood contribute to our closeness with nature and what are the interactive effects. Is access to a large forest more effective than a neighborhood full of smaller green features, such as street trees and green rooftops? And what is the actual daily minimum level of nature needed by urbanites, and in what form, to live a healthy life?

There are also a host of research questions that relate to how effective our biophilic strategies in fact are—what are the most effective planning and policies means for getting people outside? What will it take to nudge urban populations to adopt a more outdoor nature-oriented lifestyle? As well, our very understanding of the science and ecology of cities remains quite limited and there is much work to be done here as well. New research is needed to better understand the biology and life cycles of fauna found in cities and it changes or is modified in an urban setting (e.g. think of coyotes!), as well as the management implications therein. There are many, almost countless, research questions and opportunities that arise from the agenda of biophilic cities.

Much of task in the future, certainly for those in city planning and urban design, will be in offering an alternative future vision of cities and urban neighborhoods. As Stephen Kellert of Yale University has said: "We need to do more than just avoid all the bad things that we have done in terms of our adverse effects on natural systems. We also have to create the context for thriving, for development, for meaningful exchange with the world around us, and the people around us. And for that we need to restore that sense of relationship with the natural world which has always been the cradle of our creativity" (*The Nature of Cities* 2010). That vision will be of dense, sustainable, walkable cities, and places that are also full of nature, and are profoundly restorative, magical and wondrous. *Biophilic Cities.*

Figure 3.5   **The High Line Park in New York City provides a linear garden and park in the heart of Manhattan. Formerly an elevated commercial rail line, the park provides an unusual vantage point (and respite and calm) in this busy, energetic city**

References

Carson, Rachel. 1956. "Help Your Child to Wonder," *Woman's Home Companion*, July, 25–7.

Kellert, Stephen. 2006. *Building for Life: Designing and Understanding the Human-Nature Connection*. Washington, DC: Island Press.

King County, Washington. 2008. *King County Biodiversity Report*.

The Nature of Cities. 2009. Film directed by Stephen Kellert.

New Housing, New York Legacy Project. 2007. *Phipps-Rose-Dattner-Grimshaw Selected to Develop City-Owned Site in South Bronx*, press release, January 17.

NYC.gov. 2008. "Mayor Announces Plan to Reduce the Use of Tropical Hardwoods." February 11. Available February 17, 2009.

Putnam, Robert. 2001. *Bowling Alone: The Collapse and Revival of American Community*. New York: Simon & Schuster.

Wilson, E.O. 1993. "Biophilia and the Conservation Ethic" in *The Biophilia Hypothesis*, edited by S. Kellert and E.O. Wilson. Washington, DC: Island Press.

Chapter 4
A Long View at High Speed

Andrew Ballantyne

The film *Koyaanisqatsi* establishes surprising effects of alienation and empathy by the technically fairly simple means of running time at the wrong speed.[1] It is a wonderful film, which fuses beautifully photographed images with a compelling musical score. Other films have done that much. The artificiality of the film-making process is such that normally the triumph of a film is to leave the audience with the feeling that they have been a witness to something that more or less really happened: people did things, emotions were genuinely felt, and the audience was able to witness and empathize. *Koyaanisqatsi* is unusual in that its events do not unfold at human speed, and although humanity is often on the screen there is no emotional engagement with individuals nor anyone who could be called a protagonist. The film was made in 1982 under the direction of Godfrey Reggio, and the music, which is the film's only soundtrack—there are no sound-effects and no dialogue—was by Philip Glass. We see landscape speeded up, its clouds roiling and evaporating, sunlight flickering, shadows moving, sand dunes drifting. It is as if we can see the landscape taking shape before our eyes. The camera's gaze is indifferent to whether it is looking at natural landscape or cities, and the atmosphere continues across both, calmly and without comment. Other things are slowed down, so we can see what is happening with a clarity that would normally be impossible. A wave breaks in slow motion, so that its undulations are as graspable as the sand dunes, and the debris from the explosive take-off of a Saturn V rocket floats gently through the air. Some of the most compelling sequences show an urban grid with traffic moving through it, red lights moving away from us, white lights towards us, stopping at junctions and then starting again. We all know what that feels like from the point of view of the urban traveler. There are rules and codes, and a destination that we will eventually reach, despite the stopping and starting along the way. We have our music with us, and maybe someone else in the car having a conversation. In the film all individuality and human feeling is drained away, and the mechanical aspect of the process is brought to the fore. The lights move like blood cells stopped and started by valves, the human agency that we know about becomes invisible, and as they are speeded up so much the rhythm of our ordinary life is not longer to be felt there. There are images of people waiting to buy rail tickets, waiting in line, being served, moving on; and people going up and down escalators. We know what it feels like to engage in these activities, and it may try our patience, but here we see only the mechanical pattern of the behavior, which looks like a physical flow with predictable dynamics. Whatever I might feel myself to be as an individual, if I am participating in the system that is on display here then I am a molecule in a flow, and it is that aspect of me that matters.

In architecture we have an ingrained habit of considering buildings and cities at different scales depending on the size of the site: maybe 1:1250 for a terrain, 1:500 for the outline organization of a complex building, 1:100 for a house plan, 1:50 for arranging the furniture, 1:20 to full-size for detailing the joinery. If instead of scaling the size we scale the time, then we start to apprehend new aspects of the things around us. Our personal experience is limited, but we speed things up then we can grasp a sense of trajectory. On a geological timescale where we see the rocks taking shape like slowly breaking waves, life forms do not really show up; but imagine a film made from one still shot of a human taken with each generation. If we were to start taking the photos 6 million years ago, at the estimated time of the last common ancestor of apes and humans, and estimated that each generation succeeded the next every 25 years, then we would have a film with 240,000 frames. If it ran at 24 frames a second then the film would be 167 minutes long. *Koyaanisqatsi* runs for 87 minutes. *Apocalypse Now* lasts for 202 minutes. Homo Sapiens Sapiens would be comfortably identifiable for the final 5.5 minutes of the film, hunting and gathering and making tools, but would only start on agricultural activity and the production of settlements in the last 17 seconds. The oldest buildings that we

---

1 *Koyaaniqatsi*, directed by Godfrey Reggio (1982), music by Philip Glass.

know would start to show up during the last eight seconds. The last 2,000 years would pass in 3.3 seconds. At this rate of change even the most traditional societies see progress, and modern industrial society seems very sudden, producing its most widespread effects in the last fraction of a second before the credits roll—a subliminal glimpse would be all we would see of the world we know (Diamond 2012).

Nobody really knows how evolution works, but we have picked up various instincts, habits and reflexes in our past that normally escape conscious analysis. I do not have to think to make my heart beat. Somehow my heart knows that that is the thing to do. I know that I have to sleep, but I do not know why. There is no point in arguing with my body about this: I just know that it is one of the things I must manage as I go about my life. I can rationally decide that now would be a good time to sleep, and could even decide that I will never sleep again … and see where that gets me.

The near relatives of humans, whom we do not consider to be of the same species, but who must at some point have shared some ancestry, seem to have thought in a way that was much more dominated by habit. They could certainly make tools and may well have made dwellings of some sort. Birds' nests and some mammals' burrows might give us some clues about how dwellings can be made in an instinctual habit-driven way. In trying to understand the thinking of early humans and near humans such as the Neanderthals, paleontologists need a theory of mind. It is imagined that as individuals we go through stages of development that in the distant past we went through as a species, or as a succession of species (plural). The patterns of behavior that might be found in adult Neanderthals might be present in modern toddlers, but attached to toddlers' goals. Modern adults find repetition boring, but toddlers love it. We have very little evidence to support conjectures about the behavior of Neanderthals, but their stone tools seem to have undergone very little change during the 100,000-year span when they might have been produced. What was it like to be a Neanderthal? Life would have been lived very much "in the present," with little sense of the past and little speculation about the future. Everyday consciousness would have been of the type that we recognize from when we are doing a routine or much-practiced activity, where it has become ingrained and habitual, such as driving a car on a familiar journey or playing a well-rehearsed piece of music. The Neanderthals thought in highly compartmentalized ways, and the archaeological remains of their sites show that tool-making, butchering, and social interaction were conducted in spatially distinct locations (Mithen 1996: 155). The early modern-human sites show these activities overlaid on one another in the same space.

The defining development in the minds of modern humans seems to have been a new capacity for transferring ideas from one part of the mind to another. The Neanderthals' minds were, it seems, compartmentalized in such a way that they were inclined to develop different kinds of intelligence in different parts of the mind, where they could develop to a high degree but without a development in one part informing the other parts. We can still do that. Linguistic intelligence develops separately from technical intelligence, social intelligence and natural history intelligence. However, in a modern human connections are made by consciously thinking about the things in different parts of the mind—which could well have found their way in by way of unconscious experience or intuition, or even perhaps by way of inherited instinct—or habits learnt so early that they feel as if they are innate. This "thinking about" goes on in what we would now call the conscious mind, and it is that consciousness that the Neanderthals lacked—or at least had it in a much more limited way than Homo Sapiens Sapiens, who was therefore much more creative and adaptable.

Without an art world there are no "works of art" as we know them, but some figurative paintings survive from as early as 30,000 years ago, at the Chauvet cave where they were protected from weathering and lost from view. We have no idea how many such paintings were lost. Nor do we know what was their role in the social group that produced them. Categories like "religion," "magic" and "superstition" also belong to much later times, but it took time and effort to develop the necessary skills and their production was evidently found to be worthwhile. An early object that was highly worked (for no tool-like purpose that we can imagine) was made 30,000–33,000 years ago and was found in fragments in 1939 at Hohlenstein-Stadel in Germany. It is a 30cm-high figure, carved from a mammoth tusk, and shows a standing person with a lion's head. Although it stands as the earliest such find, it does not look like a beginner's work. The hands that crafted this with flint tools would not be doing their first work on ivory, and there were presumably many lost works in perishable wood that rehearsed the form, which might have been traditional by the time that this example was carved, or might have been the idea of the carver. It may have been made to be venerated, or to be destroyed. Perhaps grasping it gave a hunter courage and stealth, turning him into a lion, helping to awaken those attributes in himself. It is striking that although it is naturalistic to the extent that its features are clearly recognizable and well made; it is a model of a creature that has never existed in nature, and the instant one sees it one knows that it is human work. The archaeological record has not yet turned up much "decorative" work that is older—some beads, including some in ivory that were carved to resemble shells, have been dated to 40,000 years ago. These people were scavengers and moved about. If they formed attachments to precious objects then the objects would have to be portable. There would have been little scope for specialization. Maybe it would be recognized that someone was stronger or more ingenious, sang better or carved better, but in everyday life everyone would have had to join in with things and would have had at least an idea of how things were done, and probably a practical ability to do them.

Relatively recently Adam Smith explained how the division of labor—specialization, and the development of a high level of expertise in a very limited skill—increases by a factor of thousands the efficiency and productivity of the people involved in a process (Smith 1776). His classic example was the making of pins. Our ice-age hunter-gatherers were still a long way off making pins, even inefficiently, and they were a long way off having the kind of social structure that could allow for significant specialization.

The relations of cause and effect are always problematic in an evolutionary process. In retrospect one can see things working towards a significant threshold-event, but it was certainly not visible in advance and was certainly not the goal towards which people were working. It is clear that humans were already being inventive and doing characteristically human things long before the end of the Ice Age with the global warming that marks the end of the era that geologists call the Pleistocene, about 11,500 years ago. Our current era is known as the Holocene, and it seems as though the global warming were a precondition for the development of human flourishing, and looking back one follows the other as if there were a relation of cause and effect. Just as water predictably comes to the boil when heat is applied and behaves in a way that we would not anticipate had we not seen it before, so with the addition of heat the groups of humans started behaving differently. Instead of going out to forage for food, they started producing it: growing crops and husbanding animals, initially as a supplement to hunted and foraged food, but then with the farmed food as their principal sustenance. The changes were so gradual that any individual who lived through this era would have thought that things were just continuing in the same way that they always had. In retrospect, replayed at high speed, it looks like a revolution (Christian, 2004: 209–10). Agriculture began independently in various parts of the world, and news of its advantages spread around. The relatively intensive production of crops and tending of herds brought with it a non-nomadic way of life. Settlements were formed and they grew. Çatalhöyük, one of the oldest and most-studied settlements is often called a village, but with 8,000 inhabitants at its peak, it was among the largest settlements on Earth at the time (Balter 2006); 7,000 years ago in Mesopotamia there were "large towns" with about 1,000 inhabitants, and developments would happen at a particular place not so much because of natural topography but because of interconnections with other towns (Christian 2004: 262).

A settlement of such a size allows for some specialization of roles. Not everyone need work in the fields, and if a society is going to develop the ability to work metals, weave fabrics and make pots, then it will need specialists. The rate of change since then has been breathtaking. People kept having ideas about how things might be better, and sometimes they implemented them. They did not always live in the towns, but they great changes were made through the agency of towns and the contacts that were made possible through them. The people who produced metals were itinerant. They needed to travel to the places where the ores were to be found. They would heat up the rocks so as to make the metals flow out of them, and then trade them in the town. The farmer's efficiency was increased by the plough, but the plough could not be made without access to the materials available only through the town. Irrigation systems watered the crops so that they were no longer at the mercy of unreliable rainfall. Above all the flow of information and ideas followed trade-routes, which were sometimes importantly waterways. The Tigris and Euphrates rivers bounded fertile land that was known in Greek as Mesopotamia (between-rivers) now in Iraq, which acted as a cradle for urban culture. The Nile became a super-highway for an extraordinary centralized state, some 900km long, but only a few wide, as the fertile ground that was irrigated by the river was bounded by desert beyond that. Greek civilization grew up around the Aegean, and the Roman Empire round the

Mediterranean—their principal support for long-distance communication. In China there were parallel but independent developments, based on systems of roads across the vast land-mass.

The connections between people echo the kind of connections that are made in the modern human mind which distinguish that mind from the Neanderthals' mind. Our new type of conscious thought wanders off when it is faced with repetition. We start to do things automatically and if we are doing something routine that does not fully engage our thought, we can have conversations, think about the evening's meal or plan travel arrangements. One likes to think that the Neanderthals would have found these routine tasks completely satisfying, but we get restless. We delegate the dull tasks to others if we can, and nowadays there is often a machine to do the work. In early societies the moves were intuitive as indeed they often still are. We are drawn to the company of some other people and find our interactions with them socially and intellectually stimulating. Sometimes that is fruitful, but often the new idea makes its appearance later, on reflection in solitude, but if anything is to come of it one must connect again with a social realm. In the modern world this can often be through writing, with ideas prompted as if by conversation with someone who lived perhaps hundreds of years ago. A vast number of discrete incremental steps brought us to this state of affairs, but now that they have been taken the means of communication seems to be quite natural and it is used intuitively. Children growing up now, surrounded by electronic media, communicate in ways that would have seemed to their great-grandparents like telepathy, and they can seem to be indifferent to the difference between the conversation being conducted with someone in the next room or on a distant continent. The technical means of communication have developed, but the instinct to communicate is deep rooted. It is present in all humans, but is developed by individual circumstances: reinforcement and encouragement in the family, years of deliberate schooling, informal social interactions etc. It can be derailed by trauma.

Buildings appear late in the line of development. There are traces of fire long before there are traces of discernible buildings. Caves were used as shelter, not only by humans (bears used the Chauvet cave) but they can never have been the norm as they are too scarce. For early scavengers maybe a fire and some animal skins would have given a level of security and comfort that was good enough—or even if not good enough, was all that could be had. The places where traces of buildings first appear seem to be where food supplies were so abundant that a permanent base could be established. These places were rare before the adoption of agriculture, so buildings as we know them are mainly the product of the last 10,000 years. Minor earthworks, timber constructions and portable shelters leave no archaeological trace, but pottery does—and there are finds of fired clay that have been dated back to 28,000 years ago. The major attempt to translate the understanding of evolution-derived instincts into modern aesthetic theory is Jay Appleton's prospect-and-refuge theory of landscape, which suggests that we find comfort and satisfaction in a landscape when we are in an enclosed space that feels safe and which offers an extensive view of terrain (Appelton 1996). Grant Hildebrand has discussed these ideas in relation to architecture (Hildebrand 1999).

I find these ideas convincing and they correlate with my own experience. When I was looking for somewhere to live I began by asking estate agents about the houses they were trying to sell, which were invariably classified according to criteria that did not seem to me to be apposite. As an architect I expect that when I move into a house I am going to want to change it. I do not expect to find a place that is already decorated in the way that I would want it to be, and it is quite likely that I will want to remove walls and reposition windows, so the precise configuration of the place would not be an issue. The thing that it is impossible to change is the view, so it is important to me to get that right. So when estate agents asked me what I was looking for, I explained (deadpan) that I was looking for a place where I could see the shadows of clouds moving on hills. This invariably produced a pause by way of response, and then my favorite come-back (also delivered deadpan) was "I'll put that down as two bedrooms." If we have an inherited longing for such a view, then it is an indictment of the property-selling business that it is not part of their thinking. In the end I did find a house with such a view: I am working in it now, and I found it without the help of an agent. The view does give me profound satisfaction of the type that Appleton and Hildebrand describe, perhaps indeed because it is information-rich with the kind of information that I would want if I were a hunter-gatherer scanning the view for prey (Barkow et al. 1992). I notice that sometimes when I sit outside with this view before me, there is about 100m away to my left a kennel-dwelling hunting dog, who seems to be sitting contentedly looking into the distance, and maybe responding to the same instincts.

For my work, however, I have a different window on the world. I am surrounded by books, some of which are functionally necessary for my writing, but the bulk of which are actually experienced as a reassuring presence. I have the feeling that I can reach for their content when I feel the need for it, and because they are my books there is a good correlation with my interests and lines of inquiry. However, the other element that seems vital for the sense of well-being here is the internet connection. Telecommunications have been an important part of life for one generation, perhaps two, and the internet has ingrained itself in our lives with surprising rapidity. Television is a mass medium that feeds us a supply of general news and entertainment, but the internet will accept our own questions and gives us a more personally directed view of information. It will also help us to address social needs, so one remains connected with the world of ideas, friends and colleagues. Engagement with it is a sublimated version of engagement with the hunter-gatherer's prospect. If I am hunting for and gathering information, then being given this access to it actually addresses the same primitive instinct as does contemplating the view. Its use feels utilitarian, whereas the contemplation of the view is now classified as aesthetic as I do not have any practical need to engage with anything that I would learn about from the view. By contrast I might miss the fact that the internet connection has an aesthetic aspect, precisely because it is useful, in the same way that I might have missed the aesthetic value of a view when I was surveying it in the hope of seeing food. Julia Kristeva has speculated that our relationship with our dwellings is so intense that dwelling in steel-and-glass cities might give us new neuroses (Kristeva 1993: 29). Probably, though, the prospect-and-refuge formula is more important. If we are genuinely secure and have a richly informed view of the world, then the specific materiality of the buildings is less significant. Some neighborhoods are more secure than others. Some countries are safer places to live in. I am less likely to develop neuroses in a steel-and-glass building with a good concierge and views over parkland than I am in a traditional adobe dwelling in a city where gun-crime is out of control. Note also that Kristeva's anxiety was expressed back in 1993, before mobile communications and the internet were a routine part of the fabric of everyday life. The blank uncommunicative facades are simply inexpressive: they do not express the alienation of the people who live behind them, but mask a wealth of social interaction that has no architectural expression. It also no doubt masks some alienation and neurosis.

The rate of change has changed. For hundreds of thousands of years so far as we can tell people managed to survive and maybe inventively outwitted the competition, but left no record of changing culture. Then decorative beads appear, and thousands of years later the sculpture of a lion-person and paintings in caves; 20,000 years after that there are the first signs of agriculture and the conditions were put in place for settlements in which there could be specialization. In the 10,000 years that have passed since then have seen the living conditions of many humans change astonishingly. Once the idea had been had, people noticed that there was something good about living in settlements—at least that is what the people who settled noticed. Others remained nomadic and developed in a different way, but anyone who is reading this book is likely to have a home to go to. Settlements were not invented so as to make possible the division of labor and technological progress, but these things were among the consequences of settlement. The number and the size of settlements grew. The number of people grew more rapidly after settlement, because more children could be supported. Scavengers would have had to carry their infants (McNeill and McNeill 2003: 27–8).

We continue to head for the cities, even if we are not born there as most people now are. We are drawn there with the hope of prosperity or status, and because the number of machines now operating in the countryside has diminished the number of agricultural workers that is needed. The dwellings in the European countryside are often occupied by people who work in a city, and therefore functionally these dwellings are part of the city (Ballantyne and Ince 2010: 1–27). It is in the city above all that we encounter and learn respectfully to deal with people who are unlike ourselves and our immediate family. In the distant past such encounters may have been rare, but such skills and the values that they reflect are important now and will be important in the future (Gardner 2008). Where once the drift into agriculture was relatively slow, the current adoption of new ways of life is rapid. Until relatively recently it was a normal pattern of events for children to grow up in the same place as their parents and to follow the same or a similar trade. The industrial revolution changed things, especially the pace of things. Instead of working at the rate that was comfortable for a person to work, the machines could run much faster and could continue night and day. The water and then steam-driven machines of the nineteenth century were large and had moving parts that seemed powerful and expressive. The advanced machines of today and tomorrow are too small to see and do not have evocative form, but they bring us into new relations and bring about shifts in sensibility and our sense of boundaries of all sorts—physical and psychological.

The city in a machine that brings people into contact and helps them to generate new ideas and ways of life. It will continue to do that, but we are forcing the pace. Once upon a time we might have imagined that the world might continue harmoniously unchanging forever. Later we might have imagined that, having learnt a profession, we could practice it through the duration of a career. Now we have "lifelong learning," and "continuing professional development," if not mid-career changes of direction. Now we look for trends, and rather than being content to know what is happening, we try to see where it will all end and to get there before our competitors. Change is not only recognized, but institutionalized. In some places transactions may still be made after days of travel and a bartering of produce that the participants in the exchange have actually grown or made. But deals can now be made in commodities far more abstract than straightforward "money," and they be instigated by machines and repeated thousands or even tens of thousands of times in a second. In this world of machines and exchanges that remain beneath the threshold of human sensory apparatus, the means by which things are achieved become undetectable and ceases to have symbolic value in art and culture. What remains is a more or less flexible network of communications and interactions, which join up to make society's mind, which may not know what it is thinking because the consciousness remains in the individuals.

In *The Uses of Disorder*, Richard Sennett stigmatized the impulse to zone cities, which has often been felt by urban designers, as "adolescent" (Sennet 1970). Looking at human development at high speed, I would now want to call it Neanderthal. The Neanderthals had tidy minds, and lived tidily zoned lives, but the drawbacks are all-too-evident to us. We will continue to need secure and information-rich vantage points from which to make connections across the rest of our world, but not all our instincts will serve us well. Whatever it is that impels us to compete, acquire and build, does not seem to have an upper limit to the amount of competition, acquisition and building that seems necessary. Just a little bit more, we feel, will make us contented—and we assemble global corporations that push their machinery to its limits and they turn out to have appetites that are absolutely insatiable. Humans are now moving minerals about the Earth's surface at a greater rate than the glaciers did during the Ice Age, and it is proposed that we should call the dawning geological age the Anthropocene. Geologists themselves, however, resist the idea, because the Holocene has only just begun. In geological time the global warming that melted the glaciers is such a recent phenomenon, is so close to the rise in human culture that one would intuitively see them as cause and effect. Our instincts belong to a time long before our current patterns of life were established. At times we need to allow our reason to overrule our instincts, in the interests of the rest of society; but our instincts must be accommodated. Our buildings and cities must remain vital, and must help us to manage our instincts, as we get to understand them better. They can be dangerous and untidy, but must promote social interaction and experiment if we are to find out what is now possible.

References

Appleton, Jay. 1996. *The Experience of Landscape* (1st edn 1975). London: Wiley.
Ballantyne, Andrew, and Ince, Gill. 2010. "Rural and Urban Milieux," in *Rural and Urban: Architecture between Two Cultures*, edited by Andrew Ballantyne. London: Routledge.
Balter, Michael. 2006. *The Goddess and the Bull: Çatalhöyük: An Archaeological Journey to the Dawn of Civilization*. Walnut Creek, CA: Left Coast Press.
Barkow, Jerome H., Cosmides, Leda, and Tooby, John. 1992. *The Adapted Mind: Evolutionary Psychology and the Generation of Culture*. Oxford: Oxford University Press.
Christian, David. 2004. *Maps of Time: An Introduction to Big History*. Berkeley, CA: University of California Press.
Diamond, Jared. 2012. *The World until Yesterday: What Can We Learn from Traditional Societies?* Allen Lane: London.
Gardner, Howard. 1993. *Multiple Intelligences*. New York: Basic Books (rev. edn 2006).
Gardner, Howard. 2008. *Five Minds for the Future*. Boston, MA: Harvard Business Press.
Hildebrand, Grant. 1999. *Origins of Architectural Pleasure*. Berkeley, CA: University of California Press.

Kristeva, Julia. 1993. *Les Nouvelles maladies de l'âme*. Paris: Fayard, translated by Ross Guberman as *New Maladies of the Soul*, New York: Columbia University Press, 1995.

McNeill, J.R. and McNeill, William H. 2003. *The Human Web: A Bird's-Eye View of World History*. New York: Norton.

Mithen, Steven. 1996. *The Prehistory of the Mind*. London: Thames and Hudson Howard.

Sennett, Richard. 1970. *The Uses of Disorder: Personal Identity and City Life*. New York: Knopf.

Smith, Adam. 1776. *An Inquiry into the Nature and Causes of the Wealth of Nations*, edited by Edwin Canaan, 2 vols. London: Methuen, 1904.

Chapter 5

Creativity, Diversity and Interaction: Urban Space and Place-Making

Ali Madanipour

Within the lifetime of a generation, we have witnessed the cyclical collapse of two models of development. The first model, which involved a compromise between employers and employees, was made possible through state support. It had emerged in response to the economic crisis of the 1930s and the Second World War; but it ran out of steam by the 1970s (Aglietta 2000). In response to the crisis of this model, a second model emerged, based on free markets, privatization and deregulation, globalization and technological change, a model which in turn has been unravelling since 2008 (Barber 2009). The collapse of these two models has led to a search for a new model of development based on innovation and creativity in their broadest sense (Madanipour 2011a). The chapter outlines the significance of innovation for economic development, the role of diversity and dialogue in innovation, and the urban implications of these concepts. Rather than elite and specialist enclaves, it is argued, innovation and creativity are better served by an inclusive notion of diversity, which is partly made possible through a strong public realm.

Innovation Based on Interaction and Diversity

In the quest for new directions, knowledge has found a central place as the basis for future economic development. One of the key drivers of the European Commission's EU2020 vision is "creating value by basing growth on knowledge" (EC 2009a: 5). Within the framework of economic development, knowledge is often defined in terms of science and technology, supported through the spread of information and communication technologies. A parallel, but less acknowledged, path to economic development is through cultural and creative activities, whose significance as part of the drive for knowledge-based economic development has been increasingly recognized (DCMS 2008). Many still consider the relationship between culture and economy as hierarchical and at best tangential, privileging the economy, where the relations of production, distribution and exchange of goods and services take place and where the "real concerns" are to be found. Culture, in its different meanings from symbolic products to ways of life, is considered to be a soft subject with a secondary significance, even a byproduct of these economic relations. If anything is going to be important for these relations of production and exchange, it is assumed to be science and technology. This is why the EU visions of the future knowledge economy, the type of economy which is going to support the future of Europe, are primarily based on science and technology, as tools that can transform the productive capacity and facilitate exchange. But arts and design have now been increasingly accepted as a parallel path. While widely different, these twin paths of science and technology and arts and design coincide in the idea of creativity and innovation.

Innovation is a key principle in economic development and transformation (EC 2009b). It involves the generation of new ideas, products, and practices, which can fuel the processes of production, consumption and exchange. Innovation is taken to be a result of a process of exploration through research and development, design and creativity, as well as the reuse of existing or borrowed knowledge or application of new tools. As such, it is often the product of dialogue between different ideas and practices, a meeting of minds by different individuals, groups and organizations. Difference and dialogue are therefore at the core of innovation, which in turn is at the core of economic development. The question that we need to raise then is: what forms of difference and what forms of dialogue can lead to innovation?

What Forms of Interaction?

The first question is: what forms of dialogue are possible and desirable? Two sets of answers are identifiable. One set of answers is given by the information and communication technologies, which have facilitated the meeting of minds in new, mediated forms. The ability to transmit information at unprecedented levels and to communicate with almost anyone from almost anywhere has fuelled innovation enormously, to the extent that for some people this is the only form of innovation that does or should take place. It has given rise to the idea of intangible products, aspatial relations, immaterial economy, and even the death of the city (Quah 2002).

But we know that these processes of information and communication are not as immaterial as they are believed to be. We cannot simply hold something to be immaterial because we don't see it. We cannot see the atomic and subatomic world with our eyes; should we think that it has no spatial or temporal dimensions, while it forms the basic blocks of material reality? The production, processing, transmission, and display of data are all material processes formed of energy and matter. The people, machines, and networks that are in control of these processes are all material beings, all with spatial features of mass, location, and distance from others. These products are all produced, distributed and consumed under particular material conditions. Judging by the sheer number of material objects that people possess nowadays, the extent of consumption of material goods and the sea of waste that is produced as a result, it would be hard to call this an immaterial economy. These material dimensions often make up the urban environment, and all the evidence indicates the growth of cities, rather than their demise and disappearance, as once was rumored. Face-to-face relations and spatial concentration are still the most important forms of interaction.

Another set of answers is given, therefore, through spatial clustering. In the urban context, the answers to the question of interaction and diversity are often given through place-based solutions, which help face-to-face communication, bringing different sectors or individuals together in particular locations, hoping that a cluster of activities would be created, in which innovation becomes possible. By observing the way existing clusters emerge through individual decisions and market mechanisms, the idea is to develop new clusters by public policy. In urban development and management, therefore, interaction has been facilitated through the formation of spatial clusters and interactive institutional arrangements. In other words, if clustering can make the interaction of different minds possible, it would be seen as a pre-requisite for innovation, and so why not try to create some new clusters, hoping to develop a fertile ground for the seeds of innovation to grow. This is why we see science parks, cultural quarters, education districts and the like are created as clusters of innovation.

Therefore, these two sets of answers lay the foundations for technologically and spatially mediated dialogue, creating virtual or physical clusters, which are expected to trigger innovation in science and technology, in arts and culture. There is no doubt that they have the potential to support interpersonal communication, which is a basis for innovation, and so they have their advantages and strengths. But if we are to evaluate them properly, we need to explore and test their limits as well.

Clustering and Fragmentation

Ever since Alfred Marshall's analysis of industrial districts, the process of agglomeration is considered to be a defining feature of urban economics, whereby the location decisions of firms tend to produce specialization of urban space. Such specialization is not necessarily exclusive, and it can coexist with a range of other activities that may support it in various ways. But when this process of clustering is institutionalized through public policy, the result may become less diverse, with direct implications for productivity. The example of zoning in land use planning clearly shows this problem. By functional division of labor in land use, some parts of the city become detached from others, undermining the possibility of mutual support between different activities, and turning into more monotonous or sometimes completely unsafe or under-used areas.

The new sites of production in the knowledge economy include universities, science and technology parks, creative economy clusters, as well as homes and office clusters (Madanipour 2011a). The pressure for specialization and suburbanization has created fragmented specialist sites, while the nature of some sectors makes it undesirable for them to be separated from the life of the city. The economies of scale and the pressure for agglomeration are either produced through the market or public policy to create new clusters, in the hope that innovation would result. The core of these ideas is that clustering would generate innovation and economic development. A subtext is that clustering, which is often clearly branded and well-advertised, would generate a positive image for city marketing and global competition between cities. The relationship between the cluster and the rest of the city, both in terms of the sectors of economy and the type of workers employed, and in the spatial relations of proximity and integration or decontextualization and segregation, is often undermined in this process. "Designed clusters" may not lead to functional innovation or new investment in the city, and if they are not a part of the city's economy and society, their success, if it materializes at all, would be limited. The production of space may be only partly connected to the need for clusters, responding to the demands of the development industry rather than the knowledge economy.

Furthermore, the particular model of innovative clusters may fragment the urban space in new ways. Silicon Valley portrays a prototype for many spaces of innovation, as a pioneer that other parts of the world envied and copied. The overall spatial configuration is one of a low density spread of workspaces, surrounded by suburban housing, shopping strips and malls, and some town centers. It is primarily following the models of suburban development that evolved after the Second World War in the United States. It belonged to a particular time and culture, and the fact that it was the center of innovation in information and communication technology could be lost to a casual visitor, as its spatial organization and appearance could hardly suggest it. If you were not familiar with the names and logos of the famous companies that line the streets, you could think that you are going through yet another suburban area, where shops, offices and houses were scattered about, accessed by wide roads and large cars. This was the most cutting-edge space of creativity, and yet it was also a typical suburban sprawl, a model that grew on the basis of the availability of cheap fossil fuel and land, which characterized the post-war suburban growth.

Cultural quarters, however, often tend to be located inside cities, rather than in suburbs, as urban life is often more conducive to cultural creativity. Many local authorities have now created such clusters. Existing cultural institutions are linked and branded in these quarters, and new places for creative activities have been developed from the remnants of the manufacturing industry's decline. Questions that need to be explored, however, are: While cities have always developed clusters of different activities, can planned clusters be a force for cultural productivity? What sorts of spaces are created and how do these spaces relate to their surroundings? If they are spaces in the middle of declining inner cities or former factory sites, what strength of relationship and cross-fertilization can be expected between these areas and the surrounding parts of the city? Is physical proximity enough to generate face-to-face encounters? We know of the limits and perils of social engineering and physical determinism, whereby spatial reorganization is taken to be the primary tool for changing the social and economic organization of a society, with unavoidable failures. These policies of providing creative clusters are based on the idea of commercialization of science and culture, and of being located in designated places, two conditions to which not all practitioners wish to subscribe. Furthermore, attention by government, big business, or tourists may price out those who cluster in these areas for their low rent.

What Forms of Diversity?

The second question is about the forms of diversity that we acknowledge. A spatial response to this question has been retrofitting the urban space for the needs of a so-called creative class. But the idea of a creative elite that forms the backbone of the economy may not be accurate, as many of their activities may not necessarily involve creativity. Furthermore, the work of any elite can only be effective in connection with the support of the wider community, without which this group will not be able to operate. Overlooking the contribution of the other parts of society, however, may lead to two-tier societies, in which it may be taken for granted that gentrification is inevitable, turning a blind eye on its negative social consequences, which include bitterness and resentment by those who are priced out or simply displaced by force (Madanipour 2011b).

A hierarchical conceptualization of economy splits the society into what matters and what does not matter. In an earlier interpretation, this was a separation of the base and superstructure, privileging political economy over culture; in current economic analysis, it refers to the separation of base and non-base activities, of the creative class from the others, of the conception from execution, of the productive sphere from the consumption sphere. A primary form of split is between inward and outward looking strategies; between those that look to a globalized world to attract resources, and those that are needed to look inward to find out what the local needs are. But in all these splits, the privileged segment can only be privileged if the other segments exist. In other words, they are parts of a whole, rather than existing independently. Without the non-base, the superstructure, the so-called non-creative classes, the consumers, no economy can function. The split between important and unimportant roles in the social division of labor lays the foundation for social stratification, alienation, and exclusion. While individual differences are unavoidable, and it is inevitable to weigh different roles differently, it is the structural split that creates long-term and large-scale gaps and fractures (Madanipour 2011c).

The idea of spatial clusters appeals to economic development analysts, but not necessarily or in the same way to social analysts: an economic cluster may be a localization of specialist networks of production and exchange, and a social cluster may also be a localization of social similarity, but it may not lead to any particular form of innovation. Quite to the contrary, a social cluster may be a ghetto, an enclave which may refuse to integrate, becoming rigid or antagonistic to others. Clusters are a socio-spatial phenomenon, which may have different consequences in different contexts.

To recap, the establishment of elite clusters of innovation may have some positive results, but they may also have fragmentary impacts on society and space. So, rather than only focusing on exclusive and specialist agglomeration, inclusive interaction as a path for innovation could confront the fragmentary pressures. A broader, more inclusive approach would see the local forms of knowledge and the diversity of populations and their different cultures to be a source of innovation. Rather than a hierarchy of classes based in a collection of spatial fragments, the urban society could offer a framework for innovation, where new ideas and practices can emerge through open expression and interaction. As the source of all value is human effort, a point recognized by early analysts such as Adam Smith (1993) and Robert Owen (1991), the challenge is how to facilitate, mobilize and support human effort in all its different forms.

The inclusive approach acknowledges the role that various groups play in the economy, and facilitates their coexistence and interaction through the development of a strong public realm. The public realm, in its spatial and institutional forms, is where the different cultures that make up the urban society can relate to one another and develop new ideas and practices. This approach, however, is not without concerns (Madanipour 2010).

One problem is the domination of the public space by the proliferation of cultural products in a consumerist economy. The spatial dimension of this approach has been the development of urban spaces that stimulate consumption through leisure and retail, drawing on color, experience, events, and advertising. With the current economic problems, however, it has become clear that the consumerist model is not economically or environmentally sustainable. A question, therefore, is whether and how public spaces and cultural products can be developed; how can new ideas, practices, and products be generated that have economic value without being consumerist. Furthermore, consumption is not equally accessible, and the growing inequality in many societies (OECD 2008) leads to urban partitioning, with a range of places from rich gated neighborhoods to poor ghettos, encouraging everyone to consume and excluding those who cannot afford to have access to consumer products.

These approaches tend to draw on an instrumental notion of culture and may not engage with the underlying cultural diversity that is a feature of modern urban life. In the absence of explicit measures to confront social inequality, the spatial results may be the generation of elite enclaves, gentrified areas, and branded places, which may lead to fragmented social conditions and may not stimulate the local productive capacity in cultural and economic development.

Diversity and Identity

Diversity is a necessary ingredient in creativity and innovation. However, a limited understanding of diversity may simply result in superficial outcomes, placing emphasis on appearances, reflecting an imaginary cultural diversity that sanitizes and fictionalizes existing diversities. This can be seen everywhere in advertising and the experience economy, whereby exotic experiences are called upon to generate excitement. On the other hand, a very deep and rigid understanding of diversity becomes inward-looking, leading to forms of tribalism that are not willing to engage with others. For some, this intersection of cultural diversity and innovation may result in a sense of insecurity and loss of identity. In practice, social identity is not as fluid as consumerism seems to suggest and not as stagnant as tribalism recommends; it is not simply at the mercy of international corporations nor of ultra-conservative perspectives.

Identity is often taken to be the distinctiveness of something, but it also shows its similarities with others, both elements of a process of comparison between things (Madanipour 2009). In economic development, identity is sometimes used for branding, to show one product is different from the others in the same range. In cultural terms, there is a sense that in the process of globalization, local distinctions are being eroded and therefore the assertion of identity is needed. In cities, these economic and cultural considerations find manifestation in the development of iconic architecture and other forms of distinctiveness, from league tables to specific mottos, all feeding an army of brand consultants. But how can this outward looking quest for distinction relate to the local society's realities, needs and aspirations? How far can this approach go beyond the surface and reach the material conditions of people in places?

For many, diversity is a source of vitality, but also a threat to stability and continuity. What forms of diversity are desirable? The long struggle for diversity is rooted in response to the emergence of large bureaucracies and corporations, the universalist cultural trends, and the significance of the economic and political considerations at the expense of cultural expression. But when diversity becomes the norm, identity becomes a concern. Innovation requires new ways of thinking and acting, often through the meeting of different minds, the interface of different ideas and practices. However, such interface puts forward serious challenges to all those involved. The sense of local distinction and identity may be challenged by the introduction of new ideas, which may undermine the age-old traditions of a locality. The threat of globalization challenges localities to find a sense of identity, on how to be distinctive from others in their search for competitiveness. But identity is not just being distinctive, it also means similarity. So a sense of cultural identity in a locality revolves around how that place is different from others, but in doing so establishes how similar it is to others, expressing how it wishes to belong to a particular group.

A local pattern of activities can be a constellation with a clear identity, but without being cut off from the rest of the world. It means the balance between the necessity for looking outwards and the need to relate to and mobilize the local needs, ideas and capacities. Spatially, it means the need for contextualized clusters, embedded symbolic expressions, and democratic governance. In economically vibrant cities, diversity is a necessary but not sufficient source of success; it is the ability to mobilize social resources that lies at the core of their success. The vibrancy of this social context is closely entwined with their economic vibrancy. The cultural richness of the soil in which the seeds of innovation grow is important, but the ability to engage in collective self-rule is essential.

The problems of local versus global is the problem of power. The places at the core of the world system are also localities. In globalization, London, New York and Tokyo have occupied key places as the pivotal nodes of the process of integrating the different global economies into an increasingly integrated sphere. But even these cities are not floating immaterialities: they are local places like any other local place, with the difference that these places, or at least some of their places, benefit most from the globalization process. So the battle is not between the local and the global, as it is often formulated; it is a tension around power in all its forms: between the more powerful and the less powerful agencies and localities. Depending on their location on this gradient, they feel more or less at ease with the processes of globalization. If they are in a place where they feel they can have some control over their own affairs, they feel less threatened than places where they are overwhelmed by change and without any hope of managing it to their benefit. But as the forces of globalization have accelerated their pace, uncertainty and insecurity have prevailed, even among the privileged core players. The scale and speed of change, the extent of interdependence and therefore vulnerability, as manifest in the global economic and environmental crises, have undermined the earlier sense of confidence.

A difficult balance then needs to be struck between the need for security and continuity, and the dynamics of diversification and innovation. Difference should then be interpreted in a sense that would avoid superficial and temporary associations that do not have any particular meaning other than another form of consumption, while also avoiding the rigid affiliations that would not acknowledge others and remain within an unchanging and potentially stagnating world. It should include the diversity that exists within a population, and the diversity that emerges from the meeting of this population with each other and with others, whether face to face or mediated.

Creativity and Inclusive Interaction

Modern society is primarily urban, and cities are places of difference. From the ancient times, this diversity has been recognized, particularly in the division of labor, which assigns different roles to different people, making the urban life possible (Aristotle 1992). The search for innovation, however, tends to privilege some participants, some sectors and spaces over the others, creating disconnections between these participants and the rest of society. A narrow understanding of the process assumes that innovation takes place outside a context. Innovation, however, is embedded in the context of the city, takes place in many areas of activity, and by all levels of stakeholders. The idea that innovation is an elite specialism undermines the intelligence and the intensity of knowledge that can be found in all human activity (UNESCO 2005), amounting to cultural schizophrenia. Social difference, however, should be understood in a wide sense, which would go beyond a limited range of participants and explore new possibilities through inclusive and open forms of interaction.

The spatial and institutional form that this open type of interaction may take is the development of the public realm (Madanipour 2003). Places and institutions that can allow diverse groups to become aware of themselves and others, participate in political and cultural life, and freely explore new ideas and practices, would be an essential ingredient of this recognition of diversity. In response to the nineteenth-century economic laissez-faire and social diversity, many public institutions were developed, while a long line of thinkers, from Hegel onwards, have emphasized the significance of recognition as a social force (Honneth 1996, Bourdieu 2000, Ricoeur 2005). It is made possible through public institutions that offered opportunities for new ideas and practices, a lesson that we may need to relearn today. This force can be mobilized to develop new ideas and practices. Interactive institutional arrangements and inclusive governance can be supported and made possible through a vibrant public realm. Recognition, however, is one side of the coin, which needs to be balanced with access to resources and decision-making, through a range of measures to combat social inequality and exclusion (Madanipour 2011c). Many attempts at mixing social groups and land uses are made in the name of facilitating toleration and sustainability, but in practice many lead to gentrification: the arrival of stronger players who displace the weaker ones.

A narrow interpretation of culture may lead to the development of elite enclaves disconnected from the rest of society, legitimating gentrification and elitism, or consumerism and superficial deployment of diversity. A wider interpretation of culture as a way of life, however, would recognize diversity as an inherent feature of urban society and look for the ways in which these diverse ways can be present and have positive mutual effects. In spatial and institutional terms, this would lead to the development of the public realm, the places and processes where different ideas, practices and groups can meet. Rather than elite or functionalist enclaves, the energized and empowered public realm would be inclusive for a wider range of ideas and practices, and allow for the development of local distinctiveness as the outcome of interaction among culturally diverse populations within and between localities. Pressure for homogenization, which is a consequence of globalization, would be offset in this way by local democratic compositions with their unique social and economic features.

References

Aglietta, M. 2000. *A Theory of Capitalist Regulation: The US Experience*, new edn, London: Verso.
Aristotle 1992. *The Politics*, London: Penguin.
Barber, L. 2009. Capitalism redrawn, *Financial Times*, May 12, 3.
Bourdieu, P. 2000. *Pascalian Meditations*, Cambridge: Polity Press.

DCMS 2008. Creative Britain: New Talents for the New Economy, London: Department for Culture, Media and Sport. Available at: http://www.culture.gov.uk/images/publications/CEPFeb2008.pdf [accessed November 26, 2009].

EC 2009a. Consultation on the Future "EU 2020" Strategy, COM(2009)647 final, 24.11.2009, Brussels: European Commission. Available at: http://ec.europa.eu/eu2020/pdf/eu2020_en.pdf [accessed November 27, 2009].

EC 2009b. European Innovation Scoreboard 2008: Comparative analysis of innovation performance, Luxembourg: European Commission Enterprise and Industry. Available at:http://www.proinno-europe. eu/admin/uploaded_documents/EIS2008_Final_report-pv.pdf [accessed October 17, 2009].

Honneth, A. 1996. *The Struggle for Recognition*, Cambridge, MA: MIT Press.

Madanipour, A. 2003. *Public and Private Spaces of the City*, London: Routledge.

Madanipour, A. 2009. City identity and management of change, in C. Vallat, F. Dufaux and S. Kehman-Frisch (eds), *Pérennité urbaine, ou la ville par delà ses métamorphoses*, Paris: L'Harmattan, vol. 3, 217–34.

Madanipour, A. (ed.) 2010. *Whose Public Space?*, London: Routledge.

Madanipour, A. 2011a. *Knowledge Economy and the City*, London: Routledge.

Madanipour, A. 2011b. Living together or apart: Exclusion, gentrification and displacement, in Tridib Banerjee and Anastasia Loukaitou-Sideris (eds), *Companion to Urban Design*, London: Routledge, 484–94.

Madanipour, A. 2011c. Social exclusion and space, in R. LeGates and F. Stout (eds), *The City Reader*, 5th edn, London: Routledge, 186–94.

Madanipour, A. Cars, G. and Allen, J. (eds) 2003. *Social Exclusion in European Cities*, London: Routledge.

OECD 2008. *Growing Unequal? Income Distribution and Poverty in OECD Countries*, Paris: OECD.

Owen, R. 1991. *A New View of Society and Other Writings*, London: Penguin.

Quah, D. 2002. Matching demand and supply in a weightless economy: Market-driven creativity with and without IPRS, *De Economist*, 150, No. 4, 381–403.

Ricoeur, P. 2005. *The Course of Recognition*, Cambridge, MA: Harvard University Press.

Smith, A. 1993. *An Inquiry into the Nature and Cause of the Wealth of Nations*, Oxford: Oxford University Press.

UNESCO 2005. *Towards Knowledge Societies*, UNESCO World Report, Paris: United Nations Educational, Scientific and Cultural Organization (UNESCO).

Chapter 6
Incremental Urbanism:
The Emergence of Informal Settlements

Kim Dovey[1]

Introduction

Much has been made of the fact that most of the global population is now urban, up from about 30% in 1950 and rising. It is not so often noted that most of this new urban population has been accommodated through the expansion of informal settlements or slums in the developing world. While the urban population increased about fourfold from 1950 to 2010, the urban slum population increased more than tenfold. In other words, most new urban populations have been accommodated outside the control of the state, without the engagement of built environment professions. This is an emergent urbanism in terms of both the fact and mode of its emergence – its predominance in cities of the global South and its links to theories of 'emergence'. The first task is to recognize the magnitude of this global condition as a primary challenge facing urban studies and the built environment professions. With few exceptions, informal settlements cannot be erased and replaced – most such settlements are here to stay and the task is one of on-site and incremental upgrading. This in turn suggests a re-thinking of architecture, urban design and planning in terms of theories of emergence, self-organization and assemblage. Traditional forms of urban theory and practice – focused on formal regulation and top-down plans – have proven poorly equipped to cope with the dynamism, complexity and resilience of informal urbanism. In terms of research this requires an analysis of where such settlements emerge and why; an understanding of the morphology and dynamics of how such settlements work – the spatial patterns, construction systems, increments of change and informal codes. Finally, it requires an understanding of how the professions of architecture, landscape, urban design and urban planning might engage in such forms of practice.

Informality, Slums, Squatting

The categorization of parts of cities into 'informal' settlements, 'slums' and 'squatter' settlements, while at times useful, is generally inaccurate. While such terms are often used interchangeably they are defined in opposition to 'formality', 'livability' and 'legality' respectively. The formal/informal distinction originally developed as an understanding of the ways informal economies operate outside the formal controls of the state – untaxed and unregulated. While some degree of informality is characteristic of all parts of all cities 'informal settlements' become identified when entire neighbourhoods or districts develop outside the formal control of the state (Roy and Alsayyad 2004). The UN definition of a slum is based in criteria of livability – lack of space, clean water, sanitation, security or durable shelter (UN-Habitat 2006: 19). Squatting, by contrast, is defined by encroachment on formally 'owned' land. The label 'informal' is often applied in order to avoid the sense of lack implied by 'slums' and 'squatting', but can be seen as equally problematic with links to organized crime and the black economy. Neuwirth (2012) suggests the phrase 'system D' to celebrate the entrepreneurship and self-organization of the small-scale informal sector.

The terms 'slum', 'squatter' and 'informal' are not synonyms and there are no pure conditions of 'slum', 'squatter' or 'informal' settlements. Many dwellings within so-called 'slums' do not fit the UN definition and standards of construction can be quite high (Hernandez and Kellett 2010). Illegal tenure often becomes

---

1 Unless otherwise specified, all figures in this chapter are the author's own.

ambiguous, irregular and contested over time with emergent forms of *de-facto* tenure (Durand-Lasserve and Royston 2002). Most typical are conditions of 'becoming': slums becoming upgraded; squatters becoming tenured; informal settlements becoming formalized; formalized settlements becoming informalized. Our thinking, analysis and action on this nexus of issues needs to move beyond the somewhat essentialized concepts of slums, squatters and informal settlements to deal with these dual conditions (Figure 6.1).

Figure 6.1   Santa Marta, Rio de Janeiro, 2012. Settlement becoming formalized – note the recent funicular and formalised housing to the right, gentrification spreading upwards and banners showing resistance to eviction at the top

Incrementalism

Before I turn to these larger questions, there is a fourth term that is increasingly used as a partial synonym here – 'incrementalism'. This is a concept that describes a scale of process and form rather than formality, legality or livability. Incremental urbanism is a way of describing the process of room-by-room accretion through which informal settlements agglomerate. Incremental urbanism operates on sites without cranes, where structures span less than five metres, where materials are transported by hand and stored in the interstices of existing structures. It describes a process whereby the shape of urban morphology and public space emerges incrementally through a multiplicity of design decisions and without any prevailing master plan. It embodies a process of self-organization where negotiations between neighbours result in an informal spatial code with laneways of varying width and permeability. It is a process of intensification as rooms are added horizontally and vertically until a limit is reached at about 3–5 storeys. At such densities incremental urbanism can result in a version of the tragedy of the commons where accumulations of self-interest lead to a loss of the common interest. Escalating encroachments onto public space can lead to a lack of natural light, air and open space – the dark and labyrinthine conditions of the stereotypic 'slum'.

A key argument here is that this incremental condition of informal settlements is also the condition for their upgrading. With up to half the population of some cities of the global South housed informally, demolition and replacement has become politically and economically impossible without massive social dislocation. The key challenge is one of on-site or *in situ* upgrading through a principally incremental process – adapting the existing infrastructure, urban design and tenure over time into well-serviced neighbourhoods that are no longer 'slums'. I begin with five key arguments for incrementalism: avoiding displacement, preserving adaptability, enabling tenure security, environmentally responsive design, and aesthetic/heritage issues.

With few exceptions informal settlements occupy land that is interstitial and seems of marginal use to the formal city – waterfronts, escarpments, infrastructure easements and the leftover space of the formal city (Dovey and King 2011). Such settlements, however, are not marginal to these cities in economic terms, they are located where they are because they have access to jobs. Slumdwellers service the formal city and any strategy that suggests they be moved to cheap land on the urban fringes will fail because it exacerbates poverty and strips the city of its workforce. *Insitu* upgrading is the only way to avoid displacement. While erasure and replacement is possible on-site, informal settlements embody a particular dependence on the street and laneway network – particularly the capacity for domestic production to spill into public space with high levels of intensity and efficiency (Figure 6.2). Formalization often standardizes private space in apartments that are separated from street networks; producing access spaces that are less flexible and productive. High levels of informality enable micro-flows of information, goods, materials and practices that produce income and make life sustainable under conditions of poverty. These practices are integrated with the micro-spatial adaptations that flourish under conditions of informal urbanism – particularly incremental construction processes. In this sense informality is not to be confused with poverty; it is indeed a resource for managing poverty. A marginal increase in the private floor area of each house can be a spurious gain when it is coupled to a loss of adaptability and access to adjacent public networks.

While land tenure in informal settlements is generally ambiguous, the houses are assets that are often owned by residents who may also become landlords. Wholesale formalization often conflates upgrading with public housing, converting homeowners into tenants and leaving former tenants homeless. While public housing can play an important role and there are relatively successful projects of this kind, there is no prospect of such funding being able to address more than a small fraction of the global problem. The larger opportunity is to move incrementally from informal to formal tenure.

Informal settlements are relatively high-density, walkable, transit-oriented and car-free. They are often constructed from recycled materials with low embodied energy and passive heating/cooling. While any effective upgrading will increase consumption, to upgrade a billion slum-dwellers to the levels of CO_2 emissions prevailing in the formal city is a recipe for environmental catastrophe. Incremental transformation can be coupled to the development of models for the low-carbon city, particularly by maintaining the car-free morphologies of informality.

Finally, there are also aesthetic and heritage reasons to retain the basic morphology of informal urbanism – a difficult issue to deal with briefly while avoiding the charge of an aestheticization of poverty. While we mostly avoid speaking about what slums look like, popular images of 'architecture without architects' have long demonstrated how an informal order can emerge from a repetition of vernacular types, variegated by an incremental adaptive process (Dovey and King 2012). There are remnants of urban informality in many 'cities of the north' – effectively upgraded informal settlements – that have become global tourist attractions protected under the umbrella of 'heritage'. The public space networks of informal settlements are indeed part of the inheritance of each city, embodying a history of each neighbourhood that can be incrementally upgraded rather than erased.

There are important exceptions to the case for incremental change. Some settlements are constructed to such low standards and at such densities that they cannot be upgraded without wholesale demolition. Many are on land that needs key infrastructure to be rendered safe, accessible or livable. Some have emerged in locations where it makes no sense to upgrade *in situ* because threats from flood or unstable land cannot be mitigated. Others are located so close to railway lines that either the railway or the housing must be re-located (Figure 6.3). Such decisions, however, are highly political as well as technical; the need is for innovative solutions that do not involve surrender to the narrow logic of displacement to the urban fringes. A great deal is lost to those who most need it in a wholesale transformation from informal to formal. What is needed are tactics of incremental change geared to existing morphologies that service a larger strategy of transformational change.

The case for incrementalism, however, is not one-sided. There is no shortage of good thinkers who attribute the global growth of slums to the excesses of neoliberal capitalism under conditions of a weak state

Figure 6.2   Dharavi, Mumbai, India, 2011. Domestic and economic life is highly dependent on public space

and there are important arguments against incrementalism in this regard. As summarized by Davis (2006: Ch. 4), they are that the focus on self-help involves a blaming of the victim, that many schemes turn out to fail; that funds leak to corrupt operators; that owner-built housing is shoddy and incremental construction is inefficient; that NGOs can co-opt the interests of slum-dwellers to their own; and that self-help programs divert slumdwellers from political struggle. This is a long list and all of these arguments have a degree of truth but they do not add up to a convincing case against incremental upgrading. Informal construction is less efficient but the cost to the owner is a fraction of a formal construction contract. Corruption may be an informal flow of resources but its most damaging forms depend on large-scale flows of formal funding. While some buildings need replacement in all slums, in most settlements the majority of buildings can be effectively upgraded rather than replaced.

The important question here, however, is the degree to which the problem of the slums can be reduced to the effects of neoliberal capitalism and solved by some available alternative. One does not need to choose between critical analysis of the causes of slums and incremental tactics for their alleviation. Incremental upgrading is not a form of blaming the victim but of empowerment; it is not a diversion from political action but a legitimation of existing social insurgency. Transformational change at the global scale needs to incorporate the urban transformation that has already taken place at the incremental scale.

Figure 6.3   Manila, 2008. Informal settlements and transport infrastructure compete for public space

Complex Adaptive Assemblage

If the built environment professions are to engage with this challenge of incremental *in situ* upgrading of informal settlements, then we need to re-think the city within new conceptual frameworks. This shift can be construed as from a focus on fixed outcomes and master plans to adaptive processes, from hierarchic organization to networked self-organization, from tree-like thinking to rhizomic thought. This is not, however, simply a shift from formality to informality but rather to a between position that encompasses both without becoming an amalgam of the two. There are two bodies of theory that I want to briefly introduce here and that we might label with the terms assemblage and resilience.

Assemblage

Assemblage thinking is based on the philosophy and social theory of Deleuze and Guattari (1987), particularly as developed by DeLanda (2006, 2011). An assemblage is a whole that emerges from the interconnectivity and flows between parts. As a verb 'assemblage' focuses attention on processes of connecting – connecting people or firms to each other, producers to consumers, people to buildings, public to private space. As a noun an 'assemblage' is a cluster of interconnections rather than a 'thing'. It is akin to a 'place' in the sense that it is a socio-spatial territory with some form of identity, however fluid (Dovey 2010: Ch. 2). Assemblage is fundamentally dynamic and productive, a dynamism based primarily in horizontal networks of connectivity (pedestrian networks, information flows) yet also stabilised by hierarchical territories (policies, planning codes, laws). Assemblage theory cuts across any separation of subject and object; it is fundamentally socio-spatial with the spatial and social parts mutually constituting each other. Assemblage is multi-scalar – the room, building, street, neighbourhood, city and globe are interconnected and analysis at a single scale can be inherently blind. Assemblage thinking opposes hegemonies of scale – agency and power flow both up and down. Thick description and micro-scale urban analysis become important to reveal the ways an assemblage works. Assemblage theory is emerging as an important form of critical urbanism with key links to urban political economy but without the economic reductionism (McFarlane 2011, Dovey 2011).

A key dimension of assemblage thinking is an axis of territorialization/deterritorialization that describes the ways socio-spatial boundaries are inscribed and erased, the ways identities are formed, expressed and transformed. A territory is a stabilized assemblage, a zone of order, a socio-spatial identity, an inscription of boundaries, a settlement; deterritorialization is the movement by which territories are eroded (demolished) (Deleuze and Guattari 1987: 310–12). The use of a phrase such as 'informal settlement' is already to acknowledge a double condition of being at once 'settled' yet not formally territorialized.

Assemblage thinking is useful for understanding the relationship of formal to informal practices in the city because a range of twofold concepts that resonate with informality/formality are deployed as a means to understand assemblages – rhizome/tree, smooth/striated, supple/rigid, network/hierarchy, minor/major (Deleuze and Guattari 1987, Dovey 2010: 22–4). Informal practices are rhizomic in contrast with the tree-like strictures of urban regulation and planning; they involve minor adaptations and tactics in contrast to the major strategies of master planning; they involve informal network connectivity in contrast to hierarchical control. Assemblage thinking incorporates informality as fundamental to understanding how cities work cities and undermines conceptions of informality as an aberration or problem that can or should be erased.

Assemblage theory is essentially a form of philosophy, it involves a huge amount of jargon and requires a good knowledge of philosophy and social theory in order to even understand it. To apply such a conceptual framework to urban research and practice is a further task. With this in mind (and at the risk of multiplying this complexity) I want to suggest that assemblage theory can be usefully linked to the cluster of theories on complex adaptive systems and resilience.

Resilience

Resilience thinking of the kind I want to introduce here is based in a mix of theories of cybernetics, chaos, complexity adaptation and emergence, mostly drawn from the natural and information sciences (Gunderson and Holling 2002; Walker and Salt 2006). This body of work involves an attempt to understand the dynamics of complex systems wherein the parts are interdependent and unpredictable. The outcomes of such a system cannot be determined in advance but rather emerge from practices of adaptation and self-organization. Over time a regime with certain characteristics 'settles' down. At an urban scale of the city, district, neighbourhood or street, the emergent properties of the urban system have something in common with place identity and urban character. This emergent regime is always a mix of both formal and informal properties and practices. Unpredictability is in part a result of the fact that minor changes in one part or level of the system can have pervasive effects throughout the system; and major plans for wholesale transformation can be stymied by deep-seated resilience.

The 'resilience' of a complex adaptive system is defined as its capacity to adapt to change without slipping into a new 'regime' or 'identity' (Walker and Salt 2006). Resilience in this sense is not a static quality but a dynamic capacity to move between a range of adaptive states without crossing a threshold of no return. Yet beyond such a threshold change can escalate until the system settles into a new regime. Informal settlements often settle into forms of resilient yet dynamic stability. The phrase 'informal settlement' might more aptly be described as a negotiated settlement between informal and formal forces.

Resilience thinking offers a way of understanding how such processes might be managed with a focus on certain 'key slow variables' which have potential to push the system across a threshold into a new regime or identity. In urban terms such key slow variables may include land and rental value, economic vitality, gentrification, traffic speed and volume, building height and density, social mix, crime, public transport, governance and political will. As any of these variables changes incrementally, other parts of the system adapt.

The characteristics of a system that can increase its resilience to regime change are mostly linked to diversity and redundancy. The diversity of the system involves a diversity of possible adaptations to change while redundancy is the capacity of parts to perform a multiplicity of functions. The tendency to strive for optimal formal outcomes can reduce resilience because it leads to a loss of redundancy. A large part of what we call urban informality consists of this relatively elastic adaptability of forms, functions and spatial practices.

Complex-adaptive systems are conceived as enmeshed in cycles of change at multiple scales with four main phases of growth, conservation, release and re-organization (Walker and Salt 2006; Gunderson and Holling 2002). This cycle draws from the economic theory of creative destruction originally derived from Schumpeter and particularly influential in Marxist geography (Harvey 1982) – capital produces cycles of creative innovation that destroys existing structures and territories (cities, industries, neighbourhoods) in order to create new ones. This cycle is also congruent with the assemblage concept of territorialisation/ deterritorialization and can be linked to cycles of informal urbanization including land invasion, settlement, upgrading, demolition and resettlement. Settlements may spiral downwards into a dangerous and resilient slum; or become incrementally upgraded and formalized.

Resilience thinking suggests that such cycles of change are enmeshed in multi-scalar hierarchies called 'panarchies' where resilience is embedded in both horizontal and vertical interconnections. It follows that we need to understand informal settlements at the scale of room-by–room accretions as well as pedestrian networks, the interface with the formal city, the political and governance framework and neoliberal capitalism. The resilience of the system and its emergent properties can only be understood through a multi-scalar approach.

Emergence

Assemblage thinking emerges from philosophy and social theory while resilience thinking is more geared to the quantitative sciences, yet they are in many ways consistent approaches. Both are fundamentally multi-scalar, anti-reductionist and multi-disciplinary. There is a shared resistance to explanations that reduce the particular to the general, local to the global, or micro to macro. The complexity and adaptability of the city cannot be understood from within disciplines such as geography, sociology, urban planning or architecture. Since the term 'system' connotes both large-scale predictability, I have suggested the concept of a 'complex adaptive assemblage' as an integrating concept (Dovey 2012).

Emergence is a process where simple generative processes can create a larger scale order with characteristics that transcend its ingredients. From an urban design and urban studies perspective such thinking is not new but has key antecedents in Geddes, Jacobs and Alexander. Geddes (1915) brought an evolutionary perspective to urban morphology and Alexander's (1996 [1965]) seminal paper 'A City is Not a Tree' prefigured much recent assemblage thinking. Likewise, the seminal urban writings of Jacobs (1965) are replete with the valorization of informal connections at every scale from 'eyes on the street' to the productivity and creativity of larger urban economies.

Different forms of terminology can be involved in re-thinking the informal/formal relationship. For Portugali (2000) the self-organizing city can be seen in terms of fast and slow processes of urban change at small and large scales respectively. Larger scale slow changes (traffic, tenure, gentrification, crime, planning codes) become the parameters for smaller scale but faster changes (incremental construction, local production, micro-politics) which in turn are productive of slow change in the larger parameters. Marshall (2009) adopts an evolutionary approach to urban morphology at an urban design scale where he identifies two kinds of order that he terms 'systematic' and 'characteristic'. Systematic order is loosely defined as top-down or controlled from above – akin to the formal urban planning and design codes imposed and enforced by the state. 'Characteristic' order, by contrast, operates from below and the urban morphology emerges as a result of both.

It is now clear just how intermeshed informal and formal processes are in all urban assemblages. While there are clearly interactions between formal and informal this is not a simple dialectic; and while semi-formal alloys can form, it is not a hybrid. It is best described as a 'twofold' wherein the one is always becoming the other; informality encroaches and infiltrates the formal city (Bayat 1997) while formality frames and imposes upon the informal.

There is nothing essentially good or bad about urban informality; the crucial research questions lie in the myriad ways in which the formal and informal intersect. Much crime, violence and corruption is informal and the informal sector can operate in alliance with state and market oppression (Roy 2004: 159). The informal economy can drain the tax base necessary for effective regime change at a higher level. To understand urban assemblages, to design or regulate effectively within them, requires a complex understanding of the factors that drive regime change. We may wish to limit the forces for change (the creative destruction of demolition and displacement) or we may wish to drive the system into a new and better regime (upgrading). There is, likewise, nothing essentially good about urban resilience – corruption and poverty can be highly resilient to change. Emergence is at once social and spatial, characterized by practices of cooperation, corruption and conflict that can escalate out of control or can stabilize through informal codes. The 'tragedy of the commons' can become a resilient condition of public squallor.

Assemblage thinking is inherently multiplicitous, implying a multiplicity of methods of analysis at multiple scales and from multidisciplinary perspectives. We need to understand constructions of meaning, productions of space, socio-spatial practices, temporal rhythms, network connectivity, experiences of place and much more. Such research may incorporate approaches from ethnography, phenomenology, post-structuralism and political economy; methods may include discourse analysis, interview, observation, spatial syntax analysis, mapping, photography, archival research and many others. My own interests focus on the morphological and spatial at an urban design scale. How does the image of informal settlements impact on the public gaze and as forms of political discourse? How do informal settlements emerge within different urban niches with different degrees of visibility/invisibility (Dovey and King 2011)? How does the morphology of makeshift house types in problematic contexts mesh with political and economic ideals? How do images of informality play out in the field of urban aesthetics and what are the attractions of slum tourism (Dovey and King 2012)? What transformational strategies are adopted to manage such imagery and, how is this mediated by the political economy of place branding, upgrading and eviction?

While dramatic images of informal settlements often appear on the book covers, research on slums is often aspatial, as if the ways in which they have been designed— the detailed materiality, spatiality, density, amenity and spatial structure – are of interest only to the degree that they affirm the idea of poverty and disadvantage as a prelude to transformation. The forms of urban informality are too easily written off as superficial symptoms of larger socio-political forces. Assemblage thinking involves a non-linear logic where the order of the city emerges unpredictably from the multiplicity; spatial thinking and design thinking can incorporate such non-linear logic. The forms of informality matter to the flows of global tourists seeking out the authentic; they matter to the politicians who want such images ordered, erased or covered; and they matter in more complex ways to local middle classes on elevated freeways, behind walls and in highrise towers, for whom they are largely invisible or imagined away.

Finally, what are the consequences of such a re-think on policies and practices of urban planning and design? Some forms of governance are emerging that operate in a twofold manner across the formal/informal divide – NGOs such as SPARC in India have morphed into quasi-planning agencies in alliance with community-based organizations (Appadurai 2002, Roy 2009: 160). While there are dangers that flexibility in urban governance can be a cover for corruption and runaway deregulation, it is surely clear that comprehensive master planning will fail. This is the great challenge for the urban planning profession: how to move on from the dominant paradigm of comprehensive rational planning towards a model that accepts unpredictability without surrender to the ravages of market-led deregulation. How to plan in a manner that does not kill the vitality and productivity of the city in the drive to organize it? How to formalize the city without erasing the complexity and adaptability that produce it?

A key shift is from outcome-based to process-based design and planning. In an emergent system, the form and identity of the outcome remains provisional and contingent – an urbanism in a state of becoming. This entails a focus away from any kind of fixed outcome, design product or master plan. Designing and planning for this emergent order involves a shift in creativity from the design of fixed outcomes to the design of adaptive types, urban codes and the management of adaptive process. The city is not a machine but it is 'machinic' in the sense of a productive gearing of parts to each other; the city is not an organism but it emerges as self-organized whole; the city is not work of art but if we can better understand these forms of emergent urbanism then one of the characteristics that emerges is a potent aesthetic dimension that is geared at once to its sociality, spatiality and productivity.

References

Alexander, C. 1996 (1965). *A City is not a Tree*, in R. LeGates, and F. Stout (eds), *The City Reader*, London: Routledge, 118–31.

Appadurai, A. 2002. Deep Democracy, *Public Culture*, 14, 21–47.

Bayat, A. 1997. *Street Politics*, New York: Columbia University Press.

Davis, M. 2006. *Planet of Slums*, London: Verso.

DeLanda, M. 2006. *A New Philosophy of Society*, New York: Continuum.

DeLanda, M. 2011. *Philosophy and Simulation*, New York: Continuum.

Deleuze, G. and Guattari, F. 1987. *A Thousand Plateaus*, London: Athlone.

Dovey, K. 2010. *Becoming Places*, London: Routledge.

Dovey, K. 2011. Uprooting Critical Urbanism, *City*, 15 (3/4), 347–54.

Dovey, K. 2012. Informal Settlement and Complex Adaptive Assemblage, *International Development Planning Review*, 34 (3), 371–90.

Dovey, K. and King, R. 2011. Forms of Informality, *Built Environment*, 37, 11–29.

Dovey, K. and King, R. 2012. Informal Urbanism and the Taste for Slums, *Tourism Geographies*, 14 (2), 275–93.

Durand-Lasserve, A. and Royston, L. 2002. Introduction, in A. Durand-Lasserve and L.Royston (eds), *Holding Their Ground*, London: Earthscan, 1–34.

Geddes, P. 1915. *Cities in Evolution*, London: Williams & Norgate.

Gunderson, L. and Holling, C. (eds) 2002. *Panarchy*, Washington, Island Press.

Harvey, D. 1982. *The Limits to Capital*, Oxford, Blackwell.

Hernandez, F. and Kellett, P. 2010. Introduction, in F. Hernandez, P. Kellett and L. Allen (eds), *Rethinking the Informal City*, New York: Berghahn, 1–19.

Jacobs, J. 1965. *The Death and Life of Great American Cities*, Harmondsworth: Penguin.

Marshall, S. 2009. *Cities, Design and Evolution*, London: Routledge.

McFarlane, C. 2011. *Learning the City*, Oxford: Wiley-Blackwell.

Portugali, J. 2000. *Self-Organization and the City*, Berlin: Springer.

Roy, A. 2004. 'The Gentleman's City', in A. Roy and N. Alsayyad, N. (eds), *Urban Informality*, New York: Lexington, 147–70.

Roy, A. 2009. Civic Governmentality, *Antipode*, 41, 159–79.

Roy, A., and Alsayyad, N. (eds) 2004. *Urban Informality*, New York: Lexington.

UN-Habitat 2006. *The State of The World's Cities*, London: Earthscan.

Walker, B. and Salt, D. 2006. *Resilience Thinking*, Washington: Island Press.

Chapter 7

The City Seen:
Strategies of Coherence, Evocation and
Simulation in Urban Representation

William Uricchio

The premise of this chapter is simple: our ideas of the city, of the urban as a space, process and condition, are bound up in our modes of representation. Those modes, like representational regimes generally, articulate ways of seeing, giving "the seen" shape and form. And at the same time, they serve as evidence of ways of seeing, offering insights into the shifting conceptual frameworks that societies use to make sense of the world around them. From the last quarter of the nineteenth century through to the present, the proliferation of new technologies of seeing coincided with rapid transformations of the city, providing an opportunity to reflect on the larger processes of mediation between the city and its image, shifting the focus from the thing seen to the manner of seeing, and in the process revealing something about the frameworks through which we image—and imagine—the city.[1]

I would like briefly to consider a series of representational trends in the moving image depiction of the city, of urban space and event. In particular, I'd like to look, first, at non-fiction city films and filmed panoramas through the first decade of the twentieth century (c.1895–1920), moving images that served as the culmination of nineteenth century photographic and painterly representational practices. Second, I'll consider the so-called city symphonies of the 1920s and 1930s, films that embraced an aesthetic of the "camera eye" and sought to depict the city in a self-referential manner as an experiential kaleidoscope. And finally, I will discuss time-based city images from the end of the twentieth century into the start of our own, as manifest in algorithmic simulations of urban space and event. Although I will argue for distinct conventions or "regimes" of representation throughout, I do so fully aware of the coexistence of multiple representational traditions within such a relatively short time period. By underscoring what I see as dominant trends, I do not in any way want to deny the rich complexity that characterizes our representational environment.

Far more than a (mere) repository of urban images and thus an unwritten history of the urban encounter, the traditions I will sketch offer a shifting set of metaphors, visual organizing instruments, as well as evidence of a perceptual order based on the logics of spatial articulation. The issue is not so much the documentation of *what* visual data the images hold (although that is certainly both considerable and valuable), but rather evidence of *how* makers and viewers related to the larger world. What might we find if we step back and viewed the distinctive patterns of moving image representation and use?

Spatial and Temporal Coherence: Mapping the City

"Panorama" and "panoramic views" by title constitute the single largest entry among films copyrighted in the United States between 1896 and 1912, with the preponderance of titles referring to films registered before 1906. These films offer boat-mounted views of waterfronts; carriage-drawn shots of passing storefronts, pedestrians, and traffic; street-level tilting shots of skyscrapers, emulating a tourist's gaze; and lateral documentation of the city skyline from the tops of those same skyscrapers, as the camera pivots from

---

1　This chapter draws heavily upon and reworks an earlier article: William Uricchio, "Imag(in)ing the City: Simonides to the Sims" from *Cities in Transition*, edited by Andrew Webber and Emma Wilson. Copyright © 2008 Andrew Webber and Emma Wilson. Reprinted with permission of Columbia University Press.

a single, fixed point, covering up to 360 degrees. While some of these films deal with scenic natural vistas, the preponderance record urban landscapes from New York to Tokyo and serve as a dynamic repository of the early twentieth-century city. The last decades of the nineteenth century and first of the twentieth saw the rapid urbanization in the U.S. and western Europe, with cities from Berlin to Minneapolis doubling and even tripling in size within the space of a decade. This wondrous (and traumatic) transformation gave the city a centrality in media and the popular imagination that was manifest in abundant urban imagery, as well as literature and social surveys (thanks to the coincident rise of sociology as a discipline).

For some, these films attest to the "naïve" fascination with movement of any kind that allegedly graced the film medium's first years. For others, they stand as evidence of the early entrepreneurial organization of production, with itinerant cameramen trading in views and catering to audiences in search of sensation and an expanded view of the world. And for still others, they suggest continuities with precedent still photographic practice, replicating the vantage points and even catalogue descriptions of the postcards and views so popular at the end of the nineteenth century. I'd like to argue that these films can be seen as the fulfilment of a project mapped out in earlier, mass-deployed, non-moving image systems such as the panorama and the stereoscope. Rather than the naïve first steps of a new medium, these films represent the culmination of a much longer representational tradition, and a translation into coherent slices of time and space of that which could only previously be suggested through static compositional conceits. This highly ordered representational strategy embodied a way of seeing and, I would assert, of experiencing the rapid and often chaotic transformations in the urban landscape.

Panoramic city films explored space in many different ways—horizontally, vertically, and by tracking shots. Moreover, they charted the texture of movement itself, in the process offering new pleasures and presences than had been available to the painted or photographed static panorama. Filmed panoramas—horizontal or vertical or forward tracking—usually maintained time and space relations in a rigorously continuous manner. The emphasis on the act of seeing, on the unfolding of space in a manner that encourages the viewer to feel "really on the spot" links these films with Barker's initial appeal in his 1787 patent for a 360-degree painting, originally entitled "*la nature à coup d'oeil*" or "nature at a glance."[2]

Rather than simply presenting a wide expanse as had sixteenth- and seventeenth-century city portraitists, Barker's panorama stressed the construction of a particular way of seeing. Said Barker, "The idea is entirely new, and the effect, produced by fair perspective, a proper point of view, and unlimiting the bounds of the Art of Painting." Like some of today's amusements in London's *Trocadero* or Los Angeles' *Disneyland*, Barker conceived of elaborate strategies to lure the viewer into seeing in a particular way. The expiration of Barker's patent in 1801 opened the way for a host of other entrepreneurs to explore the "panopticon of nature." Although far removed from the original "nature at a glance," the continued deployment of the term "panorama" retained an insistence on the act of seeing linking it to the *quality* and not the *object* of what is seen. Our contemporary usage has tended to dull this connection with the act of seeing, instead shifting attention to the graphic parameters of representation, as the latest panoramic format snapshots attest. Within a decade of Barker's introduction of the term panorama, it was being used in book titles to refer to comprehensive coverage—for example, *The Political Panorama* (1801), *The Panorama of Youth* (1806), and *Literary Panorama* (1806).[3]

One might wonder why films constituted largely by forward tracking shots were included within the same conceptual realm as traditional panoramas, since one of the fundamental characteristics of the painted panorama (360-degree or moving) regards the image's fixed distance from the spectator. The forward track, moving towards the vanishing point, would seem to shift the *extensive* relations mapped out by the traditional panorama to a set of *intensive* relations—an ever closer inspection of spaces first seen at a distance. I suggest

---

2   A copy of Barker's 1787 patent may be found at http://www.edvec.ed.ac.uk/html/projects/panorama/barker.html/.

3   This is not to deny that the term panorama also referred to the object seen. In 1842, the *Illustrated London News* began to market in print form the kinds of images of nature, exotic locations, and epic events that for the previous 50 years had been institutionalized in the panorama. Shortly after its start, the *News* published an etched, two-page version of Antoine Claudet's "collosseum view" photograph of London (7 January 1843). But while image was marketed as a collector's item, the metaphoric dimensions of the shift from one site of seeing (the panorama) to another (the illustrated press) remain striking.

that such films were consistent with Baker's original use of the term, and that moreover, this underscores the notion of the continuity of space that underlies the filmed panorama's deployment.

But perhaps more to the point, the films also seem to have served as explorations of the space mapped out by another late nineteenth century rage—the stereoscope. The illusory third dimension evoked in the stereoscope and responsible for its status as one of the most important elements of pre-cinematic mass visual culture, is entered and probed by these films. These films occupy a cross-point between the two very different experiences of spatial continuity mapped out by the panorama and the stereograph. And in so doing, they are consistent with a larger understanding of time, space and the world that had not changed much since Newton's pronouncements. The same grand ordering principles served as the point of reference for all of these technologies, so it is not surprising that their projects were fundamentally related. Correlations might even be drawn to the grand narratives so characteristic of nineteenth century sociological representations of the city: consider the unified explanatory paradigms of Henry Sumner Maine (law); Adna Weber (location); Fustel de Coulanges (religion); and Karl Marx (production). Like the stereograph, panorama, or panoramic film, they privilege particular parameters of representation, charting the world viewed through that lens in a systematic and expansive manner. While the notion that panoramic city films resonate with the city's great structuralist thinkers goes beyond the bounds of this chapter, the two domains partake equally in Barker's notion of the importance of the quality of seeing in a particular manner.

Fragmentation and Evocation: City Symphonies

Even as the film medium took form, and throughout the years when the mapping strategies just described dominated film production, change was afoot in the larger world. The scientific domain of physics, and with it the understanding of how the world worked and the inexorably linked project of how the world was represented, was in a growing state of crisis (consider the work of Mach, Heisenberg, and Einstein); in sociology, grand narratives gave way to the interaction-based, multi-variable models of Georg Simmel, Max Weber, and the Chicago School (Park, McKenzie and Wirth); and in painting, the tradition of realism was under siege by impressionists, cubo-futurists, and expressionists, all exploring new ways of giving form to their experience.

In sharp contrast to the previous representational tradition's concern with mapping, with tracing spatio-temporal continuities, with their intertwined notions of the city as a space and the medium as a window on the world, a new generation of moving images shattered that window and reassembled the pieces in order to give form to their notion of the city as experience. Skewed perspective and violent changes in scale, simultaneous perception of different sites and objects, multiple points of view of surging masses and buildings, the imposition of rhythms and accentuation of formal elements, all served as the vocabulary that artists, photographers and filmmakers drew upon for their evocation of a new experience.

More radical than even the painterly tradition of the Cubists or Italian Futurists, the efforts of Dada photomonteurs such as Hanna Hoch, John Heartfield, Paul Citroen, and Raoul Hausmann literally fragmented the photographic surface, and with it any claims the medium might have had to a coherent epistemology, recomposing the shards into new compositions, and freely mixing scraps of time, space, and perspective (Citroen's 1923 montage, *Metropolis I*, is emblematic in this regard). Powerful assumptions regarding the photographic image's indexicality were confronted, subverted, and in the process, newly constructed images foreground their own mediality in powerful ways unavailable to painters.

City films begin to pick up on this strategy with Paul Strand and Charles Sheeler's *Manhatta* (1921), a film constructed around radical shifts in angle and perspective, explicitly informed by the compositional conceits of the cubo-futurists, with whom Sheeler had extensive roots. Lázló Moholy-Nagy's *Dynamic of the Metropolis: Sketch for a Film also Typophoto*, written in 1921–22 and published in 1925 (*Bauhausbucher* 8), served as a manifesto for a more far-reaching vision of the experiential articulation of the city than *Manhatta*. Although never realized as a film, Moholy-Nagy's project envisioned a city film that sustained over time the temporal contradictions, compressions, and juxtapositions suggested in photomontage. Moholy-Nagy packed his "sketch" with all of elements that would reappear several years later in the city symphonies: sharply contrasting compositions, the explicit invocation of temporal markings (tempo, fortissimo), and an embrace of the notion of *gesamtkunstwerk*. And, since the sketch was never filmed but only appeared in printed form, he also pressed the medium of print into his vision of urban experience through the use of creative typography.

But the *locus classicus* of this new way of representing the city appeared in 1927 with Walther Ruttmann's *Berlin: Sinfonie einer Grossstadt*. With roots in the post-Expressionist realist art movement, *die neue Sachlichkeit*, and informed by the work of photomonteurs, *Berlin*, like Moholy-Nagy's sketch before it, departed from traditional notions of narrative and instead relied on the structure of a day in the city. The film evokes the city as a palimpsest of rhythms, experiences, and scales, in the process, rigorously excluding the vistas, monuments, skylines, and axial perspective characteristic of the urban post card trade, the stereographs and films that dominated the earlier representational tradition. One of the striking things that Berlin reveals, and that Dziga Vertov was quick to pick up on in his 1929 *The Man with a Movie Camera*, was a sense of the acoustical. Although these, along with other city films sharing in the same basic project such as Eugen Deslaw's *La Nuit Electrique* (1930) and Wilfried Basse's *Markt am Wittenbergplatz* (1928) were silent films, they evoked sound as much through visual reference to sound sources (telephones, radios, bells, steam whistles, car horns), as through an awareness of the image's potential to engender a sense of synaesthesia in its viewers. Significantly, both Ruttmann and Vertov were early experimenters with radio, with Ruttmann's 1930 sound collage, *Weekend*, serving as an acoustical counterpart to his *Berlin* film. From this perspective, the nomenclature of *city symphony* captures both the reference and technique of the many usually silent films clustered at the end of the 1920s and start of the 1930s that understood the city in musical terms ranging from rhythms to cacophony. That this historical juncture also witnessed the introduction of sound into film and the mass acceptance of radio as a medium with its own distinct representational parameters helps to situate this dramatic shift in the city's cinematic depiction.

The project of these non-fiction films has little to do with recording or documenting urban space, or with creating a sense "as if being on the spot," at least with regards to physical location. Instead, they offer an instrument for evoking the city as dynamic, and like the modernist project generally, they offer insights into a perceptual order that embraced the materiality of the medium both as a means and end. Experience of the city as the ebb and flow of competing forces and perspectives, as complexity and contradiction (to echo Robert Venturi's notion of the modern), emerges as its defining character. The visual landmarks of famous buildings or well-established vistas that distinguished Paris from Berlin from New York for an earlier generation of image-makers are here abandoned, and with them, even the stability of orientation and representation provided by simple panoramas, tracking shots, and tilts. The camera eye, seeing sights, assembling rhythms, and constructing myriad juxtapositions, constructs a very different subjectivity from that bound up in the stable, single viewing position of the panoramic tradition. Indeed, it is an impossible viewing position, or at least a viewing position that is impossible to humanly embody or literalize "as if being on the spot." It evokes the richness of experience and the dynamic of the metropolis in ways that fundamentally redefine the notion of the city to be documented, in the process calling upon distinctively modernist deployments of the medium.

Simulation: Games and Augmented Reality

The digital turn has enabled a litany of well-rehearsed possibilities in the domain of representation, though it continues to surprise with its networked affordances and its blurring of the line between production and consumption. Terms such as "virtual" and "interactive" have acquired fresh meanings, and the logics of remediation have resulted in a tension between on one hand, a repurposing of the new in the framework of the old, and on the other, the exploration of new and as yet unformulated expressive capacities. If one accepts the repurposing argument, one can certainly find ample evidence of digital technologies being used to support all of the visions discussed in this chapter. The panorama, and with it the notion of a coherent block of time and space accessible from a unified subject position, can be found anywhere from online 360-degree views of existing cities that the viewer can control, to game spaces such as *Grand Theft Auto* where one's character inhabits a seamless imaginary urban environment. And the notion of a reflexive and evocative experience representing multiple and conflicting points of view (the city symphony approach) can be found in the rhizomic structures of the internet, where hundreds of thousands of competing visual perspectives of a given city link together through social tagging and compete for our attention in domains such as Google Image Search, Flickr and Photosynth.

Downloadable applications such as Photosynth, to take one example, aggregate hundreds of location-tagged photographs into a near-seamless whole, providing a visual space that the viewer can navigate in three dimensions. But moves beyond the project of the city symphony in offering ways to consider such issues as collaborative authorship of the image, unstable points of view, and the repositioning of subject-object relationships. Points of uniqueness are sought out and built upon by the program's algorithms—and not those perceived by the viewer. The viewer is in turn free to explore an extensive and dynamic image-space unconstrained by (and indeed, without access to) an authorized or "correct" viewing position (in contrast to the strict perspectival regimes of the early city films. Other examples, such as certain augmented reality (AR) applications, work by "recognizing" particular spaces and, through the use of computationally enhanced viewing screens, superimposing new images over real space. In this case, a system of virtual spatial annotation depends upon the "correct" positioning of the viewer (and portable computing device) in the world. The virtual image gives the viewer access to an encoded and location-based domain of signification, augmenting her encounters with the world and potentially transforming the meaning of its sights. This situation-dependent experience stands in direct contrast to the fixed and linear evocative strategies of the "city symphonies." The two examples of Photosynth and AR stand in a rough reciprocal relationship, one loosening our spatial moors and leaving us to wander within a deep, wide and constantly changing image-space ripe with multiple meanings; the other using the requirements of the image to fix our physical place, offering overlays of information and specific meaning. Both cases turn on differing notions of algorithmic intermediation, a reconfiguration of subject-object relations, and new dynamics for the generation of meaning and value.[4]

These deployments might be read as repurposing old technologies (e.g., photography) to serve new purposes, but the fit by no means offers a one-to-one correspondence with earlier textual instantiations. Significant differences in agency, for example, reposition apparent similarities in concept and graphic form; and the weight of history bears heavily upon the accrued meanings of a particular application or expressive tradition. While the panoramic webcam or dynamically assembled photomontage might seem the formal equivalents of much older analogue practices, such fundamental contextual repositioning renders these examples perhaps referential, but ultimately quite distinct in meaning and implication. The alternative to the repurposing scenario, the exploration of new and as yet unformulated expressive capacities, offers a more promising approach. And it seems capable of drawing upon and activating previous representational traditions, rather than simply claiming radical novelty. I would like briefly to exemplify two very different directions that these (moving image) technologies can take, both regarding the city and its (possible) memory. Berlin-based Art + Com's *The Invisible Shape of Things Past* (1995) offers an exploration of the representation of time in virtual space and the navigation through time in virtual reality.[5] The project enables users to transform historical film sequences (time-based information) into interactive, seemingly three-dimensional virtual objects. These objects, in turn, are positioned on flat maps representing a particular time and space (say, Berlin, 1920). One can immediately see the various films made of the city over a certain period of time as a set of spatialized objects occupying an otherwise flat map.

The transformation of cinematic images into virtual objects is based on the visual parameters of a particular film sequence (movement, perspective, focal length): the individual frames of the film are lined up along the path of the camera as it is transferred to virtual space. The angle of the individual frames in relation to the virtual camera-path depends on the perspective of the actual camera. The outer pixel rows of the frames defines the skin of the film object, thus rendering a simple tracking shot into something like a shoebox with a photographic image (the opening frame) on one end. Navigating into the image, the tracking shot begins, running its course until the viewer is deposited on the other side of the "box." A fixed-point 360-degree

---

4   I have written about these applications elsewhere, and so will not develop them here. My point is simply to include them as exemplary of a larger shift in how we represent and understand the city, consistent with those examples that I will develop. William Uricchio, "The Algorithmic Turn: photosynth, augmented reality and the changing implications of the image".

5   http://www.artcom.de/en/projects/project/detail/the-invisible-shape-of-things-past-1/.

panoramic film in this system would look more like a wheel of cheese. A mapping protocol is available that permits the user to stack the accumulated images produced year by year over any period of time and chart patterns of interest and intersection. Comparing, say, a map from 1920 with one from 1940 shows the persistence of Unter den Linden as a site of interest, allows users to compare and contrast both physical points of view and the impact of historical developments on the street and its buildings, and serves as a robust tool for assessing cultural trends and archival holdings. Meanwhile, a virtual information architecture is also available that permits us to step inside the image box, and to see inside the walls of filmed objects, experiencing space and representation in heretofore unimaginable ways. The implications of this latter tool for notions of point of view are intriguing.

The meta-view of a city's film history afforded by *The Invisible Shape of Things Past* both draws upon past signifying practices, indeed, literally re-calling them, and at the same time re-casts them and their significance. Like the earlier shift from coherent swaths of panoramic time and space and a fixed notion of the subject, to the symphonic evocation of the city as a fragmented and multiply embodied experience, this latest turn in representational conventions offers a new metaphoric vocabulary through which to order our memories and perceptions, and new tools through which we can variously manipulate and understand an accreted visual history and evolving present. And this latest turn attests to a new way of seeing, at once unarticulated by previous deployments of the moving image, and consistent with the larger shift in cultural perception, as argued by the likes of Deleuze, Virilio and Baudrilliard (to mention but one line of assessment).

Of course, other approaches abound, each in their own way making use of the new technologies' affordances and charting out new possibilities. *SimCity 3000: World Edition*, a computer game, for example, offers historical moments in four "real" cities as a simulation laboratory for the user to construct and manipulate conditions, playing God as the crude contours of a historical moment are replayed, this time with new variables. Thus, *SimCity Berlin* puts the viewer in the unenviable position of being a kind of Helmut Kohl: will the wall come down? Will it stay down? Will peace and prosperity reign? The ability to inhabit a city space in the subjunctive, to explore the implications of various choices and interventions, again offers a new tool through which to explore and, in a sense, test, various urban scenarios.

Although the present situation is in part supported by new technologies, we have seen that media technologies are ultimately not determining. So, for example, the shift from the panoramic city film to the city symphony was largely based on the same silent 35mm film technology; just as saliently, as the early work of Baudrillard, Deleuze, et al. demonstrates, key components of the current representational change were already in play well before the public appearance of digital affordances. Instead, I have tried to point to the distinctive temporalities, spatialities, and notions of experience and event that can be found in the last hundred or so years of non-fiction moving image representations of the city. Although the sites seen in New York, Paris or Berlin certainly differ, the accreted modes of seeing, of representing and fixing experience, have much in common within each of these clusters.

Representation offers a way to trace the fundamental concepts underlying and informing a distinctively historical manner of being in the world. Donald Lowe's *History of Bourgeois Perception* (1982) comes to mind, though Lowe's scope is obviously far more ambitious and his insights wider ranging. In each of the cases that I've briefly sketched, we've seen clusters of representational strategies that differ in their notions of viewing position (from unified, to multiple, to a kind of algorithmically enabled agency), their deployments of media (from "being there," to experiential evocation, to simulated interaction), their notions of time and space (coherent, fractured and relative, virtual), and even their aesthetic assumptions (from the contemplative and sublime, to the reflexive and modernist, to what for the moment might be summarized as algorithmic and programmatic, though this is a contentious stance). This approach admittedly risks missing or over-writing the specificity of individual texts, a task taken up by many other chapters in this collection; but it has the advantage of encouraging us to reflect upon a body of representation in terms of its metaphoric capacities. It calls attention to the larger ordering strategies that give public memory its contours. And it offers a way to move beyond what is seen in order to consider a way of seeing or being in the world.

References

Bousquet, Henri and Redi, Riccardo 1988. Pathé Frères. Les films de la production Pathé 1896–1914, *Quaderni di Cinema*, 37.

Foucault, Michel 1979. *Discipline and Punish: The Birth of the Prison*, New York: Vintage Books.

Lowe, Donald 1982. *A History of Bourgeois Perception*, Chicago, IL: The University of Chicago Press.

Moholy-Nagy, Lázló 1925. *Painting, Photography, Film*, Bauhaus Book No. 8; trans. Janet Seligman, Cambridge, MA: MIT Press, 1973.

Quintilian, *Institutio Oratoria* (Institutes of Oratory 95CD).

Uricchio, William 2011. The Algorithmic Turn: Photosynth, augmented reality and the changing implications of the image. *Visual Studies*, 26(1), 25–35.

Yates, Frances 1966. *The Art of Memory*, Chicago, IL: The University of Chicago Press.

PART II
Processes of Planning and Urban Change

Chapter 8
Social Capital in the Age of Megacities and the Knowledge Economy[1]

Hans Westlund

Introduction

Many industries, in particular knowledge-intense industries in their first stages of development, seem to be concentrated in certain clusters of megacities. What are the driving forces for such a development and what is the role of social capital in these spatially concentrated growth processes of the knowledge economy? What is the role of social capital in the theories that aim to explain phenomena such as clusters and innovation systems? This chapter discusses these and other questions connected to social capital and megacities.

Social capital is here defined as *social, non-formalized networks that are filled by the networks' nodes/ actors with norms, values, preferences and other social attributes and characteristics*. An important feature of this definition is that it distinguishes between the networks and the norms, values and preferences that are distributed in the networks:

> Social capital is considered as a type of infrastructure with nodes and links. The nodes consist of individuals and organizations, which establish links between each other. The construction of links is governed by the individuals'/organizations' norms, preferences and attitudes, which can thus prevent emergence of links between individuals or organizations as well. In the links, different types of information are distributed between the nodes. From an infrastructure perspective, this distribution of information can be compared with traffic in the transport infrastructure. Social capital's impact on society depends on both its quality and quantity. The norms, preferences and attitudes of the nodes, and thereby the kind of information being distributed in the links, is at least as important as is the number of links. A 'strong' social capital can thus have preservative as well as progressive effects, depending on its qualitative characteristics. (Westlund 2006: 6)

Throughout history, space and social capital have affected each other in both cumulative and counteractive ways. *Physical* space, expressed in distance, has in general contributed to the forming of divergent social capitals within groups separated in space. The social capital of groups has been a prerequisite for group cohesion, which in its turn has reduced interaction between groups already separated by space. On the other hand, when a group or organization has been spread out in space, its social capital has contributed to diminishing the role of space in shaping and reshaping social capital. Thus, we can distinguish between social capital as a proximity-strengthening, internalizing factor and social capital as a network-building, externalizing factor, over-bridging space.

Social space, expressed in ethnicity, religion, class, etc. is in many cases an original result of physical space. The forming of in particular ethnic groups have been processes where distance has played a crucial role. However, class division is much more of a purely social process in which, if physical distance between classes occurs, it has been the result and not the cause. In the case of social space, social capital has been a fundamental prerequisite behind the cohesion of social groups and their delimitation from each other—but establishment of "critical links" between groups has also contributed to mutual understanding and conflict

---

1   This chapter is an updated and shortened version of Chapter 4 of Hans Westlund's book *Social Capital in the Knowledge Economy: Theory and Empirics* (Springer 2006), 39–50, © Springer-Verlag Berlin Heidelberg 2006. The text is published with kind permission of Springer Science+Business Media.

reduction. Thus, in the case of social space, we can distinguish between social capital as an "intra-action"-promoting, i.e. internalizing factor and social capital as an interaction-promoting, externalizing factor.

This dual role of social capital—under certain circumstances promoting spatial and group internal cohesion, under other circumstances contributing to link-building that promote spatial interaction across physical and social borders—makes social capital a much more complicated factor than the trust-building, transaction-cost-reducing factor often assumed in the modern literature. In the spatial perspective, certain component parts of social capital work internalizing and are governed by the actors in that locality/region, and other component parts give access to externalities which the local/regional actors cannot govern. A similar conclusion can be drawn from the firm's perspective. The internal social capital of a firm is formed by its management and employees and for its survival there are strong incentives to internalize firm-specific knowledge—but by location decisions and other investment the firm also builds links and relations to gain access to externalities such as knowledge and information.

From the perspective of the spatial concentration of firms and their connections to each other and other actors, the character and composition of firms' internal social capital is the first important factor. The basic activities of the firm, its type of production and products, its possession of (partial or temporary) product monopolies, its need for the input of knowledge and information, its position in formal ownership, supplier-customer networks or other dependencies, etc.—all these characteristics contribute to the firm's internalization and externalization of different actions. A firm with a great need to keep its tacit knowledge internalized—and with the resources to generate new knowledge internally—has low incentives to interact with other firms outside regular market transactions. A firm tied up in formal networks might not even be permitted to engage in certain interaction external to the network. On the other hand, a group of independent firms whose activities complement each other has very strong incentives to share knowledge and cooperate in R&D. Thus, a firm's activities, its ownership and other dependencies govern its opportunity to gain from and need to use the externalities of an agglomeration—and accordingly its location decisions. The firm forms its social capital in accordance with these needs and the social capital becomes a factor that supports and reinforces the firm's positions on the internalization–externalization scale. In this way, the firm's internal social capital is a reflected image of its external social capitals.

On the highest level of spatial agglomerations, megacities, the decisive social capitals are (1) the internal social capital of the megacity, i.e. firms' and other actors' proximity-related social capital, and (2) the social networks between the megacity's actors and the rest of the world. By definition, the internal social capital of megacities and other agglomerations must be stronger than the external—otherwise the agglomeration would be dissolved, or preserved by other forces than the social.

Externalities

The kinds of phenomena that in the economic literature are called *externalities* are the fundamental reason for a firm's choice of location and other investment in social capital. The concept of externalities dates back to Marshall (1920 [1890]) and has since then been considered as one of the most elusive and hard-formalized in the economic literature (Scitovsky 1954). Sraffa (1926) considered externalities as the only source of increasing returns under perfect competition and claimed that although externalities are external to the firm they are internal to the industry (cf. the spatial perspective above).

Based on Scitovsky's (1954) classification of externalities as either pecuniary or technological, Johansson (2004) has made a fundamental distinction between firms' *intra-market* and *extra-market* externalities. Intra-market externalities are mediated through the formation of prices, while extra-market externalities comprise links, agreements, networks and other club-like arrangements, but also information and knowledge spillovers, denominated communication externalities by Fujita and Thisse (2002). It should be noted that the establishment of links, networks, etc. are deliberate actions of a firm with the aim of internalizing transactions within the network that otherwise would have been market transactions, while the spillover externalities may be both a result of deliberate aims and unintended byproducts. Johansson (2004) also makes a difference between *proximity* externalities, within an urban region or district, and *link* externalities, being more or less distance independent. Links can be established both inside and between regions; in the latter case they are substitutes to proximity.

Several concepts have been formulated to describe and analyze the proximity- or link-based interaction between individual firms and other actors producing externalities. Here we focus on two of them. *Cluster*, a concept with a number of slightly different interpretations, has, through Porter (1990), received an enormous amount of attention in both research and policy circles. Clusters are often defined as spatially delimited industrial systems regardless of the size of the enterprises (Paniccia 2002). Much of the cluster literature, based on Porter (1990) treats clusters as purely a spatial concentration of related firms (see e.g. Enright 1998), while Porter later (1998, 2000) explicitly includes public institutions, such as government educational institutions and support services, in the definition of clusters. The vast popularity of the concept, not least in industrial policies, has resulted in "cluster" becoming become a possible denomination of almost any agglomeration of economic activity.

The term cluster sets the focus on inter-firm relations. As Johansson (2004) points out, the external relations of a firm can be of an intra- or extra-market character. The latter can be divided in two forms: (1) organized transaction-link externalities (with club characteristics) where knowledge exchange can be a deliberate aim of the relation, and (2) spillover externalities. These inter-firm spillovers can be horizontal, between similar firms imitating each other or in other ways taking advantage of the spillover externalities in "the air." But spillovers between firms in a megacity or other form of cluster can also be vertical, between an input-buying firm and its suppliers or between an input-selling firm and its customer firms. In both directions, the knowledge spillovers are byproducts of the market interaction.

While the term cluster has mainly been used for local and regional relations between firms, the concept of *innovation systems* was originally formulated for systems at a *national* level and denoted not only inter-firm relations but also links between firms and government, firms and research institutions or between all three of them. It was used for the first time by Freeman (1987) in his analysis of the economic development of Japan after World War II, where government, especially the Ministry of Industry and Trade (MITI) played a crucial role.

In the last decades the concept of *regional* innovation systems (RIS) has yielded a rapidly increasing literature (see e.g. Cooke 1992, 2001, 2003, De la Mothe and Paquet 1998, Asheim and Gertler 2004, Doloreux and Parto 2004, etc.). The regional approach on innovation systems is based on two main bodies. The first is the national innovation systems approach, based on evolutionary, non-equilibrium theories and in which innovation is a result of processes both internal and external to the firm. These processes are not only technical and economic but also social. *Learning*, through interaction, is a key concept in the innovation processes. The second body of literature is that of regional milieu, embeddedness and the role of proximity.

Formalized and Non-Formalized Interactions

The two approaches, very briefly summed up above, have one thing clearly in common: the focus on *spatial interaction* where firms are involved.

Although not always explicitly expressed, the two approaches also have something else in common, namely their acknowledgment of externalities in the form of *transfer of* (tacit) *knowledge* or *knowledge spillovers, emergence of new knowledge* and (collective) *learning* as a primary outcome of the interaction. It is in these knowledge creating and transfer processes that social capital constitutes a ubiquitous but multifaceted factor.

Following Johansson (2004) we can assume that knowledge transfers and collective learning take place through two types of processes:

1. Deliberate, formalized transaction-links, agreements, networks and other club-like arrangements between firms and firms and other actors.
2. Unintended knowledge spillovers between firms or between firms and other actors, caused by non-formalized interactions. These kinds of interactions consist of (a) vertical technical/economic interactions between firms and their suppliers and/or customers, (b) spin-offs of new firms from existing ones and turnover and exchange on the labor market, (c) horizontal interaction in the form of informal exchange of information and knowledge in the (local/regional) civil society, between individuals connected to firms or other actors.

In the first case, that of formalized transaction-links and networks, the formalization is in itself a confirmation of the firm's willingness to invest in a link with a longer duration than a pure market transaction. In contrast to the "conventional wisdom" on (spatial) clusters, the reasons for the emergence of these fixed links/networks are not the firm's wish to enjoy informal knowledge and information spillovers and other outcomes of flexible inter-actor interactions—but to *internalize* knowledge within the fixed network, often a corporate grouping. McCann and Arita claim that the cluster type of Silicon Valley is more of an exception which should not be generalized, and that the internalizing "industrial complex" type of cluster is "… typical of many firms and sectors, and in particular, of the semiconductor industry" (McCann and Arita 2004: 247). In this case, knowledge spillovers within the delimited industrial complex are internalities for the industrial complex, but still extra-market externalities for the individual firms; externalities that are both formalized and institutionalized.

It can be assumed that the motives for a link-investment are completely based on economic considerations, but the outcome of this "long-term" investment is among other things dependent on the social relations between the actors who establish, use and maintain the link. With negative attitudes to the link among these actors, incentives to use the link would be lower, and the link would yield lower returns than in the case of neutral or positive attitudes. Thus, it is in the interest of all the actors who invest in the link or network to establish a positive social capital among its users.

In the second case, the non-formalized interactions consisted of three types, each of them being able to result in unintended knowledge spillovers. The first type, vertical, technical/economic interactions between firms and their suppliers and/or customers, is a similar process to that of intended links having unintended effects discussed above, although there is no formalized link but market transactions. The purpose of these transactions is to buy input or sell output, but as a byproduct spillovers of knowledge and information may occur between the involved actors. These spillovers do not necessarily have to happen through social interaction—it may be sufficient with purely technical/economic information, i.e. the information and knowledge "built-in" in a product, a complicated order or specialized demand.[2] But knowledge spillovers without social interaction between human beings have their limitations. They are one-way, one-occasion spillovers, entirely dependent on the internal absorption and learning capacity of the firm, without any informal external dialogue or support. As the relations between suppliers and customers as a rule are non-competitive in both directions, there are normally no reasons for the involved firms to regard informal links and positive attitudes to limited informal knowledge exchange as a threat. The conclusion is that social capital facilitates this non-competitive informal knowledge exchange and that this is normally in the interests of both (all) parts.

The second type of non-formalized interactions, spin-offs of new firms from existing firms or organizations and turnover and exchange on the labor market, are market interactions with obvious effects on the spread of knowledge and information. For a cluster these market interactions are likely to have positive effects similar to those of formalized networks, i.e. they tend to spread best-practice and raise competition and average productivity. For the individual firm, the effects are dependent on whether the interactions are vertical or horizontal, if the firms are leading or lagging, and on the time horizon.

Another form of non-formalized market interactions having an impact on knowledge spillovers is labor market turnover. On a perfect regional labor market, labor is distributed so that maximum productivity is achieved. On an imperfect labor market, the rule is: the larger the labor market, the better the matching. Workforce turnover is not only inflows and outflows of knowledge but also of social capital. Just as each firm has an incentive to optimize its blend of knowledge adapted to its activities, so it has an incentive to optimize its blend of social capital. A workforce with the optimum blend of social capital has the optimum amount and combination of external and internal links and values and attitudes adapted to the firm's activities. Such a workforce is more likely to be found in megacities and other spatial agglomerations of higher order. The conclusion is that labor market externalities consist not only of access to labor with the right knowledge but also the right social capital.

---

2   Japanese firms' "reverse engineering" up to about 1990 is an excellent example of *deliberate* knowledge spillovers, without social links, through study of products produced in the West. However, the learning processes in the Japanese firms were highly dependent on an *internal* social capital adapted to these tasks.

The Civil Society

The third and last type of informal knowledge spillovers is also the most intangible of the intangible externalities. The informal exchange of information and knowledge in the (local/regional) civil society, between individuals connected to firms or other actors, is a form of horizontal, extra-market interaction, whose extent and content is dependent on the size and diversity of the agglomeration, the types of economic activities located there and the existing social capital of the civil society. Most of these correlations are almost self-evident: the amount of knowledge increases with the agglomeration's size; the economic activities and their diversity influence the content of knowledge and information, etc. The factor whose connections to knowledge externalities need an expounded discussion is civil society's social capital.

A civil society is basically something that is formed and maintained by people during their non-productive time. Voluntary public and club activities and other leisure activities are also what civil society's social capital is focused upon. The networks and values of business life, i.e. of production, play a mainly hidden role in a civil society. In line with the fundamental differences between production and consumption, business life and civil society are based on different principles and belong to different spheres of human activities, with different networks and different norms and values. However, as the two spheres are populated to quite a considerable extent by the same people, i.e. the productive population, there are naturally certain informal interactions between them. These interactions can be divided into two types: (a) those mainly based of norms, values, attitudes, etc.; and (b) those where these values, etc. have developed into the links and networks of a group of individuals.

The first type of interaction comprises general approaches of the importance of "spirit" and similar attributes to the economic development of a region. Putnam's (1993, 2000) view of the impact of civic society on the economy and Florida's (2002) view of creativity as the factor constituting the important difference between a region's economic performance are examples of such spatially connected approaches. Also Schumpeter expressed opinions on the influence of the attitudes of a social environment towards entrepreneurship when he pointed out that:

> the reaction of the social environment against one who wishes to do something new ... any deviating conduct by a member of a social group is condemned, though in greatly varying degrees according as the social group is used to such conduct or not ... This opposition is stronger in primitive stages of culture than in others, but it is never absent. Even mere astonishment at the deviation, even merely noticing it, exercises a pressure on the individual. The manifestation of condemnation may even come to social ostracism and finally to physical prevention or to direct attack ... (Schumpeter 1934: 76–7)

It is reasonable to assume that the attitudes of the social environment that have an impact on the production environment in general are formed in interplay between the two spheres. A stable production sphere fosters stable attitudes in the civil society and vice versa. The old industrial regions of the world show up many examples of how this stability of business life and civil life created safe and predictable conditions for stable growth. On the other hand, when the industrial crisis came in the 1970s, these regions lacked the ability to change and, with Schumpeter's words, "do something new."

The other type of interaction in civil society with implications for business life is a result of the general values of the social environment, in which the values of communities, groups or sub-communities have developed into links and networks. While a community can in principle be based merely on some kind of shared values, the step towards the formation of informal networks of groups or sub-communities means more stable relations between certain actors of the community—and a way to partly avoid general opinion's reactions. A megacity as such provides a potential solution to the problem of gaining from the change-promoting elements of social capital and avoiding the restricting elements. This potential solution is based on the fact that megacities tend to foster the emergence of diverse groups and sub-communities, based on ethnicity, religion, industry and also interests. Florida (2002) and other scholars on creativity stress the importance of this tolerated diversity of megacities and regard the interfaces between these groups as an importance source of creativity, innovations and economic development.

Within a group or sub-community that is positive to innovations, an entrepreneur can find the support he needs to "do something new." Outside this sub-community, the entrepreneur can pick-up certain information and knowledge of other groups, being that this knowledge is not too tacit and internalized. In this way, a megacity can provide the entrepreneur with access to the social capital that support his activities the most, and provides the best access to useful tacit knowledge. At the same time individuals in the established industries can maintain their communities, with their values and networks, without being confronted with the new.

Tentative Conclusions

From the analysis above it is possible do draw some tentative conclusions.

There are a number of different reasons for firms to cluster and/or locate in megacities, from pure labor market reasons to the need to become embedded in an entrepreneurial environment, from a wish to internalize knowledge and R&D in a closed network of actors to a wish to gain from flexible inter-firm relations and knowledge spillovers. The current literature on clusters and similar phenomena has to a large extent focused on a few of these motives, mainly those related to tacit actor- or space-specific knowledge and its spillovers between firms and other actors. Even if we leave aside the pure market-related reasons for clustering in megacities, there are important reasons behind clustering that are seldom observed and analyzed. One such reason was found in McCann and Arita's (2004) study of semiconductor clusters: companies' needs to internalize vital tacit knowledge and R&D within a small group of close partners (and shut out potential competitors). Proximity facilitates not only external spillovers but also internalization.

It is highly probable that the individual firm will find several, even contradicting reasons for clustering in megacities. Regarding knowledge and information, the cluster may on the one hand give the opportunity to form closed partnerships in which vital tacit knowledge can be internalized. On the other hand, the firm may simultaneously be snapping up "semi-tacit" information and knowledge spillovers.

Both these motives are probably relevant for knowledge-intense industries; in which almost all investment consists of R&D and investment by definition is extremely sensitive to leaks of vital knowledge. Thus, each firm has strong incentives to internalize its vital knowledge to as few external actors as possible—and to bind these actors with strong ties. However, a firm also needs input of more general relevant information about the industry, and this information is fastest and most easily available through personal contacts, which in its turn is facilitated by proximity to these contacts. In this way, a megacity cluster has the potential to satisfy both these apparently contradicting needs of a firm.

The different motives for clustering contribute to the forming of different social capitals within firms, within formal or informal groups of actors and within megacities. What these social capitals have in common are a certain proportion of values and links that internalize specific knowledge and uphold the firm's/group's solidarity, *combined* with a certain proportion of values and links that make the external exchange of non-vital information possible. The respective shares of the internalizing and externalizing components are dependent upon a number of factors discussed above, such as the firm's size, type of production and its knowledge intensity, formal and informal external dependencies, the market, etc.

The knowledge being spilled over and exchanged in the processes analyzed above is to a varying degree tacit, i.e. it is partly non-formalized and dependent on informal links where attitudes and values govern both how it is generated and how and to which actors it is spread. In this way, social capital is a crucial factor in knowledge creation, knowledge internalization and intentional and unintentional knowledge exchange and spillovers.

Knowledge-intense industries in their first stages of development consist mainly of small firms with R&D as their main activity. Their smallness makes collaboration with other firms and research institutions a necessity. Firms in their stage of development are often dependent on public support in the form of R&D grants, venture capital etc. and public sector institutions may also act as the "demanding customer." Thus, the "golden triangle" of collaboration between companies, research institutions and government seems highly relevant to the success of these industries. This means that the growing industries of the knowledge economy have a need to develop a more complex social capital compared with established, traditional industries. This need seems easiest to fulfill in megacities.

References

Asheim, B. and Gertler, M. 2004. Understanding Regional Innovation Systems. In Fagerberg, J., Mowery, D. and Nelson, R. (eds), *Handbook of Innovation*. Oxford: Oxford University Press.

Cooke, P. 1992. Regional Innovation Systems: Competitive Regulation in the New Europe, *Geoforum*, vol. 23, 365–82.

Cooke, P. 2001. Regional Innovation Systems, Clusters, and the Knowledge Economy, *Industrial and Corporate Change*, vol. 10, 945–74.

Cooke, P. 2003. Regional Innovation and Learning Systems, Clusters, and Local and Global Value Chains. In Bröcker, J., Dohse, D. and Soltwedel, R. (eds), *Innovation Clusters and Interregional Competition*. Berlin, Heidelberg, New York: Springer.

De la Mothe, J. and Paquet, G. (eds) 1998. *Local and Regional Systems of Innovation*. Amsterdam: Kluwer.

Doloreux, D. and Parto, S. 2004. *Regional Innovation Systems: A Critical Synthesis*. Discussion Paper Series No. 2004-17, Maastricht: United Nations University, Institute for New Technologies.

Enright, M.J. 1998. Regional Clusters and Firm Strategy. In Chandler Jr., A.D., Sölvell, Ö. and Hagström, P. (eds), *The Dynamic Firm: The Role of Technology, Strategy, Organization and Regions*. Oxford: Oxford University Press, 315–42.

Florida, R. 2002. *The Rise of the Creative Class: And How It's Transforming Work, Leisure, Community and Everyday Life*. New York: Basic Books.

Freeman, C. 1987. *Technology and Economic Performance: Lessons from Japan*. London: Pinter Publishers.

Fujita, M. and Thisse, J.-F. 2002. *Economics of Agglomeration*. Cambridge: Cambridge University Press.

Johansson, B. 2004. *Parsing the Menagerie of Agglomeration and Network Externalities*. CESIS Electronic Working Paper Series, Paper No. 2. Available at: www.infra.kth.se/cesis/research/workpap.htm [accessed October 9, 2013].

Marcusen, A. 1999. Fuzzy Concepts, Scanty Evidence, Policy Distance: The Case for Rigour and Policy Relevance in Critical Regional Studies, *Regional Studies*, vol. 33, 869–84.

Marshall, A. 1920 (1880). *Principles of Economics: An Introductory Volume*, 8th edition 1920. London: Macmillan.

McCann, P. and Arita, T. 2004. Industrial Clusters and Regional Development: A Transaction-Costs Perspective on the Semiconductor Industry. In de Groot, H.L.F., Nijkamp, P. and Stough, R.R. (eds), *Entrepreneurship and Regional Economic Development: A Spatial Perspective*. Cheltenham: Edward Elgar, 225–51.

Paniccia, I. 2002. *Industrial Districts: Evolution and Competitiveness in Italian Firm*. Cheltenham: Edward Elgar.

Porter, M. 1990. *The Competitive Advantage of Nations*. Basingstoke: Macmillan.

Porter, M. 1998. Clusters and the New Economics of Competition. *Harvard Business Review*, vol. 76, November/December, 77–90.

Porter, M. 2000. Location, Clusters and Company Strategy. In Clark, G.L., Feldman, M.P. and Gertler, M.S. (eds), *The Oxford Handbook of Economic Geography*. Oxford: Oxford University Press, 253–74.

Putnam, R.D. 1993. *Making Democracy Work: Civic Traditions in Modern Italy*. Princeton, NJ: Princeton University Press.

Putnam, R.D. 2000. *Bowling Alone: The Collapse and Revival of American Community*. New York: Simon and Schuster.

Schumpeter, J.A. 1934. *The Theory of Economic Development*. Cambridge, MA: Harvard University Press.

Schumpeter, J.A. 1950. *Capitalism, Socialism, and Democracy*. 3rd edition. New York: Harper.

Scitovsky, T. 1954. Two Concepts of External Economies, *Journal of Political Economy*, vol. 62, 143–51.

Sraffa, P. 1926. The Laws of Returns under Competitive Conditions, *Economic Journal*, vol. 40, 79–116.

Westlund, H. 2000. *Social Capital in the Knowledge Economy: Theory and Empirics*. Berlin, Heidelberg, New York: Springer.

Chapter 9
Cities of Culture and Culture in Cities: The Emerging Uses of Culture in City Branding

Gregory Ashworth and Mihalis Kavaratzis

What Are We Talking About?

The various emerging urbanisms discussed in these chapters are notable for their diversity but have a number of discernible common threads, among which are new urban objectives, new communication media that contribute towards a different relationship between consumers and urban services and amenities, a new governance linking citizens and their governments, and new intensified competitive arenas both within the city and between cities, often on a global scale. There are evident changes in context, the urban setting whether physical and spatial or the economic and social environment in which it is set, in process, the way change whether intentional or not occurs and in outcome, the urban cityscapes and experiences that derive from these processes. Although none of these can be confidently labeled as trends, in the sense of clearly understood trajectories leading to envisaged outcomes, yet it is clear that two ostensibly quite different phenomena play central roles in almost all of these changes. These are culture and place-brands both of which are broad, often all-encompassing ideas, which need immediate specification.

It is not our intention to describe all aspects of culture in cities and the many ways culture, however defined, is used nor to discuss all the ramifications of place marketing and place-branding. Such a task would be impossible. But it is our intention to focus upon the intersection of the two, namely how culture, in a number of its manifestations is increasingly being used in the construction of place-brands.

Branding in Cities

All cities, and the services they provide, exist within markets, whether implicitly or explicitly, and most urban places have long engaged in forms of promotion within these markets, if only through flags, nomenclature, armorial bearings, slogans, traditional events, civic ceremonies and the like, which embody and reflect the aspirations of citizens, users of the city services and place management authorities. A brand is initially the shaping of a distinctiveness that uniquely identifies a product among others. The brand is more than an identifying name as it embodies a whole set of physical and socio-psychological attributes and beliefs which are quite deliberately associated with the product (Simoes and Dibb 2001). As such ideas were transferred from the commercial world into the realm of cities a set of terminology, tools and methods has been devised that is now commonplace in the agendas and activities of local authorities. The assumptions that the place is a product, its users are consumers and its governments are producers are certainly questionable and complicate the application of the branding instrument to places (Kavaratzis and Ashworth 2005). The generally acknowledged—if contested—purpose of all activities that can be classified under place-branding is the forging and projection of a desirable, distinctive place character (Braun 2008) that will appeal to visitors and investors and that will assist in place identification while differentiating the place from other places (Kavaratzis 2004). The brand is currently thought to be a network of associations that people hold with the city (Zenker and Beckmann 2013), which helps them make sense of the city and what it means.

Significant agreement has been reached regarding some of the fundamental issues that surround city branding. For instance, it has become clear and it is widely accepted that city branding involves much more than the simple tactics of visual identity materialized in logos and slogans for places in their eager attempt to communicate to the outside world their uniqueness (e.g. Anholt 2007). At the same time, there is a growing discussion around the significance of the place's various stakeholders (e.g. Kavaratzis 2012). There is also considerable agreement that place-brands are inexorably connected to the notions of place identity, place image and place culture (Kalandides 2011), although the exact nature of this relationship has not been clarified. We focus here on one of these issues, namely the relation to culture.

Culture in Cities

The word culture has multiple and quite different usages. It includes a bewilderingly wide range of, often vaguely delineated, forms and activities. An inventory of meanings and approaches or the futile attempt to define culture is outside our scope here. Instead, we focus on the uses of culture in contemporary cities based on a core that most people and their governments recognize as "cultural." Cities, of course, have been places where culture has been produced and consumed almost since their beginning. However, previously culture was seen as a merit good, produced and consumed from the surplus when more essential needs had been met. Now it is treated as a resource for development, including economic, and even as a development strategy in itself. "Economy and culture were once regarded as 'self' and 'other'; they are now seen to be linked, co-constitutive or seamlessly intertwined" (Castree 2004: 206).

There are many reasons why culture is used within urban development either strategically or tactically, to the extent that it often appears that you "just add culture and stir" (Gibson and Stevenson 2004). A cursory list of some of the possibilities would include the following uses of culture:

1. There is the traditional function of providing consumable cultural experiences. The benefit is in the first instance aesthetic but this can be extended to a broad based idea of urban amenity, enhancing locational values for many non-cultural functions. Simply we do not wish to live, work or recreate in a cultural desert.
2. Secondly, there is the use of culture as a resource, rather than a consumable, in the local cultural industries of the "creative city" (Landry 2000) with its own distinctive economic geography of production (Evans 2001). The increased use of culture within urban economies has been associated with the necessity to diversify the economic base, specifically in many instances to compensate for job losses in manufacturing (Kunzmann 2004), and more widely the accompanying loss of urban purpose and élan in post-industrial, service-oriented cities facing new competitive challenges.
3. Thirdly, and overlapping with the above, there is the idea of attracting creative individuals, the so-called "creative class" (Florida 2002), who are assumed to be talented, dynamic, upward moving, people who may work in the creative industries, narrowly defined as the cultural producers, or, more broadly are attracted to the city because they receive a psychic profit from associating with other such people and the places they inhabit. They in turn by their presence add to the attraction of the place for many other, often non-creative, activities. The term "creative class" is perhaps dangerously over-generalized and we will return to this below.
4. Fourthly, tourism, or in cities more accurately written as tourisms, includes a spectrum of interest ranging from direct cultural consumption as the primary motive for the visit, through incidental consumption as ancillary motive for dominantly non-cultural tourisms, to just the value endowed by culture to a more generalized background amenity and atmosphere.
5. Finally, and a common overarching support for all of the above uses, is the use of culture as an expression of locality and thus assertion of local identities. Local culture is assumed to be by definition unique to the locality, and thus confers this quality of uniqueness upon the place-product distinguishing it from its competitors.

Although there is much in common between the various uses of culture outlined above, there is an often spurious assumption of mutual support between these different uses. All may be dependent upon evolving place-images but not necessarily upon the same image. Creative industries have significantly different location requirements than for example theatre or museum districts. However the point here is that culture, so defined and used in these instrumental ways for wider purposes, is necessarily strongly related to place-branding, specifically how a place sees itself or wishes to be seen by others.

How Is It Done?

There are four recurring techniques employed, all of which are rooted in different ways in culture, which are undertaken in diverse combinations, responsive to local contexts, and aspirations and usually as part of wider policies, including more conventional local spatial planning controls and programs.

Technique 1: Signature Structures

The physical structures and forms of the city are to a large extent under the control of local planners and managers and indeed changing the physical appearance of the local environment is not just the easiest approach, it is sometimes the only effective intervention open to local governments. Thus the shaping of the visual qualities of spaces, paving, street furniture, buildings and even whole districts are an available instrument of place-branding. The term "signature" suggests the task of conveying and validating a unique identity, through structures, distinctive through both their very physical visible presence and the public functions they house. The term "flagship" is attached to officially designed structures intended to convey statements about cities and the governments that erected them. They are flagships of much more general policies and ideas than the possibly utilitarian functions they accommodate. If nothing else such actions are a clear, visible signal inscribed on the public space of the city, that something is happening and that the government is doing something.

The fundamental choice in such "flagship buildings" is whether this should be expressed through the *avant garde* or historicist forms. The former proclaims contemporary creativity, experimental flexibility and a confident embrace of the future: the latter continuity, durability, the maintenance of traditional values and connection with the past. But both need to be noticed and memorable to the point where sight of the structure immediately evokes the city. In both, artistic quality is less important than noticeability and even notoriety. In its most strident expression it results in what has been termed hypermodernity (Go and Govers 2010), where size alone demands attention, as with Burj Khalifa and similar buildings in Dubai.

An extension of flagship building is the attempt to shape whole wider signature urban districts of distinctive design elements in a total streetscape. Structures, spaces, and even minor features of street furniture, paving, and signage together state that this is a distinct and recognizable urban district, which plays a role as signature for the city as a whole. In some cases the district is intended to convey a political message but this can easily be augmented with cultural functions, declaiming that the city and its government have strong cultural credentials. Museum districts have become something of a planning cliché, even in, or perhaps especially in, cities whose principal activities and image have little to do with culture. The late nineteenth-century archetypes were South Kensington, London, or museum district Amsterdam but a more recent example would be Frankfurt Main, which has chosen to augment, or compensate for, its image as European financial center with its *Museumsufer*.

That signature structures are principally branding exercises is illustrated by the well-known Guggenheim museum (designed by Gehry) in Bilbao. A museum, however arresting, was no solution to the reemployment or regeneration of a decayed industrial town (Evans 2006). It is also unlikely that it could provide much stimulus to the local creative scene. However, as an instantly successful re-branding exercise, to the extent that mention of the town now immediately evokes the museum, it was critical in a strategic realignment by establishing confidence. "The key point is that the model is believed to be effective and thus acts as a talisman supporting the self-esteem of residents and a place image attractive to exogenous investment" (Ashworth and Graham 2012).

Technique 2: Hallmark Events

The staging of events and festivals is a way a city can demonstrate to itself and to a wider world its organizational capacity to do it and, through the content, its commitment to a particular activity or function. Such events are as often political, sporting or commercial as cultural and may range in scale from global mega-events to small local festivals. Equally they may be a continuing feature of "festival cities" (Edinburgh, Salzburg, Bayreuth, etc.) whose image, and much of whose local economy, depends upon their staging of events held to act as a catalyst for development. This is unlikely to be effective unless it is part of a clear strategic direction. Place managers may view such events as an effective means of encouraging a local appreciation of cultural production, whether local or not, and showcase the place's potential for cultural creativity and contemporary cultural production to outside markets. The objective at its simplest is just the assertion that the city exists; secondly that the city is important enough to stage such an event; and only thirdly the association of the city with the event's content. Although a few places have been remarkably successful in using cultural events in this way, in reality most cities organize a multitude of events of different scale, content and purpose, whose very diversity adds little in itself to the place brand.

The "European City (after 1999 'Capital') of Culture" designation of the European Union epitomes this emphasis on events as well as the link between culture and branding. The epithet bestowed now (2013) on 49 cities, ostensibly involves culture, as artistic experience, but has as its implicit yet exclusive goal a re-branding exercise. The stimulation of culture is not the goal, nor is it often especially important for cultural consumption in such cities but it is intended as an instrument stimulating wider urban development, principally through its value in propagating place-brands both outside the city and even more important as a self-branding exercise aimed at creating a new local self-perception and élan. This explains the intense competition among cities for the designation, the high local expectations it evokes and the not infrequent failure to fulfil these expectations (Hakala and Lemmetyinen 2013).

Technique 3: Personality Association

The forging of an association between a place and a named individual in the expectation that the necessarily unique qualities of the individual will be transferred to the place, which thus enhances its own individuality, is a commonly employed technique (Ashworth 2010). Success depends upon ease of recognition of the selected personality by the targeted consumers, the feasibility of linking the person to the place, the longevity and durability of the individual's fame and the appropriateness of the qualities or achievements of the person to the objectives of the place-branding exercise. Personalities drawn from the creative arts often prove more suitable than others. Past cultural production provides a rich quarry of possibilities and such a choice proclaims not only that this place is different but also that it has been culturally creative. Visual artists, including painters, sculptors and designers are especially suitable because of the physically visible and internationally intelligible nature of their work, which if possible should be recognizably distinctive if not eccentric. The idiosyncratic designer Antoni Gaudi was very successfully used by Barcelona in the 1990s to help change the city's brand from serious industrial to light-hearted cultural. This success had many imitators with varying impact and longevity (Delft/Vermeer; Glasgow/Mackintosh; Vienna/Hundertwasser). Musicians or writers are also widely used, especially if the musical or literary work can be related directly to the place in some way (Joyce/Dublin; Mozart/Salzburg; Brontës/Haworth). This goes further than the marking of "x lived here," it is an attempt to make person and place inseparable with each contributing attributes to the other.

However, fame is transitory, not least with the popular appreciation of culture. Places may successfully associate themselves with people, styles or historic periods whose appreciation has faded or whose qualities no longer attune with the times or the objectives of the brand. However useful in previous centuries, does Edinburgh still want to be the city of John Knox and the Calvinist covenanters, now that a free-thinking, creative hedonism is more fitting to its contemporary self-image than a conscientious, steadfast piety? Place–personality associations that have outlived their usefulness may prove difficult to alter or erase from consumer consciousness. In this respect artists with long-established popular reputations pose less risk than historical or political figures and contemporary celebrities.

Technique 4: Creative Colonies

If museum districts represent a historicist perspective, the idea of the living artists' colony represents contemporary creativity with which the city may wish to be associated. However, the role of the state in the creation of such districts is ambiguous. There are cases where government has been the initiator of such colonies, typified by the establishment of the invited commune of state-supported artists and designers at *Mathildehöhe*, in Darmstadt in 1899 under the patronage of the Grand Duke of Hesse. More usually such colonies occur spontaneously as artists cluster in places that seem to offer convenient locations, atmospheres in which artistic freedom can flourish at a particular time (for example Taos, New Mexico; St Ives, Cornwall). It is often the absence of government, with its imposition of planning restrictions and social conventions that is a *sine qua non* of their emergence. The development trajectory of such creative clusters subsequent to their spontaneous creation (which could be called the "Montmartre path") is their discovery first by the cultural cognoscenti, then those who appreciate associating with the artistic "atmosphere," followed by the cultural tourist drawn by mentions in the tourist guidebooks, and finally by city governments who begin to devise plans and policies for shaping and regulating a "creative district" not least as an enhancement of the city brand. By which time of course the "creatives" have long departed elsewhere, leaving behind only a lingering ambiance saleable to tourists.

In New York this trajectory of "creative districts" has long been evident. The "SoHo cast iron" district moved from offices and textile workshops to abandonment and vacancy in the 1960s, occupation by young artists and designers, historic designation in 1973 and "discovery," leading to upmarket loft residences, shops and cafes. More recently the "Meatpacking" district lost its function in the 1960s, became a neighborhood for alternative lifestyles, followed by a recent gentrification accelerated by the opening of the "High Line" linear park using derelict elevated railways, in 2009. Such cases and many more worldwide suggest a spurious inevitability. Loss of function, abandonment and vacancy may be followed by demolition and redevelopment as often as by reoccupation and revitalization headed by "creatives." The role of serendipity is illustrated by Temple Bar, Dublin where vacancy led to a plan for demolition and redevelopment as a bus station in, which was abruptly reversed to renovation and rehabilitation allegedly as a result of a conversation between the prime minister and the EU Commissioner for Culture, leading to Dublin's designation as European City of Culture in 1991.

Limits, Pitfalls and Emergent Lessons

None of the above techniques are likely to be successful on their own. All are likely to be applied in some combination with each other and with the important addition of wider spatial planning, infrastuctural investment and development projects as well as much that could be labeled public relations. As it is argued in the chapters of this volume for all types of planning and design, these culture and branding related modes of interventions are usually effective only as products of a more complex infrastructure and strategic planning. They both shape and are shaped by the economic, social and spatial processes of structural change (what in this book is called "Emergent Urbanism"). In this context, a series of limitations, contrary effects and pitfalls can be discussed stemming from all the above techniques and to the use of culture within city branding. While a thorough discussion cannot be undertaken here, we outline three main issues.

The first relates to the effectiveness and even appropriateness of all such techniques and to the costs they incur. There have been many successes, especially in the strategic realignment of urban futures, which have become renowned and much imitated archetypes, some of which have been mentioned here. However, the actual impacts are often based upon little more than optimistic assumptions and fortuitously randomly chosen instances. Culture as asset exists and is seen as beneficial but the expression of the "city of culture" in the public realm may function as a visible symbol of either reassurance that governments care and are acting or as an irrelevance when other, more urgent needs are not addressed. Apart from questioning the effectiveness in achieving their stated objectives (see Colomb 2011), there may also be negative social side-effects (e.g. Miles and Paddison 2005) and possible social divisiveness (e.g. Swyngedouw and Baeten 2001). While such risks sound rather unlikely for the "personality association" technique, they are certainly evident in the remaining techniques, particularly so in the "signature districts" and "creative colonies." The potential reverse effects are very significant. In many cases the "creatives" were just the precursors of the gentrifiers, which lead ultimately to the expulsion of the original inhabitants (e.g. Evans 2006) or at least their disinheritance. Evans' (2001: 172) memorable phrase, "the artists are the storm-troopers of gentrification" graphically underlines the sequence, although "Trojan horse" concealing the entry of the real-estate brokers (Zukin 2010) is an allusion suggesting less premeditation.

A second issue relates to the elusiveness of both the creative class and the creative districts that are supposed to lure them. On the one hand, those are, as indicated above, susceptible to change and fashion. On the other hand, there is a crucial inherent challenge in governments attempting to tap into those; almost a paradox associated again mostly with the techniques of creative colonies and signature structures but also with events. Indeed the flexibility and rapidity of change, typical of many cultural producers mean that once the district receives a mention in local planning policies as a "creative district," and ultimately in the tourist guide books as a "must see" attraction, then it has already transformed into something else. The involvement of the government is a catalyst for loss of authenticity. The creative class could be young experimental artists, with associated experimental lifestyles, and limited financial resources, seeking out available, cheap and flexible neighborhoods with an absence of planning ordinances or social controls. These are the "gritty" neighborhoods, a term whose meaning evolved in the course of the 1980s from abandoned and lawless to inspiring and "edgy" (Zukin 2010) and especially accommodating, through its absence of regulations zoning residential and workplace functions. Although governments play little role in their initiation, deliberately or more usually through oversight, their transformation into the more manicured and ordered cultural districts of the gentrifier or the tourist inevitably attracts the involvement of local governments. Typical would be the case of Christiania, Copenhagen, originating as a squatter settlement on abandoned military land in 1971. It was grudgingly tolerated by the authorities as an informal self-governing commune, and in its latter years something of a *Lonely Planet* tourism attraction, until increasingly "normalized" after 2004 by the authorities because of their discomfort with its anarchic lifestyles.

A third issue relates to the right to enter the decision-making process. The question is "who gets to decide whose culture will be the one used and for what purposes?" Interests in decision-making are many and conflicting and not all noble. Decision-making thus becomes either slow and cumbersome or suspicious (Greenberg 2008). Ultimately, it is rather dubious interests that seem to prevail. Swyngedouw and Baeten (2001: 835) warn that one of the consequences of this is, "the often non-democratic and opaque organisation and decision-making procedures at these scales of governance turn them into implicit or explicit elite playing-fields that permit shaping territorial trajectories in the image of dominant and hegemonic elite coalitions." If the culture is seen as that of an elite, whether local or global, then residents may resent the colonization or usurpation of their culture.

We have undertaken above an examination of the uses of culture within place-branding and have attempted to raise significant warnings. To conclude, the question, "can culture be harnessed in the service of place-branding?" can be answered with a confident and self-evident affirmative. The answers become less clear and confident when the question is "How should it be done?," "Will it be successful?" and "What are the wider consequences of doing it?" The only lesson of global experience is that there is no universally applicable model. The only injunction is to proceed with the creation of the city of culture with a caution based upon awareness of the uniqueness of cities, sensitivity to the singularity of the local and as much foresight as possible.

References

Anholt, S. 2007. *Competitive Identity: The New Brand Management for Countries, Regions and Cities*. Basingstoke: Palgrave Macmillan.

Ashworth, G.J. 2010. Personality association as an instrument of place branding: Possibilities and pitfalls. In G.J. Ashworth and M. Kavaratzis (eds), *Towards Effective Place Brand Management*. London: Edward Elgar, 285–303.

Ashworth, G.J. and Graham, B.J. 2012. European cities: Culture and economy. In D. Stone (ed.), *Oxford Handbook of Post-War European History*. Oxford: Oxford University Press, 582–98.

Braun, E. 2008. City marketing: Towards an integrated approach. ERIM Ph.D. Series in Research and Management, 142, Erasmus Research Institute of Management (ERIM).

Castree, N. 2004. Economy and culture are dead! Long live economy and culture! *Progress in Human Geography*, 28(2), 204–26.

Colomb, C. 2011. Culture in the city, culture for the city? The political construction of the trickle-down in cultural regeneration strategies in Roubaix, France. *Town Planning Review*, 82(1), 77–98.

Evans, G. 2001. *Cultural Planning*. London: Routledge.

Evans, G. 2006. Branding the city of culture: The death of city planning? In J. Monclus and M. Guardia (eds), *Culture, Urbanism and Planning*. Aldershot: Ashgate, 197–213.

Florida, R. 2002. *The Rise of the Creative Class*. New York: Basic Books.

Gibson, L. and Stevenson, D. 2004. Urban space and the uses of culture. *International Journal of Cultural Policy*, 10(1), 1–4.

Go, F. and Govers, R. 2010. *International Place Branding Yearbook 2010*. Basingstoke: Palgrave Macmillan.

Greenberg, M. 2008. *Branding New York: How a City in Crisis was Sold to the World*. London: Routledge.

Hakala, U. and Lemmetyinen, A. 2013. Culture is the message: The status of cultural capital and its effects upon a city's brand equity. *Place Branding and Public Diplomacy*, 9(1), 5–16.

Kalandides, A. 2011. The problem with spatial identity: Revisiting the sense of place. *Journal of Place Management and Development*, 4(1), 28–39.

Kavaratzis, M. 2004. From city marketing to city branding. *Place Branding and Public Diplomacy*, 1(1), 58–73.

Kavaratzis, M. 2012. From necessary evil to necessity: The role of stakeholders in place branding. *Journal of Place Management and Development*, 5(1), 7–19.

Kavaratzis, M. and Ashworth, G.J. 2005. City branding: An effective assertion of identity or a transitory marketing trick? *Tijdschrift Voor Economische en Sociale Geografie*, 96(5), 506–14.

Kunzmann, K.R. 2004. Culture, creativity and spatial planning. *Town Planning Review*, 75(4), 383–404.

Landry, C. 2000. *The Creative City: A Toolkit for Urban Innovators*. London: Earthscan.

Miles, S. and Paddison, R. 2005. Introduction: The rise and rise of culture-led urban regeneration. *Urban Studies*, 42(5/6), 833–9.

Simoes, C. and Dibb, S. 2001. Rethinking the brand concept: New brand orientation. *Corporate Communications: An International Journal*, 6(4), 217–24.

Swyngedouw, E. and Baeten, G. 2001. Scaling the city: The political economy of "glocal" development—Brussels "conundrum." *European Planning Studies*, 9(7), 827–49.

Zenker, S. and Beckmann, S.C. 2013. My place is not your place: Different place brand knowledge by different target groups. *Journal of Place Management and Development*, 6(1), 6–17.

Zukin, S.D. 2010. *Naked City: The Death and Life of Authentic Urban Places*. Oxford: Oxford University Press.

Chapter 10
The Field of Urban Composition[1]

Mark C. Childs[2]

Shaping the collective form of our settlements is an ancient and evolving practice. Neolithic villages and the earliest cities show intentional design in site selection and development, collective infrastructure, public spaces, and the patterning of collections of buildings and spaces (see Marcus and Sabloff 2008). These practices, of course, continued and were elaborated in historic time (see Kostof 1991, 1992), a number of approaches to creating a discipline arose in the twentieth century, and there has recently been an upsurge in the literature (Childs 2010). However, I argue in this chapter that the field is still emerging.

At the beginning of the twenty-first century in the United States, "urban design" is the usual but contested and unsettled term for the field. Some argue that it is a frame of mind, an interdisciplinary practice, a discipline parallel to other design disciplines, or an overarching field that includes various disciplines and practices (Vernez-Moudon 1992, Lang 1994, Krieger 2006). Figure 10.1 diagrams these alternative conceptions, and the sidebar sketches definitions of critical terms.

Moreover, the term "design" does not cover the all the major academic/professional methods of intentionally shaping settlements. Six verbs have been the core practices of intentional settlement-making—to plan, design, engineer, develop, build, and preserve. Of course each of these methods engages sub-methods such as coordinating, researching, or curating, and other activities such as legislating, judging, financing, taxing, conquering, and story-telling have been used as methods to intentionally shape our built landscapes and have shaped them as consequences of other motives. However, the disciplines and practices have focused on their individual methods to the extent that the names of the disciplines are based on the verbs—we are planners, engineers, preservationists, and developers—and the term "designer" frequently replaces "architect." I propose to add a seventh verb, *to compose*, to embrace the six practices and all other methods we use to intentionally shape the physical form of settlements.

There are two major ways that fields are organized. Health, Law, Theology, and Women's Studies, for example, center on a topic. On the other hand, Engineering, Mathematics, and Photography are organized around a suite of methods. A college of Urban Composition would be akin to the former, a college of Design with the latter. I propose that just as the field of Health encompasses a set of methods to address the goal of human health, the field of Urban Composition should center on a set of goals about settlement form.

Thus I propose the term Urban Composition to gather the settlement-composing disciplines and practices into a field to promote cross- and supra-disciplinary thinking, scholarship, best practices, and certification defined not by the use of *a* method but by the application of multiple methods in order to compose vital settlements.

This semantic change is not simply a pedantic exercise but can help clarify goals and methods whose development and refinement will be critical to meet twenty-first century concerns. The impending sea level rise, changes in rainfall, other climate change consequences, and the continuing trend toward worldwide urbanization make it crucial to understand how to compose our settlements. How can we successfully defend, move or abandon settlements while maintaining or improving their vitality?

Of course, earlier problems such as citywide fires, endemic urban diseases, and slums also called for systemic changes in the composition of our settlements and remain concerns. The practices developed in response and their successes, excesses and secondary consequences are part of our body of knowledge.

---

1   This article draws upon, revisits, corrects, recalibrates, and expands upon my previous work, in particular Childs 2010 and 2012.

2   Unless otherwise specified, all figures in this chapter are the author's own.

AS DISCIPLINE

AS INTERDISCIPLINARY PRACTICE

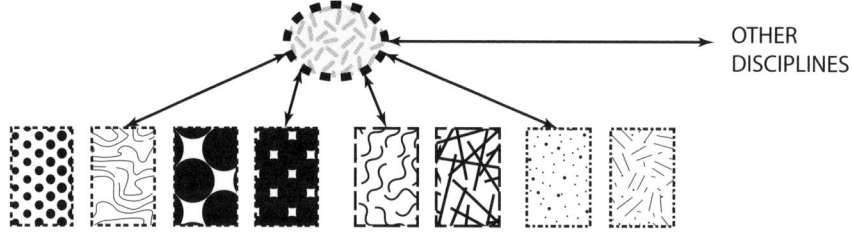

OTHER
DISCIPLINES

AS SHARED KNOWLEDGE

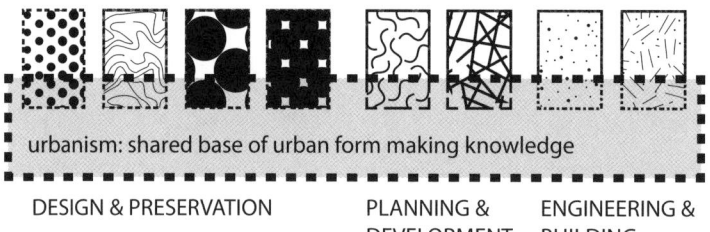

urbanism: shared base of urban form making knowledge

DESIGN & PRESERVATION   PLANNING &   ENGINEERING &
                            DEVELOPMENT   BUILDING

Figure 10.1 (above)   **Alternative conceptions of urban design field**

Figure 10.2 (right)   **Definitions of critical terms**

The literature is riddled with opaque language. Much of this is undoubtedly due to the difficulty of the concepts, the confusion of multivalent common language with delimited expert language, or the poetic struggle to invent new designs and ways of seeing. However, too much opacity appears to arise from a desire to mystify or from a lack of consensus. Disciplinary language will continually be contested. Refining language is part of how we refine thought, and to build an open community of inquiry we need to attempt to define clear terms. This article refines and restates some of my previous attempts at cogent definitions.

Discipline and Profession

The terms "discipline" and "profession" are mutable and convoluted. They have elaborate, often contradictory and intertwined semantic histories (see Freidson 1986). The definitions and constellations of "professions/disciplines" are evolving cultural constructs that have been actively shaped by academics and practitioners as well as by larger political-cultural shifts, and cross-cultural comparisons are difficult (see Freidson 1986 and 1994, Bender 1993, Macdonald 1995). However, "[i]n the United States, for the last century, the [overall] map of disciplinary social structures has been remarkably constant" and since the mid twentieth century this alignment has spread to many other parts of the world (Abbott 2001, 122). We have had a stable social agreement that there are, for example, a field of biology and a profession of architecture.

The literature associates a number of practices with a robust discipline/profession, such as (1) a shared body of knowledge or practices about an overarching line of inquiry stewarded by an academic discipline and academic journals; (2) peer review and shared reflection; (3) work autonomy; (4) colleague-based review rather than governmental regulation; (5) licensure with continued study; (6) commitment to high standards of achievement and conduct and a code of professional ethics; (7) a shared sense amongst members that the activity is "a central life-interest which provides its own rewards … something that may on occasion be considered to be play" (Freidson 1994, 200); and (8) a prime purpose of rendering a public service (see Larson 1978, Freidson 1986, Brown 1992, Jackson 2010). An established professional discipline then is an academic department dedicated to a subject area, a profession is a licensed occupation at least as part of whose activities serve a public purpose, and together they meet a plurality of the above criteria.

Field

Among many other meanings, the American Heritage Dictionary defines "field" as, "A topic, a subject, or an area of academic interest or specialization. Profession, employment, or business" (1992, 677). I use the term "field" to encompass a set of related professions and disciplines that share an overarching line of inquiry and practice, such as "how do/should/can we promote human health?" In the United States, the field of health sciences for example typically includes departments and professions such as surgery, psychiatry, obstetrics, immunology, nursing, pharmacy, etc. There is likely active disagreement about the meaning, scope or details of the line of inquiry and practice, but it is a shared argument. Frequently different professionals in the field work together, as do doctors, nurses and epidemiologists; or landscape architects, civil engineers and planners.

A mature professional field (1) shares a discussion about an overarching line(s) of inquiry and practice; (2) has a fairly uniform organization across multiple universities with a set of constituent disciplines and majors that are linked to their professions, which are themselves robust; (3) has a national academic organization; and (4) has a national market for professors (see Abbott 2001, 132). One way to conceive of a field is the group of people whose work is to elaborate, argue about and share a common language; set standards of scholarship and practice; and seek to achieve a set of systemic goals.

The field of urban composition (or urban design) does not meet these criteria. Yet, there has been significant growth in urban design departments, journals and books, and the creation of organizations that have some of the characteristics of a national organization, such as the National Academy of Environmental Design in the United States.

Urban

In everyday speech, "urban" suggests a place with a density of people, although dictionaries simply define the term as "of, relating to, or located in a city" (American Heritage 1992, 1964). However, for our purposes, I suggest that we define "urban" as referring to a density of interactions between independently created built forms that leads to or supports a set of public services. Thus, because it was designed by a single entity and because it is an entertainment venue rather than a public realm, the main street of Disneyland is not as urban as the early-twentieth century main street of Marceline, Missouri on which it was modeled.

We should be careful not to unthinkingly equate a high density of built form interactions with a good built environment but rather examine the place against a set of private and public services. The collective character of assemblages of built forms can run the spectrum from inspiring, sustainable, enriching places to disenabling, disheartening, and unhealthy slums. Moreover, just as there are many types of great conversations, parties, or jam sessions, there are many kinds of great settlements. Oxford and Istanbul are appreciably different great urban places.

Composition

"Compose" comes from the Old French meaning to put together. The American Heritage Dictionary defines compose as "1. To make up the constituent parts of; constitute or form … 2. To make or create by putting together parts or elements …." (1992, 387). Thus "composition" calls attention to the fact that our settlements are made of individual parts typically planned, designed, engineered, developed, built, and preserved by multiple different parties.

This is not to imply that the scope of urban composition is limited to disaster prevention and repair. Central concerns continue to be the built world's influence on everyday public services such as health, safety, and welfare, as well as the inspirational, poetic power of place.

Organizing the field—restructuring its conceptual framework; defining terms; articulating a line of inquiry and public services; working toward a consensus on core skills, methods, and modes of evidence; and creating vital national and international academic organizations—will aid the ability of the professions/disciplines to work in concert, and will provide a foundation to address the urgent issues of the physical form of our settlements.

Conceptual Model of the Field

To play in an orchestra, a bassoonist needs to be steeped in music, have technical skill, know how to co-create a performance, and actively participate in the group's "ennobling task" (see Leavitt and Lipman-Blumen 1995, Marotto et al. 2007). This scale of skills echoes the various definitions of urban design diagrammed in Figure 10.1, and the model for the field of Urban Composition diagrammed in Figure 10.3 incorporates this scale.

In this model, "urbanism as a frame of mind" is incorporated by the idea that all the disciplines within the field share a base set of learning objectives about composing settlements and a system of principles (an "-ism") about how each discipline participates in the field. We all need to be "steeped in the music." My book *Urban Composition* is intended as an introduction to a portion of this shared material (Childs 2012).

Urban design as district design is incorporated as a design/planning/engineering/development discipline parallel to other professional degree-granting disciplines. This discipline should include faculty from multiple disciplines, just as architecture faculties have typically included historians, structural engineers and others. The design of urban and suburban districts is an established professional practice in the United States and elsewhere and multiple masters'-granting programs exist. Developing national certification and establishing

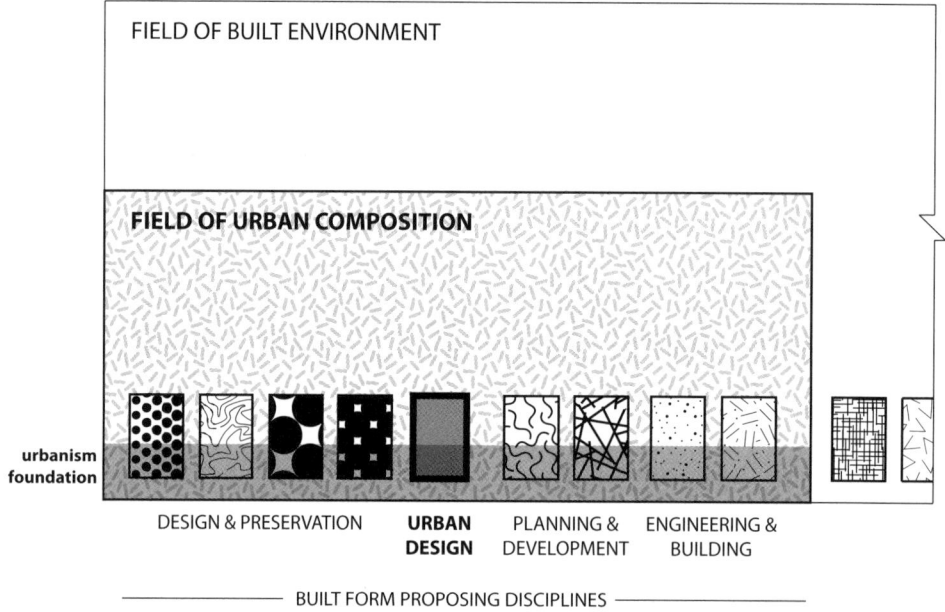

Figure 10.3   Conceptual model of the field

an inclusive disciplinary organization that hosts conferences and debates curricula and best practices would help create a more coherent discipline/profession.

Other potential masters' programs in the field of Urban Composition might include regional infrastructure and land use composition, urban industrial design (street furniture, utility equipment, etc.; for example see the Danish Royal Academy Master's program of Industrial Design in Architectural Contexts), or rural design (see Thorbeck 2012).

Urban design as an overarching field is renamed "Urban Composition" to focus on the goal of settlement-making rather than a single method such as landscape design or engineering, and thus to embrace settlement-making disciplines whose major mode of composition is not design (e.g. planning, civil engineering). This model proposes post-masters degrees (Ph.D., certificates, post-professional masters, continuing education, etc.) in Urban Composition, which allows for cross-training and supra-disciplinary scholarship and investigation of the systems and practices of settlement composition.

The term "school of the built environment" embodies a similar concept. However, it implies a broader scope including disciplines that do not propose to shape settlements, such as urban history. In institutions that have a hierarchy of school/college/department, perhaps a college of urban composition would be within a school of the built environment. However, the name is not a substantial concern as long as the settlement-composing disciplines are gathered together.

Develop an Overarching Line of Inquiry for the Field

The World Health Organization defines health as "a state of complete physical, mental and social well-being and not merely the absence of disease or infirmity" (WHO 1948). The members of the professions argue about the nuances and boundaries of the field. Should the field stop at human health or is our health best understood as part of the health of the biosphere? Nevertheless, there is a general agreement about the overarching goals and lines of inquiry of the field, and licensing boards have adopted and enforce definitions of practice. Following is a draft overarching line of inquiry for the field of urban composition: How can, do, and should we compose the physical form of our settlements to best support civilization, while being responsible to the biosphere, within the dynamic political, economical, social and technological contexts of each proposal?

The "should," "civilization," and "responsible" components of this question require a set of normative principles or criteria. One of the attributes of a profession is having a prime purpose of rendering a public service (Freidson 1986). The public services of a professional field aim to fulfill or support public interests. The design of buildings that resist the spread of fire to neighboring structures, for example, is a public service of architectural design. A central argument for governments to license professionals has been that, with the acquisition of the professional body of knowledge, best practices, and a code of ethics, professionals can better provide both private goods and public services than non-professionals (see Macdonald 1995, Freidson 1986, 1994). Moreover, governments give professional organizations control over entry into the profession and oversight of members on the grounds that these organizations are in a better position to judge best practices and egregious failures than untrained bureaucrats. This professional self-government requires a robust dialog about the profession's public services.

As a matter of professional ethics and credibility, I argue that professionals should aim to go beyond merely not endangering public health, safety, and welfare to actively supporting a set of public services.[3] Academic and professional bodies should give awards for projects and firms that provide exemplary public services (for an example see www.seed-network.org), and perhaps censure for projects that egregiously miss the mark. Building on the model of LEED certification, perhaps the field should offer certification in other public services such as community health, environmental justice, and composition of public space.

---

3   For an example of a passive construction of public services, the U.S. and Canadian professional organization The Council of Landscape Architectural Registration Boards states, "Licensure is a formal recognition that an individual has demonstrated sufficient knowledge, skill and ability to practice the profession without endangering the health, safety, and welfare of the public." Available at: https://www.clarb.org/Students/Pages/WhyLicensureIsImportant.aspx (accessed January 29, 2013).

Providing both public services and private goods is a critical professional skill. Sometimes the goals align. Vaccines, for example, both prevent individual disease and increase public health. Sometimes they conflict. Doctors may quarantine a patient with active tuberculosis against her will, or zoning regulations may prevent the development of a slaughterhouse next to residences. Often cases are complex and hazy, requiring professional imagination and judgment.

In *Urban Composition*, I proposed the following public services:

1. stewardship of our biotic contexts and built heritage;
2. public health and safety;
3. economic health including collective infrastructure;
4. a vital public realm that supports and represents conviviality and civil society;
5. enabling creative milieus for the pursuit of happiness, creativity and wisdom (see Hall 1998, Landry 2000, Florida 2002, 2005);
6. elaborating a poetically rich *genius loci*;
7. openness to debate about this list and acknowledgment that there are limits on the ability of built form to achieve these goals. (Childs 2012: 19)

In *Good City Form* (1981), Kevin Lynch proposed a set of rigorously conceived dimensions of city form performance:

1. vitality—support for human life;
2. sense—"the match between environment, our sensory and mental capabilities, and our cultural constructs";
3. fit—"the adequacy of the behavior settings, including their adaptability to future action";
4. access—the degree to which the form of the settlement enables reaching a variety of places and services;
5. control—the degree of control of built forms by "those who use, work, or reside in them."

and two meta-criteria that apply to all of the above:

1. efficiency;
2. justice (1981: 118).

There is significant overlap between these two frameworks. However, public services offer a different viewpoint than dimensions of performance. Lynch writes of his dimensions "It should be possible to connect these characteristics to the important goals and values of any culture, at least through a chain of reasonable assumptions" (1981: 113). My list is an attempt to begin a discussion of our goals and values.

Lynch's two meta-criteria should be applied to my list of public services. This addition then incorporates work like Dolores Hayden's *The Power of Place* project. This project worked to address the fact that only 4 percent of the cultural-historic landmarks in Los Angeles were associated with women's history and 2.3 percent associated with groups other than Anglo-Americans—an issue of the justice of the narratives of place (Hayden 1997: 86).

A slight reframing suggests that the public services of many other disciplines should be meta-criteria for good city form—justice, economy, human health and safety, biosphere health, and ethical public discourse. Urban composition's central public services then could be framed as curating our built and natural heritage, composing the public realm, and elaborating poetically rich places.

Core Skills

What should be (1) the core skills in "urbanism" that all students in the urban composition fields share, (2) the expert skills in the discipline of "urban design" that significantly differentiate these practitioners from others, and (3) the major lines of inquiry for advanced degrees in urban composition? The answer helps define the discipline(s) and field and provides benchmarks to improve and teach them. Using the National Architectural Accreditation Board's format and definitions of "understanding" and "ability" (NAAB 2013), I offer the following to prompt debate.

"Urbanism" learning objectives for all disciplines in the field should include:

- Collective Form Making: Understanding how individual and incremental design actions can help compose collectively made forms such as "main street," "uptown," or "the garden district."
- Public Services: Understanding theories and manifestos about goals for good urban form.
- Orchestration: Understanding models for collaboration across disciplines, across administrative structures, with community groups, and with multiple economic sectors (non-profits, governments and agencies, for-profit corporations, individuals).
- Solving for Pattern: Understanding basic systems thinking.
- Working with editors: Understanding the interaction of individual case-by-case design with systemic composition such as zoning or sewer service boundaries.
- Gathering and using evidence: Basic ability in community consultation, prototyping, beta-testing, post-occupancy evaluations, and theory testing.

"Urban design" learning objectives should include:

- Urbanism: Ability in all the urbanism skills.
- Theory of Orchestration: Understanding theories of coordination and collaboration.
- Copy-editing: Ability to establish means to review, manage, and coordinate the work of individual designers.
- Commissioning: Understanding methods of hiring, coaching and mentoring designers, planners, engineers, artists and others for an urban design project.
- Venue development: Ability to propose a design and development strategy for an urban design, including establishing design, engineering and financing tools, management structure, and choreography of development. For example, this work could include creating a set of building and street types, a phasing plan, and/or an infrastructure financing plan for a development.

"Urban composition" lines of inquiry should include:

- Systems Analysis and Stewardship: Evaluation of the practices used by professionals in urban composition disciplines, including their intended and unintended consequences and the interactions of multiple practices.
- Format development: How can we create and evaluate tools to coordinate individual projects so as to achieve collective goods? Examples include the tools called "historic districts," "form-based codes," and the National Main Street Center's four-point main street program.
- Cross-training: How should we develop opportunities for practitioners to improve their skills in another discipline?
- Regional and national composition: In the United States and other countries without a national composition practice, how do/can/should issues of regional composition, including regional and national land management, and analysis of national actors such as infrastructure creators, financing markets, tax designers, and chain store designers, be addressed? In countries with established or emerging national composition practices, regional composition may be included in urban design, planning, or a separate discipline.

National Organization(s)

National academic and professional organizations have been central to the establishment and continuity of professional fields (Burrage et al. 1990). These organizations can provide forums for dissemination and debate of scholarship and practices, political and social advocacy, and a venue for hiring. Part of the strength of the Congress for New Urbanism is its conferences, awards, publications, certification program, collaboration with other organizations, and other activities. Historically, the *Congrès International d'Architecture Moderne* (CIAM) and the early twentieth-century American Civics Association were similar strong agents shaping the goals and tools of urban design. Currently, professional organizations in the United States such as the American Public Works Association or the American Society of Landscape Architects and other academic and civil society groups serve similar roles for their particular disciplines.

However, we are missing a bridging organization that engages the full spectrum of urban composition. The emerging National Academy of Environmental Design (www.naedonline.org) or an expanded Urban Land Institute (www.uli.org) could serve this role in the United States.

So What?

If the field of urban composition as sketched above were clearly established, what might we gain?

Not all colleges with city-making disciplines will or should be organized around urban composition. Design colleges, for example, that include everything from graphics and fashion to landscape architecture and urban design can organize around the public services, ethics, and lines of inquiry of a broad definition of design.

The work of transforming existing programs to the urban composition model will depend on the composition of the existing cluster of disciplines (e.g. a school with architecture, landscape architecture, planning and real estate may more readily adopt this model than a school of architecture and fine arts), the interests of the current faculty, and a myriad of other factors. Civil engineering may never separate itself from a college of engineering, and perhaps just as architecture programs frequently hire structural engineers, urban design programs may incorporate civil engineers, or a new (sub)discipline of infrastructure urbanism can be instituted. There are costs, lost opportunities, and questions of status in any significant realignment of a school. Yet both the internal structure of disciplines/professions and the constellation of disciplines is continually changing. Moreover, the multidisciplinary nature of city-making has engendered multidisciplinary firms and alliances of firms, and creating schools of urban composition could have the following benefits.

Teaching urbanism to all the settlement-making disciplines aims to improve multidisciplinary work and the concinnity of our settlements. For example, if civil engineers, as an integral part of their work, consider how street form composes the public realm, is part of a biologically complex watershed, frames the design of adjacent buildings, and influences land values, then they may propose vital streets rather than merely roads for moving cars. A shared set of skills and understandings should also reduce disciplinary blinders such as those illustrated when designers dismiss a proposition as "planning" or "just engineering" rather than integrating the proposition with a design proposal.[4]

Continuing to build a distinct urban design discipline should provide means to evaluate and establish best practices and to clarify the private and public services and ethics of urban design. Forging a national consensus on learning objectives and criteria for licensing should improve the public value and reputation of the discipline. This discipline could lead in the creation of resilient, environmentally sound and healthy districts.

Reorganizing colleges around urban composition rather than individual methods of settlement-making provides the environment to evaluate the full spectrum of settlement-making practices, consider emerging issues such as those posed by climate change, promote supra-disciplinary scholarship, and offer cross-training. Responding to sea level rise will involve the full spectrum of compositional skills—planning and policy; design and engineering; private, public and non-profit development; building and preservation; and other methods. Developing organizations, scholars and practitioners dedicated to integrating these skills could be essential to developing robust remedies.

Moreover, this model promotes a sense of inclusiveness. Rather than concentrating on independent skills, it focuses on multiple skills applied to a goal—the continual (re)creation of vital settlements.

---

4   I have frequently heard this dismissal from design students, and too often from faculty and practitioners.

References

Abbott, A. 2001. *Chaos of Disciplines*. Chicago and London: The University of Chicago Press.

Bender, T. 1993. *Intellect and the Public Life*. Baltimore, MD: The Johns Hopkins University Press.

Brown, J. 1992. *The Definition of a Profession: The Authority of Metaphor in the History of Intelligence Testing, 1890–1930*. Princeton, NJ: Princeton University Press.

Burrage, M., Jarausch, K. and Siegrist, H. 1990. An actor-based framework for the study of the professions, in Michael Burrage and Rolf Torstendahl (eds), *Professions in Theory and History*. London: Sage Publications.

Childs, M. 2010. A Spectrum of Urban Design Roles, *Journal of Urban Design*, 15(1), 1–19.

Childs, M. 2012. *Urban Composition*. New York: Princeton Architectural Press.

Florida, R. 2002. *The Rise of the Creative Class*. New York: Basic Books.

Florida, R. 2005. *Cities and the Creative Class*. New York: Routledge.

Freidson, E. 1986. *Professional Powers: A Study of the Institutionalization of Formal Knowledge*. Chicago, IL: University of Chicago Press.

Freidson, E. 1994. *Professionalism Reborn*. Chicago, IL: The University of Chicago Press.

Hall, P. 1998. *Cities in Civilization*. London: Weidenfeld and Nicolson.

Hayden, D. 1997. *The Power of Place*. Cambridge, MA: MIT Press.

Jackson, J.A. 2010. *Professions and Professionalization: Volume 3, Sociological Studies*. Cambridge: Cambridge University Press.

Kostof, S. 1991. *The City Shaped*. New York: Little, Brown.

Kostof, S. 1992. *The City Assembled*. New York: Little, Brown.

Krieger, A. 2006. Where and How Does Urban Design Happen, *Harvard Design Magazine* Spring/Summer, 64–71.

Landry, C. 2000. *The Creative City*. London: Earthscan.

Lang, J. 1994. *Urban Design: The American Experience*. New York: Wiley.

Larson, M.S. 1978. *The Rise of Professionalism: A Sociological Analysis*. Berkeley, CA: University of California Press.

Leavitt, H.J. and Lipman-Blumen, J. 1995. Hot Groups, *Harvard Business Review*, 73(4), 109–16.

Lynch, K. 1981. *Good City Form*. Cambridge, MA: MIT Press.

Macdonald, K.M. 1995. *The Sociology of the Professions*. London: Sage Publications.

Marcus, J. and Sabloff, J.A. (eds) 2008. *The Ancient City: New Perspectives on Urbanism in the Old and New World*. Santa Fe, NM: School for Advanced Research Press.

Marotto, M., Roos, J. and Victor, B. 2007. Collective Virtuosity in Organizations: A Study of Peak Performance in an Orchestra, *Journal of Management Studies*, 44(3), 388–413.

NAAB 2013. Conditions for Accreditation. Available at: http://www.naab.org/accreditation/2009_Conditions.aspx (accessed July 2, 2013).

Thorbeck, Dewey. 2012. *Rural Design*. New York: Routledge.

Vernez-Moudon, A. 1992. A Catholic Approach to Organizing What Urban Designs Should Know, *Journal of Planning Literature*, 6(4), 331–49.

WHO 1948. *Preamble to the Constitution of the World Health Organization as Adopted by the International Health Conference*, New York, June 19–22, 1946; signed July 22, 1946 by the representatives of 61 States (Official Records of the World Health Organization, no. 2, p. 100) and entered into force on April 7, 1948.

Chapter 11
The Subject of Place: Staying with the Trouble

Jonathan Metzger

It appears, however, to be something overwhelming and hard to grasp, the topos [place].

Aristotle, Physics, Book IV[1]

Places haunt us, and we haunt them.

Nigel Thrift, Steps to an Ecology of Place

What makes a place *a place*? A question that has eluded thinkers, from Aristotle to some of the leading social scientists of our age. Intuitively it can be sensed that "place" belongs to a different register or modality of existence than other geographic signifiers such as "space" or "site." As Kim Dovey (2010: 3), has put it: "In everyday life we all know what place means, even if we do not experience particular places in the same ways. There is a crucial difference between the terms space and place in everyday language. To ask 'what kind of place is New York?', may generate a variety of answers but this question has a sense that 'what kind of space is New York' does not." Relatedly, social scientists and philosophers have for decades been engaged in sometimes heated debate regarding how to conceptually distinguish between "places" and "spaces" (for an introduction, see Agnew 2011).

It thus appears as if places exist in registers of intensities that are wickedly challenging to grasp or enumerate, to put into words or agree upon a definition of, to map or sketch exhaustively—at least without committing a serious fallacy of unwarranted reduction. Place-phenomena nevertheless appear to be crucial to be aware of in any endeavor to understand the complex entanglements of social realities, perhaps particularly for those active in so-called "place-making" professions, in which Dovey (2010: 3) claims that taken-for-granted understandings of the concept presently underwrite "some dangerous practices" (Dovey 2010: 3).

For the past 50 years or so, the most common way in academic research to grapple with the challenging ontological status of place has been to render the concept operationalizable as either an "objective" entity, that is: as part of the "furniture of the universe," or as a "subjective," individual human sentiment or private experience. In the first case, which could be called an *objectivist reductionism*, place is rendered manageable through an objectivistic reduction which removes from attention all the aspects of places that are apprehended as "soft" or "subjective." In the second case, what could be called a subjectivist reductionism, place is instead made intelligible through a turn away from the world and solely into the internal realm of individual human psyches.

The question I wish to pose in this chapter is how we can find ways to begin to re-conceptualize place in a manner that, with the words of Donna Haraway (2010), "stays with the trouble" of the entangled ontological complexity of the phenomenon of place instead of forcing us to succumb to unwarranted reductions. A conceptualization that may be of help in highlighting just how the concept of place appears to transverse the ingrained but highly artificial subject/object-divide which is latent in much of Western thinking. Instead I hope to showcase some of the intellectual tooling that may be of help in tracing the intertwinement, or even mutual constitution, of the "subjective" and "objective," as well as the "material" and the "social," which complex ontological phenomena such as places may help to open our eyes to. Borrowing words from Dovey, we can hopefully find some ways to explore how to "move beyond a false choice between place as pre-given or as socially constructed" (Dovey 2010: 6).

The proposition that I wish to offer is that we do not approach place as either a subjective or objective entity, but rather as a relation that enacts both subjects and objects, what Karen Barad—drawing on Niels

---

1   Translated by C.H. Seibert, extracted from M. Heidegger, Art and Space, *Man and World* 6, 1973, 3–8.

Bohr—dubs a *phenomenon*, or what Michel Serres calls a *quasi-object*. These are concepts that purport to highlight the existence of things material and really-real indeed, but at the same time always inextricably bound up with sensing subjects—without prematurely circumscribing who or *what* such a subject might be. I will be drawing upon the thinking of these two philosophers of science, as well as partially on the philosophy of Alfred North Whitehead, as resources to help staying with the trouble of place. I will do so through weaving them into a broader relational-materialist sensibility to generate an ontological speculation—not stating that "this is the way things are," but rather asking: what happens if we think of these things this way instead? Or, again with the apt words of Donna Haraway, exploring "what comes into the world that way, whether one chooses to throw ones lot with it or not" (Haraway 2013).

From Cartesian Dualism to Relational Materialism

As intimated above, "place" is a philosophical and social scientific concept with an intellectual pedigree countable in millennia. In this context, there is unfortunately no room for a deeper investigation of the history of the concept (see instead e.g. Casey 1997, Cresswell 2004, Massey and Thrift 2003). Most academic writing on place, while displaying distinct variances in the level of nuance, broadly falls within either the objectivist reductionist or the subjectivist reductionist folds. For instance, much of the classical work in the field of environmental psychology could easily be placed in the first category (see Stedman 2003: 674), defining "real" places as essences-above-and-beyond human experience, while influential thinkers in the humanistic geography-movement such as Yi-Fu Tuan generally have posited places as subjective or inter-subjective essences-in-experience, thus clearly falling into the second (see e.g. Tuan 1977).

The crucial problem with all the variants of either objectivist or subjectivist reductionism in relation to place is that they are both helplessly stuck in a solidified and unquestioned Cartesian dualism, positing subjects and objects as fundamentally different and separate ontological entities. Thus, even though, at an early glance, they may appear to be diametrically opposed positions, upon closer scrutiny they rather appear as two sides to the same coin, for whom the disagreement only pertains to which side of the coin the phenomenon of "place" should be sorted on. This "debate" has degenerated into a never-ending and since long stale-mated turf battle on a mutually recognized battleground. As Karen Barad has noted, according to this dualist set-up, the only alternatives on offer appear to be "the naïveté of empiricism or the same old narcissistic bedtime stories" (Barad 1998: 827).

This intellectual stalemate was partially broken, or rather bypassed, with the strong wave of relational geography that emerged in the late 1990s and early 2000s. The scholars associated with this movement primarily positioned themselves against humanistic and discourse-oriented geographers, whom they criticized for excessive subjectivism and anthropocentrism leading to a loss of attention to the material aspects of spatial entities and processes. Leading relational geographers such as Doreen Massey and Nigel Thrift instead argued that spatial entities, such as places, can best be understood by focusing on the relations that constitute them—further understanding these relations as being always both social (or rather "associational," cf. Latour 2005) *and* material (see e.g. Thrift 1996, Massey 2005a). Their perspective was thus fundamentally *relational-materialist*, heavily drawing upon developments in so-called Actor-Network Theory (see Massey and Thrift 2003 and further Law 1992).

Abandoning the unproductive quarrel over whether to locate place on either the "social" (subjective/ inter-subjective) or "material" (objective) side of a taken-for-granted divide between these, the relational geographers instead proposed that it may be more fruitful to investigate how agency is produced in the world through the constant interweaving and co-affectation of elements that are normally categorized as belonging on either side of this divide, but which upon closer examination turn out to be fundamentally entangled in the unfolding of worldly events. The basic unit of investigation instead became the *heterogeneous assemblage*, skirting any a priori distinction between the social or material aspects of the unfolding of worldly events (or discursive, cultural, economic, technological, etc. either for that part).

The relational approach to place thus built upon an intuition that we can only ever gain an understanding of places by empirically studying how human and non-human elements interact and mutually affect each other in the world, that is—by studying the relations between humans and non-humans in a specific environment *agnostically*: without prejudice concerning how the mechanics of mutual affectation between those elements which are generally categorized as "material" and those defined as "social," "symbolic," or "discursive," will play out (see also Callon 1986).[2]

Bringing the Subject of Place Back In

Relational geographers managed to side-step the fruitless quarrels of the various reductionist takes on place through conceptualizing places as "thrown-together" and entangled "bundles of trajectories" always concomitantly both "social" and "material" (Massey, 2005a: 119, 142). Nevertheless, Stenner (2008) raises a caution regarding aspects of relational geography through highlighting some problematic aspects relating to the thorny issue of subjects and objects. Effectively, Stenner argues that relational geographers such as Thrift are at such pains to combat what they perceive to be the anthropocentric excesses of humanistically inclined geographers that they are at risk of throwing out the baby of the subject with the bathwater of unwarranted subjectivism through a "too hasty dismissal of the concept of subjectivity as such" which risks a "return to a bleak anti-subjectivism" (Stenner 2008: 92; see also Dawney 2013).[3]

Taking Stenner's argument to the particular concept of place, we may pose the question that if places are bundles of heterogeneous, socio-material relations—what holds these bundles together and grants them identity and coherence *as places*? That is: what is it that enacts particular places as entities with some level of integrity or identity, instead of just endlessly interwoven, partially connecting socio-material patterns stretching through space and time? According to Stenner, we can never get a grasp of questions such as these without bringing the subject "back in" to our analysis, but at the same time doing so in a way that does not privilege *a priori* some subjectivities over other—which might in turn demand a thorough re-definition of the concept of "subjectivity" itself. Stenner draws primarily upon the philosopher Alfred North Whitehead to make this argument, and we will have reason to return to it, but first it might be gainful to turn to a philosopher of science who has particularly engaged with the role of subjectivity in the context of a broad relational-materialist sensibility.

Karen Barad is a feminist philosopher of science trained as a quantum physicist. In her scholarly project she develops and (for good and bad) philosophically formalizes some of the crucial insights of groundbreaking relational materialists such as John Law, Donna Haraway and Bruno Latour (see e.g. Haraway 1994, Latour 1994, Law 2000). In addition to these thinkers, her main inspiration is physicist Niels Bohr and his rendition of the concept "phenomenon," which is very different from the classical phenomenological definition. Barad writes that to Bohr, the primary epistemological unity—the unit that is graspable in knowledge—is not "independent objects with inherent boundaries" but "phenomena" consisting of both subject-effects and object-effects in "dynamic relationality" (Barad 2003: 819). Or as Barad elaborates, "phenomena do not merely mark the epistemological inseparability of 'observer' and 'observed'; rather, *phenomena are the ontological inseparability of agentially intra-acting 'components.'*"

Thus, to Barad, it is only in the phenomenon—in the relation between elements—that elements become endowed with concrete properties. It is only in relations that "form takes form" and "content becomes content" of the elements in relation: "In other words, relata do not preexist relations; rather, relata-within-phenomena emerge through specific intra-actions. Crucially then, intra-actions enact *agential separability*—the local condition of *exteriority-within-phenomena*" (Barad 2003: 819). In Barad's elaboration of Bohr's philosophy, "becoming" not only takes precedence over "being" as the fundamental state of things, but also: these "things" only become enacted and recognizable as such in specific webs of relations. Meaning that "objects" only become objects in relation to other elements relating to them in a "subjective" way as part of a phenomenon-event in which "'part' of the world becomes determinately bounded and propertied in its emergent intelligibility

---

2   It appears as if some leading researchers within the field of environmental psychology have also begun to approximate a relational understanding of places, see e.g. Stedman 2003, Davenport and Anderson 2005.

3   The fairness of this critique qua Thrift's work specifically is certainly debatable. It may well be that the general angle of argumentation in e.g. Thrift (2007) is in the spirit sketched by Stenner, but Thrift is also at pains to point out that "dropping the human subject entirely seems to me to be a step too far" (2007: 13).

to another 'part' of the world" (Barad 2003: 821). Thus conceptualized, phenomena evince the "inseparability of 'objects' and 'agencies of observation'" (Barad 1998: 96), further implying that "'Subjects' and 'objects' do not preexist as such, but are constituted through and within particular practices" (Barad 1998: 106).

Far from any type of stable essences, Barad rather conceptualizes subjects and objects as relational effects: as "objects for subjects" and "subjects in becoming with objects," in specific events or series of interlinked events of more or less lasting durability. This way of conceptualizing the subject/object relation also resonates deeply with the revolutionary *process philosophy* proposed by leading mathematician Alfred North Whitehead already in the early twentieth century, but broadly forgotten until its timely revival in recent years (see e.g. Stenner 2008, Stengers 2011). Whitehead calls subject/object generating-phenomena "actual occasions" (Whitehead, 1929/1978). In an actual occasion, a graspable "image" of the world is generated (or "prehended") from the flow of immanent materiality through an emergent sensing/synthesizing, but also positioned, subject.[4] To Whitehead, objects (or "objectifications")—as discrete and bounded entities—are prehended or sensed aspects of the universe that are always an effect of an instantiation of subjectivity within the universe (i.e. of a subject placed neither above nor beyond it).[5] From such a perspective, "subjectivity" becomes understandable as a specific, positioned "perspective" on the world, a particular nexus of sensing the world at a unique occasion—a partial view of the whole that at the same time makes up a part of the whole (cf. Latour et al. 2013).

The relational-materialist world of Barad and Whitehead, which in many ways intersect with for instance that of philosopher Gilles Deleuze (see Stenner 2008 and e.g. Hillier 2007, Dovey 2010), is a world in which beings and entities constantly generate images of the world and each other, thus enacting each other as objects in the world—a world in which beings and entities thus constantly "read" each other in a eternally ongoing, ever-present, "material semiotics" (cf. Haraway 1988). Where to draw the boundary of what constitutes part of the sensing and the sensed, the subject and the object—and the entangled nature of all the elements of a phenomenon and intersecting object/subjects, is a question of deep (onto)political dignity, which will be further discussed below. But first it is important to explore how this novel ontological 'take' may contribute to refresh our understanding of the phenomenon of place.

Place *as place*, seen from a subject-recognizing relational-materialist position, is both neither and more than "objective brute matter," as the objectivist reductionists would have it, or "subjective projected sentiments" as per the subjectivist reductionists. Rather, place as a phenomenon becomes defined as the full gamut of spatially positioned interrelated subject/object becomings in which intra-acting elements are endowed with identity and integrity, and thus generate spatial entities through which "the many become one and are increased by one" (Whithead 1929/1978: 21) in a process through which disparate elements in space, Massey's "thrown-togetherness," becomes "bounded and propertied in … emergent intelligibility" (Barad 2003: 821). Or in other words: becomes joined together as an articulated place through the integrative, synthesizing function of an instantiation of subjectivity-objectivity which senses the world in situated ways and generates specific images of the world.

Nevertheless, this is not a philosophical idealist argument claiming that places are "mere social constructions" that can be altered at a whim. Rather, it is a recognition that phenomena such as places become in heterogeneous arrangements of variously patterned "stuff" in the world, thus they are not completely "subjective," but still: they always appear as phenomena for a sensing and imaging subject (or ensemble of subjects), where "subjectivity" is one of the products of the phenomena that generates both "objects," such as places, as well as the subjects more or less attached to them.

---

4   Whitehead (1929/1978: 61ff.) teases out the complexity of the notion of "imaging" in a way that is difficult to do justice to in the present context. It is important to note, though, that to Whitehead any apprehension of the world is in a way an "image," e.g. in more complex organisms also individual organs in a body generate "images" of its surroundings, which are then further processed in the brain into a type of composite (or "impure") image of the world. This idea resonates with both the material-semiotic sensibility of, for instance, Donna Haraway, and also with the philosophy of the image developed by Gilles Deleuze (see e.g. Deleuze 1986–1989).

5   I am here consciously (over)simplifying Whitehead's complicated and highly nuanced philosophical terminology, thus not anyway near making justice to his elaborately laid out argumentation. I can only direct the interested reader to the original works of Whitehead for a fuller introduction to his original and creative philosophical vocabulary and reasoning.

From such a perspective, places appear as entities that by necessity are always very much both/and. Always both objective *and* subjective, both always "social" *and* "material" with subjects always attached in various ways to the places they sense (cf. Metzger 2013a, Latour 1999)—as well as, I will now add: both singular *and* multiple, individual *and* collective. Having touched upon the previous conceptual pairings above, it is now time to turn to the final two.

The Ontological Politics of Place

In a discussion moving more on the meta-conceptual level, but also applicable in the present context, Barnes (2008: 1552) has argued that "an idea of place will be sustained only as long as there is a community to support it." This assertion chimes well with the above discussed crucial role of subjectivity in the articulation of place as place. It also points towards the possibility that it may be gainful to understand or investigate places as a type of quasi-object, following Serres' (2007) discussion of the concept as an entity which is not a mere "marker of the subject," but which is "in the world" and to which the subject is "sub-mitted" (Serres 2007: 225ff., see further also Latour 1993: 51ff.). It is an "astonishing constructer of intersubjectivity" (2007: 227) around which subjects coalesce, "a quasi-us" coming together as an entity, "more a contract than a thing" (Serres 1995: 88).

Stating that place can be gainfully understood as a quasi-object, by no means implies that it is a little less "real" compared to other objects. Rather, it serves to highlight that just as atoms, coke bottles or nations, it is dependent on subjectivity for its articulation, to be "bounded" and "propertied," to again use Barad's terms. What Serres wishes to highlight with the concept is how an object such as a place, and the group of subjects that sense that object in similar ways, are deeply entangled. So one could say that place-phenomena always appear in the world with its subjects attached, whether willingly or not—caring or not. The important thing, in this context, with Serres' conceptualization is that it defines the quasi-object as a volatile and mutable entity, the fate of which is "calumny," as it develops in constant mutations—it is a whirlwind, twisting and turning as it is passed between its attached subjects (Serres 1995: 58).

Thus, this conceptualization of place also functions as an important corrective to a too-strong emphasis on "communities" as coalescing around place, if this term is understood with the usual connotations of harmony, stability and mutual recognition. When empirically studying articulations of place in the world, we can also see that harmonious community is far from the norm in relation to places (see also Massey 1991). On the contrary, controversies concerning the correct definition of the identity, boundaries, components and important values related to a specific place are legion. These conflicts often go far beyond the recognized "politics of place," and instead signify a deeper disagreement concerning what a specific place really *is*—what could perhaps be called the *ontological politics* of place, using a concept borrowed from Annemarie Mol (1999). In ontological-political controversies over place there is fundamental disagreement or conflict concerning the fundamental elements or properties of things in the world (i.e. "places") and how/why they come to matter, what Stengers labels as a case of *cosmopolitics*—fundamental struggles over our understanding and enactment of the world (Stengers 2010–2011). So rather than a stabilized and stabilizing "community," places instead seem too often be carried by unruly and divisive "publics," according to how Marres (2005) defines the concept as a definition of actors mutually implicated or attached to an issue or entity in one way or the other, without necessarily having any agreement on either the broader definition, nor the ramifications of the thing in question.

In relation to places, this insight signifies how a disparate group of subjects might all have concern or care for a specific place, they might all carry only partially connecting or even totally conflicting articulations of a place, so to say different articulations of the "essence" of this place (cf. Metzger 2013b). We might have competing architects, preservation activists, different groups of residents, all with different types of attachments to a particular place, and all with their very different articulations of what that place "really is." As a result, places often come across as "out there," but nevertheless hopelessly "fuzzy" or ungraspable. Annemarie Mol calls this type of thing a "multiple object," a thing which "hangs together, but not quite as a *whole*. It is more than one and less than many" (Mol 2002: 84, emphasis in original, see further Metzger and

Schmitt 2012, Metzger 2013b), it is a nexus of partially connecting and overlapping, as well as sometimes conflicting, versions of an object.

In analyzing multiple versions of place that are articulated by various subjects at a given point, an objectivist reductionist would generally consider some (or all) of the versions to be simply incorrect while arguing that there is one correct way—beyond subjectivity—as to how the place should be defined. The subjectivist reductionist would on the other hand argue that everyone is right to assert their individual version of the place, claiming that any version is as true as any other since they are all anyway just arbitrary projections of sentiment onto unknowable, mute matter. A relational-materialist perspective recognizing the role of subjectivity, drawing upon Barad among other inspirations would argue that, far from being arbitrary, places as multiple objects can rather be conceptualized as complex, malleable and sometimes volatile coming-togethers of heterogeneous elements assembled subjectively, but always also dependent on elements that become externalized as beyond or outside of neatly outlined subjects.

From such a perspective, there can be no "right" or "wrong" in the definition of a specific place or statement concerning what a place *is*, as this is never ontologically given—only versions of place with variable situationally given probabilities of becoming to some degrees stabilized and spread. In a way, different—conflicting—versions of place can thus in one way be considered as alternative worlds colliding in a specific place. This does not imply, though, that differences must always turn out to be unbridgeable in some antagonistic fashion à la Carl Schmitt. But it does imply that much is at stake in sometimes superficially banal confrontations over place, as evinced for instance by the Gezi-park protests in Istanbul in or in the less dramatic but still heated controversies over public drinking in parks studied by Bylund and Byerley (2014). Both these examples point towards the concrete specificity of *this* place, *this* park, *these* trees or benches but they also flicker in, as absent-presences or concrete presences (cf. Law 2004) the "big" questions: what is a good society? What is a good life? And further, as we wrestle with these questions, while concerning ourselves with *this* place: whose perspectives and views count? Whose definitions and values? As Barad, and also John Law, have asserted time and again—these are deeply ethical and political questions that in the end also point towards another question: who gets recognized as a valid subject of the specific context, and not a mere mute object?

Towards a More-Than-Human Understanding of Place?

Following Dovey (2010: 23) I have in this chapter made the case that places are neither self-sufficient objects nor "figments of imagination." To use a too-often grossly abused word, they can rather be considered inter-subjective entities; but only granted that in the next breath we add that they are also at the same time inter-objective and (quasi-)objective/subjective, and further granted that we are prepared to see subjectivity as a situated effect of a phenomenon rather than as an ontological constant. Simply put: places appear to be ontologically and epistemologically really *messy* entities (Law 2004)—complex compounds of entangled subject/object relations and often friction-ridden nexuses of strong attachments. Place conceptualized in the above terms is thus both fully "real" and "really-out-there," but at the same time a collectively and relationally constituted phenomenon prone to both iterative evolution and radical mutation.

But even if we fully acknowledge and embrace the fundamental ontological messiness of place—what is there to possibly learn from such a fuzzy conceptualization of an even fuzzier phenomenon, for instance for a member of the "place-making professions"? To begin with: we cannot grasp the full complexity of the phenomenon of place if we disqualify *a priori* its crucial subjective side from the analysis, but neither must we succumb to the temptation to conceptualize place as wholly subjective. The crucial question rather becomes: what subjects of place and related "versions" of place become recognized? For if subjectivity is always a relational and placed effect, there can be no "view from nowhere" (Nagel 1986) to describe place "accurately"—and any pretention at this, positing an epistemological privilege of such a sort, amount to nothing else than what Donna Haraway has derided as "the god trick" (Haraway 1988), a powerful device for claiming power. The question rather becomes: who, or what, is recognized as a legitimate subject to be taken into concern in a specific context?

Relatedly, Häkli and Kallio (2013: 6) have argued that recognition as a subject "is not just a matter of due respect or courtesy, but a vital … need." I would go one step further and claim that recognition for a subject is a question of more than that—and that being seen as an "end" rather than a mere "means" is rather an existential question, in the purest sense of that word, to be recognized as worthy of consideration and concern (cf. Latour 1998, Stengers 2005). But immediately I have to confess that I am partially misquoting Häkli and Kallio above by leaving out the little word "human" between "vital" and "need." This is a word I haven't made use of previously in the text, and consciously so, because it is of crucial concern to me to leave open the question of just who, or *what*, is recognized as a subject worthy of recognition. Even some of the most nuanced investigators of the concept of place appear to take for granted that the subject of place is always human (see e.g. Gieryn 2000: 465 and my own premature assertions in Metzger 2013a). But I think it is crucial, in an era when we have to learn to functionally coexist with a myriad of other-than-human entities the well-being of which our own well-being as a species rests upon, to ask with Massey (2005b: 356 emphasis in original): "Does place *become* place only with human engagement? … is place only place *for* humans?"

For instance to Whitehead any sensing and world-imaging entity counts as a "subject," wherefore Stenner (2008: 105) concludes that in his philosophy "It is important to recognize that the human being cannot be sharply differentiated from other highly complex forms of animal life, and, ultimately, cannot be sharply distinguished from the physical environment more generally" (and to add to that, if we take a fully relational view of the subject with the help of Barad, it may even be troublesome to attempt to rank "highly complex forms" from less complex, considering the non-givenness of the relevant boundary-drawing around subjects). Thus we must ask ourselves: can we extend the definition of the concept of place to also find ways to recognize and encompass the place-making activities of other entities and beings, so as to find better ways to (albeit sometimes grudgingly) coexist on this planet?

If we decide that this is desirable, there are many theoretical and practical avenues worthy of exploration towards such an end (see e.g. Metzger 2014a). For instance, drawing upon Deleuze and Guattari (1987), Dovey (2010) understands place as intimately linked up to Deleuze and Guattari's idea of "territory" and "place-making" to "territorialization": "a synthetic process that enables wholes to form from parts, identities from differences." But a fundamental insight from Deleuze and Guattari (1987) is that it is far from only humans that territorialize. If we are to begin to be able to grasp places as territories to which many types of subjects may be attached we will have to better learn to respectfully read the material-semiotic signals of non-humans, as for instance more radical ethologists do with animals (see e.g. Despret 2004), and we have to decide if the territorial articulations and attachments of these beings and entities are worthy of our respect and consideration. Such a new understanding of place, and the subjects of place, would point into ethically quite unexplored territory, in which we must ask ourselves whose existence and experience counts, and why—and at what costs are the decisions made? (Metzger 2014b). As Massey (2005a: 141) writes, "the throwntogetherness of places demands negotiation … in our relations with non-humans they ask how we shall respond to our temporary meeting up with these particular rocks and stones and trees. They require that, in one way or the other, we confront the challenge of the negotiation of multiplicity." To which I would add: and to do so while staying with the trouble of subjectivity, and without prematurely reducing away the elusive subject of place.

References

Agnew, J. 2011. Space and place. In J. Agnew and D. Livingstone (eds), *Handbook of Geographical Knowledge*. London: Sage, 2011.

Barad, K. 1998. Getting real: Technoscientific practices and the materialization of reality. *Differences: A Journal of Feminist Cultural Studies* 10(2), 87–126.

Barad, K. 2003. Posthumanist performativity: Toward an understanding of how matter comes to matter. *Signs*, 28(3), 801–31.

Barnes, T.J. 2008. American pragmatism: Towards a geographical introduction. *Geoforum*, 39(4), 1542–54.

Bylund, J. and Byerley, A. 2014. The fate of public space in parklife: Hopeless postpolitics and professional idiots. In J. Metzger, P. Allmendinger and S. Oosterlynck (eds), (forthcoming), *Displacing the Political: Democratic Deficits in Contemporary European Territorial Governance*. London: Routledge.

Callon, M. 1986. Some elements of a sociology of translation: domestication of the scallops and the fishermen of St Brieuc Bay. In J. Law (ed.), *Power, Action and Belief: A New Sociology of Knowledge?* London: Routledge, 1986, 196–223.

Casey, E.S. 1997. *The Fate of Place: A Philosophical History*. Berkeley, CA: University of California Press.

Cresswell, T. 2004. *Place: A Short Introduction*. Malden, MA, and Oxford: Blackwell and Carlton.

Davenport, M.A. and Anderson, D.H. 2005. Getting from sense of place to place-based management: An interpretive investigation of place meanings and perceptions of landscape change. *Society and Natural Resources* 18(7), 625–41.

Dawney, L. 2013. The interruption: Investigating subjectivation and affect. *Environment and Planning D: Society and Space* 31, 628–44.

Deleuze, G. 1986–1989. *Cinema*. London: Athlone.

Deleuze, G. and Guattari, F. 1987. *A Thousand Plateaus: Capitalism and Schizophrenia*. Minneapolis, MN: University of Minnesota Press.

Despret, V. 2004. The body we care for: Figures of anthropo-zoo-genesis. *Body and Society* 10(2–3), 111–34.

Dovey, K. 2010. *Becoming Places: Urbanism/Architecture/Identity/Power*. London: Routledge.

Gieryn, T.F. 2000. A space for place in sociology. *Annual Review of Sociology* 463–96.

Häkli, J. and Kallio, K.P. 2013. Subject, action and polis theorizing political agency. *Progress in Human Geography*, DOI: 10.1177/0309132512473869.

Haraway, D. 1988. Situated knowledges: The science question in feminism and the privilege of partial perspective. *Feminist Studies* 14(3), 575–99.

Haraway, D. 1991. A cyborg manifesto: Science, technology, and socialist-feminism in the late twentieth century. In D. Haraway, *Simians, Cyborgs and Women: The Reinvention of Nature*. London: Free Association Books, 149–81.

Haraway D. 2010. When species meet: Staying with the trouble. *Environment and Planning D: Society and Space* 28(1) 53–5.

Haraway, D. 2013. Presentation given for the John E. Sawyer Seminar on the Comparative Study of Cultures "Indigenous Cosmopolitics: Dialogues about the Reconstitution of Worlds." UC Santa Cruz, May 20, 2013.

Hillier, J. 2007. *Stretching beyond the Horizon: A Multiplanar Theory of Spatial Planning and Governance*. Burlington, VT: Ashgate.

Latour, B. 1993. *We Have Never Been Modern*. Cambridge, MA: Harvard University Press.

Latour, B. 1994. On technical mediation. *Common Knowledge* 3(2), 29–64.

Latour, B. 1998. To modernize or to ecologize? That's the question. In N. Castree and B. Willems-Braun (eds), *Remaking Reality: Nature at the Millennium*. London and New York: Routledge 221–42.

Latour, B. 1999. Factures/fractures: From the concept of network to the concept of attachment. *Res: Anthropology and Aesthetics* 36, 20–31.

Latour, B. 2005. *Reassembling the Social: An Introduction to Actor-Network-Theory*. Oxford: Oxford University Press.

Latour, B., Jensen, P., Venturini, T., Grauwin, S. and Boullier, D. 2012. "The whole is always smaller than its parts": A digital test of Gabriel Tardes' monads. *The British Journal of Sociology* 63(4), 590–615.

Law, J. 1992. Notes on the theory of the actor-network: Ordering, strategy, and heterogeneity. *Systems Practice* 5(4), 379–93.

Law, J. 2000. On the subject of the object: Narrative, technology, and interpellation. *Configurations* 8(1), 1–29.

Law, J. 2004. *After Method: Mess in Social Science Research*. London: Routledge.

Marres, N.S. 2005. No issue, no public: Democratic deficits after the displacement of politics. Doctoral thesis, Department of Philosophy, University of Amsterdam.

Massey, D. 1991. A global sense of place. *Marxism Today* 35(6), 24–9.

Massey, D. 2005a. *For Space*. London: Sage.

Massey, D. 2005b. Negotiating nonhuman/human place. *Antipode* 37(2), 353–7.

Massey, D. and Thrift, N. 2003. The passion of place. In R. Johnston and M. Williams (eds), *A Century of British Geography*. Oxford: Oxford University Press, 275–99.

Metzger, J. 2013a. Placing the stakes: The enactment of territorial stakeholders in planning processes. *Environment and Planning A* 45(4), 781–96.

Metzger, J. 2013b. Raising the regional Leviathan: A relational-materialist conceptualization of regions-in-becoming as publics-in-stabilization. *International Journal of Urban and Regional Research* 37(4), 1368–95.

Metzger, J. 2014a The moose are protesting: Conceptualizing planning politics across the human/non-human divide. In J. Metzger, P. Allmendinger and S. Oosterlynck (eds), (forthcoming), *Displacing the Political: Democratic Deficits in Contemporary European Territorial Governance*. London: Routledge.

Metzger, J. 2014b. The city is not a Menschenpark: Conceptualizing the urban commons across the human/non-human divide. In C. Borch, M. Kornberger and E. Barinaga (eds), (forthcoming), *Urban Commons: Organizing the City*. London: Routledge.

Metzger, J. and Schmitt, P. 2012. When soft spaces harden: The EU strategy for the Baltic Sea Region. *Environment and planning A* 44(2), 263–80.

Mol, A. 1998. Ontological politics: A word and some questions. *The Sociological Review* 46(S), 74–89.

Mol, A. 2002. *The Body Multiple: Ontology in Medical Practice*. Durham, NC: Duke University Press.

Nagel, T. 1986. *The View from Nowhere*. New York: Oxford University Press.

Serres, M. 1995. *Genesis*. Ann Arbor, MI: University of Michigan Press.

Serres, M. 2007. *The Parasite*. Minneapolis, MN: University of Minnesota Press.

Stedman, R.C. 2003. Is it really just a social construction?: The contribution of the physical environment to sense of place. *Society & Natural Resources* 16(8), 671–85.

Stengers, I. 2005. Whitehead's account of the sixth day. *Configurations* 13(1), 35–55.

Stengers, I. 2010–2011. *Cosmopolitics I–II*. Minneapolis, MN: University of Minnesota Press.

Stengers, I. 2011. *Thinking with Whitehead: A Free and Wild Creation of Concepts*. Cambridge, MA: Harvard University Press.

Stenner, P. 2008. AN Whitehead and subjectivity. *Subjectivity* 22(1), 90–109.

Thrift, N. 1996. *Spatial Formations*. London: Sage Publications.

Thrift, N.J. 2007. *Non-Representational Theory: Space, Politics, Affect*. London: Routledge.

Tuan, Y. 1977. *Space and Place: The Perspective of Experience*. Minneapolis, MN: University of Minnesota Press.

Whitehead, A.N. 1978. *Process and Reality: An Essay in Cosmology* (corrected edn). New York: Free Press.

Chapter 12
What is Good Urbanism?

Nan Ellin[1]

Good Urbanism Is ...

Gift-Based

Good urbanism builds upon what is integral to people and locales—their *prima materia* or DNA. It enhances places by revealing and celebrating these existing gifts, rather than focusing on deficits and problems. The gifts may include natural landscapes, buildings, neighborhoods, businesses, cultural institutions, history and cultural traditions, as well as the talents, ideas, and skills of stakeholders.

Hence, good urbanism supplants the hierarchy of needs (Figure 12. 1) with a hierarchy of gifts (Figure 12. 2):

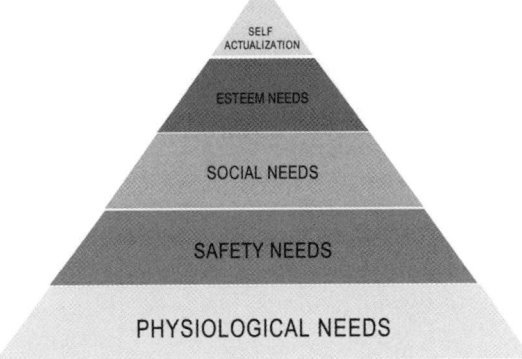

Figure 12.1   Maslow's hierarchy of needs (1943)

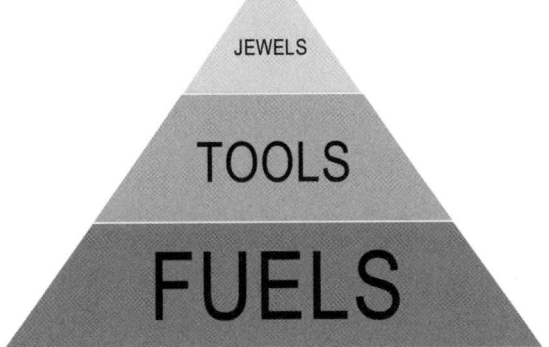

Figure 12.2   Hierarchy of gifts

---

1   Unless otherwise specified, all figures in this chapter are the author's own.

From fuels at the base (sun, water, food, wind, fossil fuels, and other energy sources) and tools above (knowledge, intuition, and skills; construction, machine, and digital tools; and communication, transportation, and building technologies), the hierarchy of gifts suggests we can extract jewels.

Good communication (writing, speaking, etc.) about places similarly begins with an appreciation for what is working, thereby offering inspiration and instruction. In contrast, the modernist genre of criticism focuses on what is not working, typically offering cautionary tales about what not to do.

Complementary

Just as complementary medicine looks at the whole person including the physical environment, a complementary urbanism looks at the whole environment, including people. Similar to complementary currencies—such as travel miles, time banking, and local currencies—good urbanism complements what is already there rather than attempt to replace it, or compete with it. It protects what is valued, enhances what may be underperforming, and then builds upon this *tabula plena* (full slate), rather than presume a *tabula rasa* (erased slate) (Figure 12.3).

Figure 12.3   **The tabula plena approach protects what is valued first, then enhances what may be underperforming, and then adds new elements informed by effective community enagagement**

Inclusive and Sideways

Good urbanism is co-creative, inviting a wide range of professionals and stakeholders to participate, welcoming them when they do, and partnering to bring ideas to life (Figure 12.4).

Figure 12.4   **Co-creation: Invite, welcome, partner**

Good urbanism is not top-down, but nor is it bottom-up. It proceeds sideways, beginning with an idea hatched by one or more people who quickly include others to refine and realize the vision so that decision-makers, urban design professionals, and communities are working together toward mutually beneficial ends. Combining the "hierarchy of needs" with the "hierarchy of assets," this rotated pyramid might look something like this (Figure 12.5).

When community erodes, an "architecture of fear" occupies the void (Ellin 1997). Good urbanism offers an "architecture of love" (Ellin 2012) that fosters community by cultivating relationships through a process that builds mutually supportive networks of people.

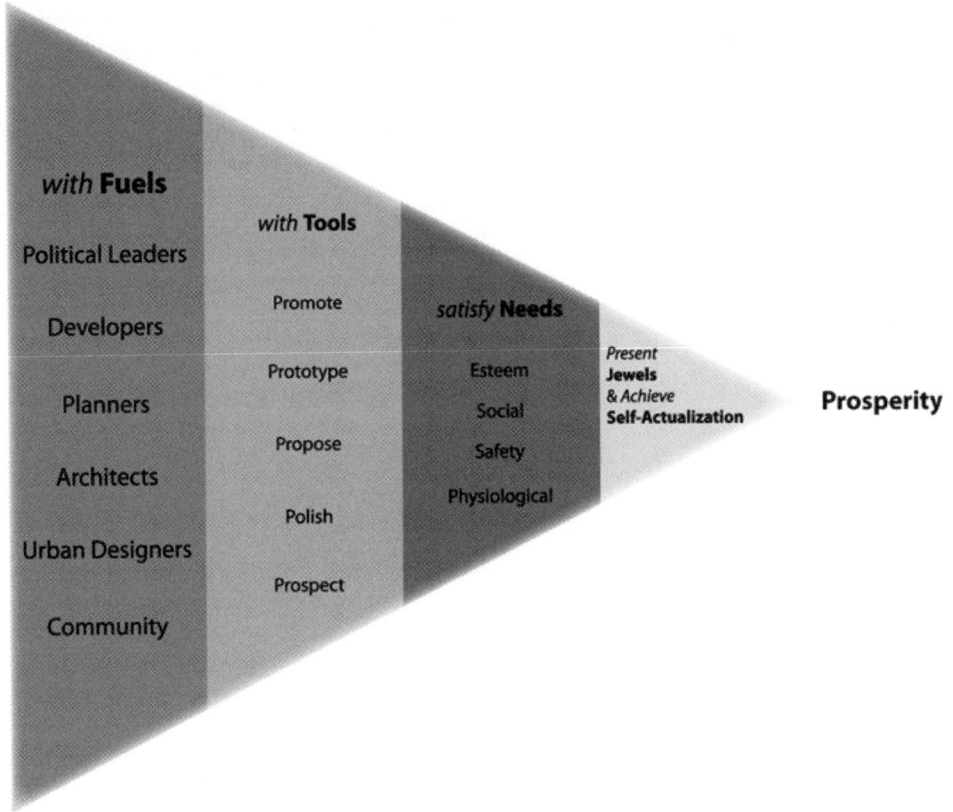

Figure 12.5   Prosperity pyramid: A sideways urbanism

Idealistic and Incremental

Good urbanism aims to create prosperous places where all people can live prosperous lives. It measures success in terms of such prosperity, rather than power, profit, and prestige. The Path toward Prosperity follows a virtuous spiral of six steps: Prospect, Polish, Propose, Prototype, Promote, and Present (Figure 12.6). It is an economy of gifts, beginning with gifts and ending with them.

Professional and Proactive

While inclusive, good urbanism relies upon the expertise and experience of professional urban designers, architects, planners, and landscape architects—typically working in teams. In addition to providing technical skills, these professionals bring an understanding of which building traditions are appropriate for any given situation—the humanist, landscape ecology, systems, and/or form-making avant-garde. Often, good urbanism draws innovatively from several traditions.

Slow, Flow, Low, and Local

Placing a brake on rapid change and the havoc it can wreak, good urbanism embraces *slow*ness, coincident with the Slow City (http://www.cittaslow.org) and Slow Food (http://www.slowfood.com) movements. Beginning with what is integral to places and people, good urbanism finds existing *flows* and goes with them, and/or

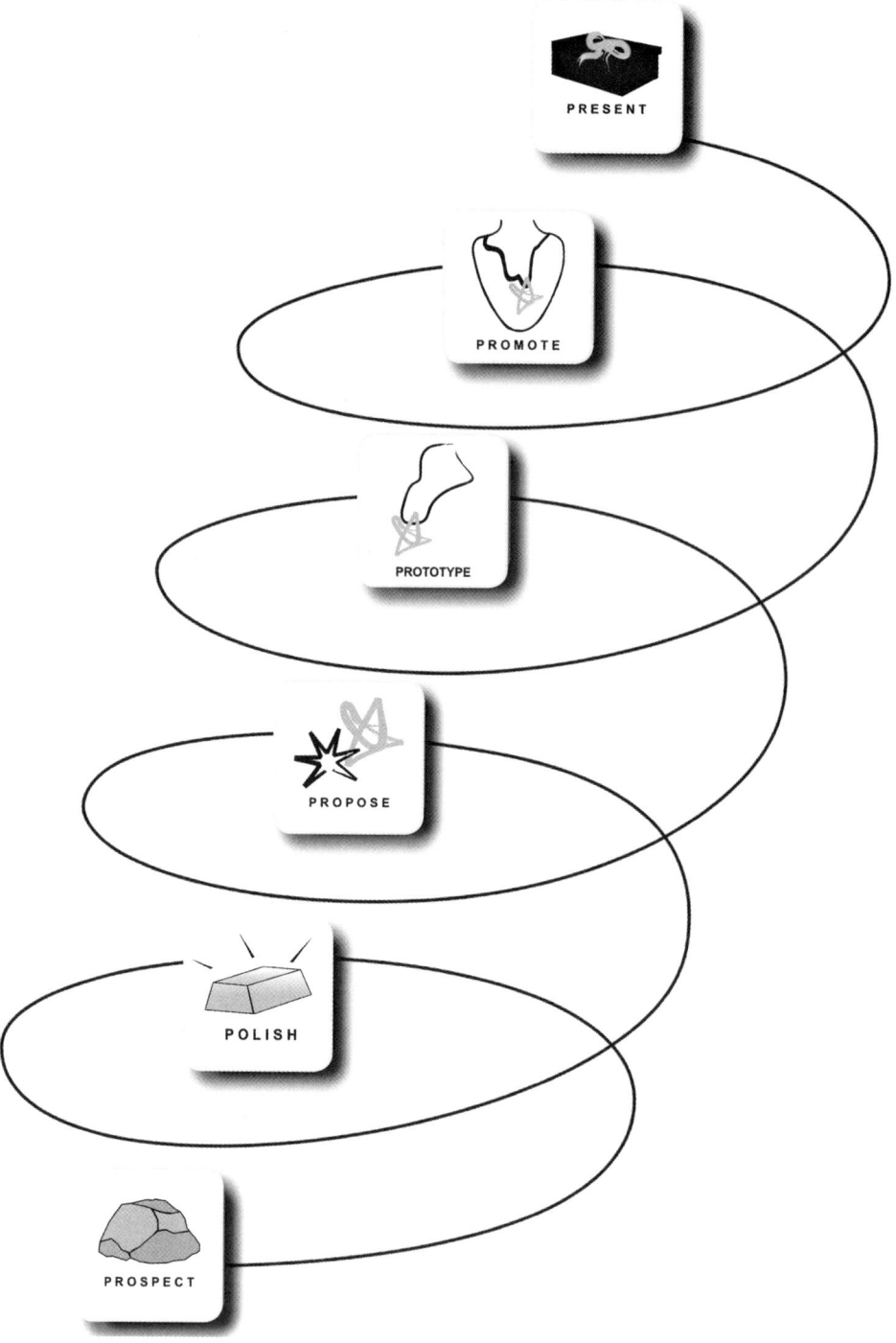

Figure 12.6   The six steps along the path toward prosperity

unblocks them to clear physical as well as social blockages, engaging in urban acupuncture. The most simple, elegant, and efficient solutions are often *low*-tech and low-impact, for instance, the use of swales, cisterns, and graywater instead of sewers and municipal water, along with urban agriculture replacing nonproductive right-of-ways, grass lawns and the purchase of produce from grocery stores. The mantra of the moment is grow, eat, shop, hire, incubate (ideas, technologies, and businesses), and generate (energy) local (Figure 12.7).

A Process as Well as a Product

Good urbanism describes both an approach to enhancing places for people and the resulting places. Those who practice it design the process, sharpening other tools of the trade and lending to a successful product. Good urbanism envisions best possibilities and rallies resources to realize them. It is not principally tactical, instead combining strategy with serendipity.

Figure 12.7   How Local Can You Go?, outside Whole Foods in Salt Lake City

Generative and Integrative

The process as well as the product creates synergies and efficiencies. Good urbanism sets a generative and dynamic self-adjusting feedback mechanism into motion, enabling clients and other stakeholders to build creatively upon their strengths in an ongoing fashion.

Part of a Worldwide Movement with No Name

The momentum currently gathering toward good urbanism figures within what Paul Hawken has described as a worldwide "movement with no name" that will prevail because it is not based on ideology, but on the identification of what is humane, behaving like an immune system (Hawken 2007) to heal social and urban malaise. Though it may have no name, some keywords and characteristics of this new paradigm are (Figure 12.8):

Figure 12.8   Keywords and characteristics of the new paradigm as word clouds

Transformative

Good urbanism can transmute problems into opportunities by revealing blessings that may be disguised and making virtue of necessity. Moving beyond sustainability to prosperity, it envisions and realizes better futures in a world that needs them now more than ever (Figure 12.9).

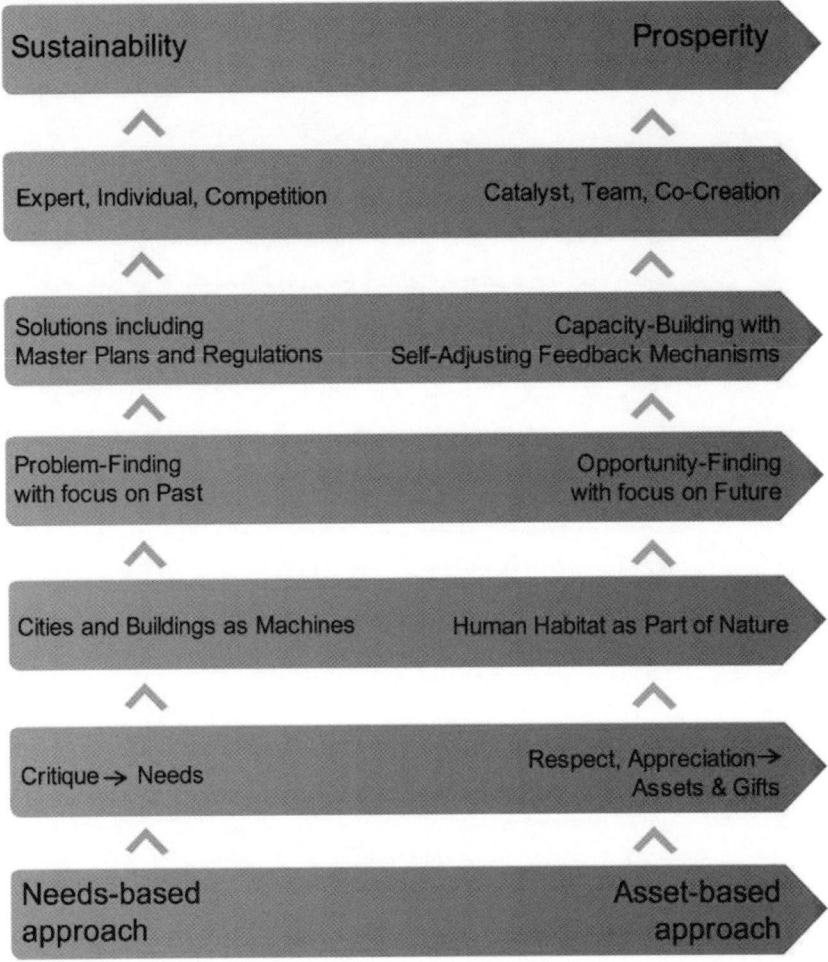

Figure 12.9   The shift from sustainability to prosperity

References

Ellin, N. (ed.) 1997. *Architecture of Fear*. New York: Princeton Architectural Press.

Ellin, N. 2012. Architecture of Love, for the *Museum of Fearology* (Michael Fisher (curator)), September 2012. Available at: http://beamsandstruts.com/articles/item/1059-the-architecture-of-fear.

Hawken, P. 2007. *Blessed Unrest: How the Largest Movement in the World Came into Being and Why No One Saw It Coming*. New York: Viking Press.

Chapter 13

The Challenge of Social Sustainability: Revisiting the Unfinished Job of Defining and Measuring Social Sustainability in an Urban Context

Andrea Colantonio

Introduction

The concept of social sustainability finds itself at an interesting crossroads. Social Sustainability has developed into both a critical tool and a key conceptual framework to assess issues surrounding the environmental, economic and social dimensions of the built and social environment of neighborhoods, communities and cities. The challenge though lies in how social sustainability is defined and then measured. There is no consensus on what criteria and perspectives should be adopted in defining social sustainability. Academics and policy-makers tend to define social sustainability as it relates to discipline-specific criteria or a specific study perspective. This thus makes a generalized definition applicable to a wide variety of disciplines and topics difficult to achieve. The challenge in defining social sustainability goes one step further when the practical application of the concept is brought into relief. Indeed, if academics and policy-makers cannot agree on a general definition of social sustainability, how can we then robustly measure the concept as it is applied to policy and practice? This is not a new challenge and indeed a review of the literature clearly demonstrates the evolution of the concept from one that was originally a dimension of sustainable development to a concept that now stands on its own.

That said, the fact remains that our understanding of this concept is still fuzzy and limited by theoretical and methodological constraints that stem from its disciplinary-dependent definitions and measurement. As a way to illustrate this point, this chapter will explore how the introduction of new "soft" themes, such as happiness, well-being and social capital, are becoming both central to the social sustainability debate, but paradoxically hampering the measurement of social sustainability.

While this "sophistication" in the definition of social sustainability mirrors the changing social needs of individuals and communities it also adds complexity to the interpretation and measurement of social sustainability. By proposing a taxonomical distinction between "hard" social policy areas and emerging "softer" research and policy making themes, the development of new sustainability metrics is increasingly focused on measuring "emerging" themes rather than on improving the assessment of more "traditional" concepts such as equity an fairness. The latter, for example, continue to be measured mainly in terms of income distribution and other monetary variables, hampering meaningful progress in the ultimate goal of assessing social sustainability. But, a review of the City of Rotterdam's (Holland) "Social Index" demonstrates how the city has developed an innovative index to measure the social evolution of local neighborhoods.

Thus, the aim of this chapter is threefold. First, it provides an overview of the challenge to defining social sustainability. Second, this chapter outlines the changing nature of measurable indicators, introducing a taxonomical division between "hard" and "soft" themes and between traditional and emergent social sustainability indicators. Finally using the example of the City of Rotterdam's Social Index, the chapter explores how emerging social sustainability indicators are used to measure a neighborhood's sustainability.

Defining Social Sustainability

Our understanding of social sustainability is rooted in, on the one hand, the debate about the social implications of environmental issues and on the other, as a component of the sustainable development debate of the 1960s and 1970s. It was only in the late 1990s that social issues were taken into account and the sustainability agenda broadened. While social sustainability's growing recognition has spurred an emerging body of literature, as noted above, there is no general definition that both academics and policy-makers can agree on. That said, Weingaertner and Moberg (2011) argue that there appears to be an underlying common understanding of what social sustainability is underpinned by a set of key themes—social capital, human capital and well-being. It is Littig and Griessler (2005) who argued that the under-theorization of social sustainability has resulted in approaches to the social sustainability concept being grounded in a more practical understanding that mirror current political agendas. As a result of this approach, social sustainability can lend itself to a range of divergent goals—be it the urban social sustainability of the built environment (Bacon et al. 2012); the sustainability of companies and products (Dempsey et al. 2011); or sustainable development within the "ecological footprint" concept (Rees and Wackernagel 1996).

Yet, as Sachs (1999) notes, at a fundamental level, it is still unclear whether the concept of social sustainability means the social preconditions for sustainable development or the need to sustain specific structures and customs in communities and societies. Moreover, the relationship between the different dimensions of sustainable development—"sustainabilities"—are still unclear. Assefa and Frostell (2007), for example, argue that social sustainability is the finality of a development whilst economic and environmental sustainability are both the goals of sustainable development and the instruments to achievement it. Similarly, Hardoy et al. (1992) dispute interpretations where social sustainability is defined purely as the social condition necessary to support environmental sustainability. The challenge is thus that social sustainability as a concept becomes something that can be applied to any policy issue without the necessary intellectual rigor to provide a meaningful framework for analysis. Nonetheless Table 13.1 outlines the number and variety of definitions that do indeed exist.

For Sachs's (1999) social sustainability is interpreted as a socio-historical process rather than a static state because of the open ended historical process of socioeconomic development. This process depends, in part, on human imagination, projects and decisions subject to both the constraints of the natural environment and the burden of the living past. From Sachs's social sustainability is fluid. It is not a zero-sum game, where something is either sustainable (one) or not (zero). Littig and Griessler's (2005: 72) sociological interpretation emphasizes the importance of both "work," which is emblematic of the German sustainability discourse, and "needs" as defined by the Brundtland Commission (1987). Similarly, Biart (2002: 6) highlights the importance of the "social" in social sustainability for the sustainable development of societies.

Table 13.1   Examples of definitions of social sustainability

A strong definition of social sustainability must rest on the basic values of equity and democracy, the latter meant as the effective appropriation of all human rights – political, civil, economic, social and cultural – by all people	Sachs (1999: 27)
… a quality of societies. It signifies the nature-society relationships, mediated by work, as well as relationships within the society. Social sustainability is given, if work within a society and the related institutional arrangements satisfy an extended set of human needs [and] are shaped in a way that nature and its reproductive capabilities are preserved over a long period of time and the normative claims of social justice, human dignity and participation are fulfilled	Littig and Griessler (2005: 72)
[Sustainability] aims to determine the minimal social requirements for long-term development (sometimes called critical social capital) and to identify the challenges to the very functioning of society in the long run	Biart (2002: 6)
Development (and/or growth) that is compatible with harmonious evolution of civil society, fostering an environment conducive to the compatible cohabitation of culturally and socially diverse groups while at the same time encouraging social integration, with improvements in the quality of life for all segments of the population	Polese and Stren (2000: 15–16)

Yet, his analysis is void of any reference to the physical environment, which opens him up to the common criticism that sociology has often suffered, namely its failure to include the physical and non-social realm in any analysis (Omann and Spangenberg 2002). Polese and Stren (2000: 15–16) provide a more comprehensive definition of social sustainability that focuses especially on urban environments. They emphasize the economic (development) and social (civil society, cultural diversity and social integration) dimensions of sustainability, highlighting the tensions and trade-offs between development and social disintegration intrinsic to the concept of sustainable development. Unlike Biart, Polese and Stren acknowledge the importance of the physical environment (e.g. housing, urban design and public spaces) within the urban sustainability debate. In the context of urban areas specifically, Ancell and Thompson-Fawcett (2008), amongst other authors, point out that social sustainability definitions that include and emphasize social equity and justice have the potential to assist cities in evolving to become "good" places by facilitating a more equitable distribution of resources.

Recent work from Bramley et al. (2006, 2009), contends that social sustainability depends upon several aspects of community and neighborhood life, which include (i) interactions in the community/social networks; (ii) community participation; (iii) pride/sense of place; (iv) community stability; (v) security (crime). Along similar lines Manzi et al. (2010) argue that the social sustainability of urban areas overlap with three "grand policy ideas" including social exclusion, social capital and governance.

By contrast, from a narrower housing and built environment perspective, Chiu (2004) identifies three main approaches to the interpretation of social sustainability. The first equates social sustainability to environmental sustainability. Here social sustainability depends on specific social relations, customs, structures and values, representing the social limits and constraints of development. Chiu (2004) refers to the second interpretation as "environment-oriented," which are the social preconditions required to achieve environmental sustainability. Here social structures, values and norms can be adapted to enable individuals to maximize their activity within the physical limit of the planet. Thirdly, the "people-oriented" approach focuses on reducing social exclusion and conflict through the equitable distribution of resources. Chiu (2004) adopted the second and third approach to demonstrate how social conditions, social relations, housing quality and the equitable distribution of housing resources and assets are key components of sustainable housing development.

Going one step further, from a policy perspective, the Berkeley Group in the United Kingdom commissioned researchers to define a concept of social sustainability that could be used to measure a range of factors that influence local quality of life and the strength of a community (Bacon et al. 2012). For them, social sustainability combines a design of the physical environment with a focus on how the individuals who live in and use the space relate to each other and function as a community. According to their study, if done well, the development of the built environment provides a strong social and cultural life, opportunities for people to participate in their community and scope for both the built place and the community to evolve.

Despite the range of definitions and approaches to social sustainability, for the purpose of this chapter, social sustainability can be envisioned as a continuum in which different levels of social sustainability exist depending on a mix of "hard" and "soft" social factors, ideals and aspects concerning *how* individuals and communities live with each other. At an operational level, social sustainability stems from key thematic areas ranging from capacity building and skills development to environmental and spatial inequalities (see Colantonio 2007 for a complete list). In this sense, social sustainability blends traditional social policy areas such as basic needs, equity and health with issues concerning participation, social capital, the economy, the environment and more recently, happiness, well-being and quality of life. Thus, given the cross-disciplinary nature of social sustainability, a better understanding of the meanings and interpretations of social sustainability are essential.

The Changing Nature of Measurable Indicators and Its Impact on the Research of Social Sustainability

A review of the key themes explored thus far suggests that the more traditional themes of equity, poverty reduction and livelihood have slowly been either replaced or are meant to complement more intangible and less measurable concepts such as identity, sense of place and the benefits of "social networks." Table 13.2

illustrates this broad shift from analyzing "hard" themes towards the increasing inclusion of "softer" concepts into the sustainability discourse.

Due to the speculative nature of social sciences, and the emerging mix of hard and soft themes in the social policy debate, the challenge is the ability of researchers to scientifically understand the inter-relationship between hard and soft themes in order to identify optimal social targets and objectives to be pursued with the objective of delivering socially sustainable places. Indeed, the multiple combinations of hard and soft themes coupled with the disagreement over their meanings hinder the scientific identification of what is and what is not socially sustainable. More dangerous yet, ill-conceived assumptions and theories concerning the elements conducive to social sustainability can potentially lead to the implementation of inadequate social policies. A classic example of this peril is represented by the assumption that higher income automatically fosters more socially sustainable communities by, for example, reducing crime or boosting personal and communal satisfaction.

However, there is evidence in EU cities that low-income communities can be more satisfied with their area than higher income communities (Blom 2009), thus making the whole community more social-sustainable because of increased levels of bonding with and attachment to of local residents to their area. Thus, social sustainability-oriented policies geared only toward increasing household income in disadvantages communities should be used in combination with other policies addressing other pressing local social issues.

Table 13.2   Traditional and emerging social sustainability key themes

Traditional	Emerging
Basic needs, including housing and environmental health	Demographic change (ageing, migration and mobility)
Education and skills	Social mixing and cohesion
Employment	Identity, sense of place and culture
Equity	Empowerment, participation and access
Human rights and gender	Health and Safety
Poverty	Social capital
Social justice	Well-being, happiness and quality of life

As new themes emerge, new indicators for measurement emerge as well. Historically, long lists of indicators were established to describe the complexity of sustainable development, with a special focus on the environmental dimension—Therivel (2004) demonstrated that two-thirds of sustainability indicators addressed environmental concerns alone. Over time, the more technical list of indicators has expanded to include social indicators. The long lists of indicators have since been simplified and reduced to a set of core indicators (Hens and De Wit 2003) which are "bundled" into sustainability themes, objectives and guiding principles.

In terms of social sustainability metrics, Colantonio (2007) argued that the evolution of indicators illustrates how older indexes prioritize the basic needs component whilst indicators developed more recently seem to emphasize the importance of governance, representation and other institutional factors (see Colantonio 2007 for a review of this evolution). In older indexes the elements taken into account were technically weighted together with other dimensions of sustainable development in an attempt to deliver an integrated approach to sustainability. However, in later sustainability indicators, the final decision about trade-offs is de facto left to "sound judgement" as well as leadership and communication skills (Egan 2004). Thus, the "community" and the "local level" have re-emerged as the main operational space for assessing sustainability (see recent study by Bacon et al. 2012). Over time, there has been a shift from analyzing sustainability using purely statistic-based indicators toward hybrid sets of indicators that mix quantitative and qualitative data.

Broadly speaking, a review of recent developments and trends in social sustainability assessment and measurement also suggests a broad distinction between "traditional social indicators" and "social sustainability indicators," summarized in Table 13.3. According to this categorization, it can be argued that traditional social indicators are used for the analysis of discrete issues accessible to specific methodologies related to individual themes that are linked to targets rather than objectives. The indicators are often selected by experts in national and regional statistical offices who focus on targets and outcomes which results in a static analysis of national and regional social phenomena.

By contrast, social sustainability indicators are concerned with the integration of multidimensional and intergenerational issues inherent to the notion of sustainability. The selection of indicators is informed by sustainability principles and objectives, which stem from a deliberative and reiterative participation process involving a wide array of stakeholders and local agents. Moreover, sustainability indicators are *process indicators* in that they analyze the processes through which sustainability principles and objectives are defined, themes agreed upon and solutions implemented. They allow the monitoring of the actual implementation of a project or a phenomenon and assess the progress towards specific objectives in a more interactive way than traditional social indicators.

Table 13.3   Characteristics of traditional social indicators and social sustainability indicators

Traditional social indicators	[Emerging] Social sustainability indicators
Static	Intergenerational and incorporating uncertainty
Predominantly quantitative	Hybrid
Product	Process
Descriptive	Strategic
Mono-dimensional	Multidimensional
Target oriented	Principles and objective driven
Top-down selection	Deliberative and reiterative selection

This is perhaps best exemplified when looking at how poverty is "measured" from a "traditional perspective" as opposed to a "social sustainability perspective." Poverty is traditionally measured in the UK using an income threshold (i.e., the proportion of individuals living in households whose income is below 60 percent of the national median) by calculating how many individuals in a household fall below the threshold (Townsend and Kennedy 2004). By contrast, from a sustainability perspective, poverty would be measured using a more complex measure which incorporates other elements such as ill-health, inadequate housing and limited access to basic services in a multidimensional index that integrates the processes and factors conducive of poverty. These include, for example, marginalization, inability to access education or poor quality housing. Yet, from an operational perspective, there are problems with this measurement approach. For example, current integrative frameworks still do not allow a meaningful aggregation of a diverse range of metrics. Keirstead (2007), for instance, argues that it is not clear how fuel poverty and quality of life data can be combined into a single social sustainability metric. Even if data can be normalized and weighted, it proves difficult to aggregate social, environmental, economic and institutional metrics in a composite index that can be compared at both spatial and temporal levels. But there is another important point.

The question is how to come up with an indicator to measure across these very desperate and different topics? Ultimately, these are indicators of different things—some indicate causes, others outcomes while some are the consequence of social sustainability. Counting them all in one measure is like counting apples and oranges. Furthermore, how should the importance or "weight" of these different factors be balanced? Is the design of the park, for example, more or less important than the management of it? This assumes that we can measure and compare all these things accurately at the individual level at the same moment in time.

The development and integration process of indicators is hindered further by the shift in the social sustainability discourse from an in-depth analysis of hard themes towards the inclusion of soft themes, as reviewed earlier. As a result, new sustainability indicators are increasingly focused on measuring these emerging themes rather than improving the measurement of the more traditional concepts such as equity and fairness. For example the Office for National Statistics (ONS 2011) has recently included four questions on subjective well-being in the ONS Integrated Household Survey (IHS) with the objective of creating a trusted set of indicators which will help to understand and monitor national well-being and happiness. Indeed in the UK the Conservative government elected in 2010 is updating New Labour's guidelines that relied on the measurement of equity using an analysis of income and relative prosperity, as outlined in the UK Green Book, for the appraisal of government policies, plans and projects (HM Treasury 2005).

Moreover, the tendency to favor the investigation of softer themes at the expense of perfecting the measurement of more established social sustainability indicators is demonstrated in the development of more recent sustainable development indicators. For example, the sustainable development indicators released by the UK government in 2007 (ONS and DEFRA 2007) contains a Sustainable Communities and a Fairer World cluster of indicators, addressing social sustainability concerns. This cluster suggests several indicators to assess different aspects of sustainable communities, including well-being, life satisfaction and happiness. However, it does not recommend any index to deal with the interlinked subjects of social justice, equity, fairness and cohesions (ONS and DEFRA 2007: 96). Similarly, a study commissioned by the EU Parliament (EP 2007) to examine the implementation of the Sustainable Communities approach in the EU concluded that fairness cannot be adequately measured through existing indicators and that further work is needed in this area.

An Example of Emerging Social Sustainability Indicators: The Social Index in Rotterdam

Despite the theoretical and practical challenges to monitoring the social evolution of places, this section illustrates the practical example of the "Social Index" (see Figure 13.1), which is a composite index launched in 2008 by Rotterdam municipal authorities to monitor the social quality of the city's poorest neighborhoods.

The index collects and aggregates data concerning four main dimensions of Rotterdam's areas and their residents: (i) *personal abilities* (language skills, health, income, education); (ii) *living environment* (level of discrimination, housing, public facilities, safety, etc.); (iii) *participation* (going to work/school, social contact, social and cultural activities, etc.); and (iv) "*bonding*" (mobility, "feeling connected," etc.) (Leidelmeijer et al. 2007). The index produces a score between 0 and 10, which has four main purposes, including measuring the social quality of a place at a given time, showing and comparing the differences between 64 of the 80 districts of Rotterdam, providing a baseline for the assessment of policies, and analyzing the strengths and weaknesses of each neighborhood in relation to the dimensions included in the index (Koppelaar 2009, Leidelmeijer et al. 2007, Gemeente Rotterdam 2008). The index, which is calculated yearly, comprises statistical (30 percent) and survey (70 percent) data.

Since the first Social Index report was published in 2008, the City of Rotterdam has published three subsequent annual reports. The most recent report was published in 2012 based on data collected in 2011. While the Social Index is relatively new, there can be little doubt that this index embodies some of the main characteristics of emerging sustainability indicators reviewed in Table 13.3. Indeed, the Social Index is a multidimensional and hybrid indicator in the sense that it endeavors to aggregate different social sustainability themes together through a mix of qualitative (survey to measure participation and bonding) and quantitative data (official statistics for the assessment of, for example, living environment and personal abilities) analysis. In addition, data for the calculation of the Social Index is gathered at the neighborhood level with the objective of providing an overview of how people live together, participate in local community activities and feel connected with each other (RIGO, 2007). This brief analysis of the Social Index highlights the main methodological and theoretical issues involved in the measurement of social sustainability (at the local level). Further it provides an opportunity for policy-makers and practitioners alike to reflect on the key rationale and methods that should be adopted to conceptualize the evaluation of local, national and international social policies.

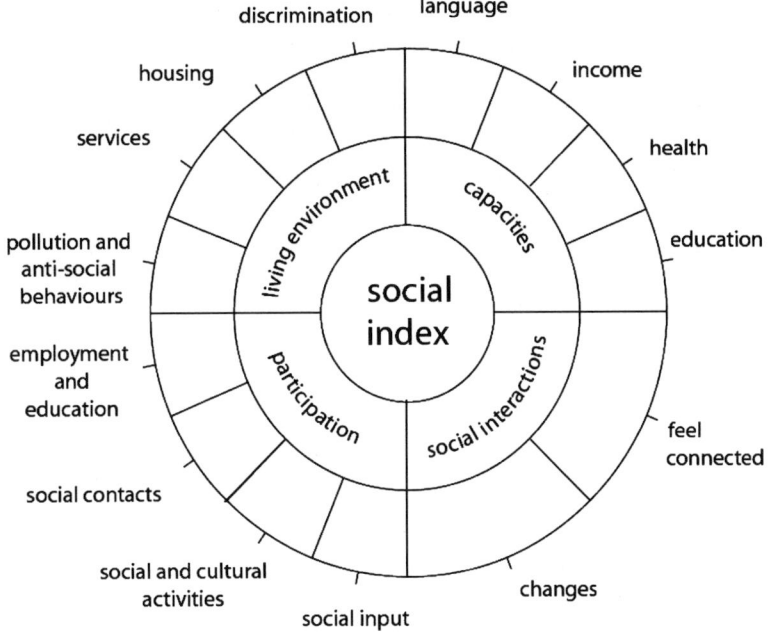

Figure 13.1   The social index

Source: Translated and redrawn by Colantonio from Gemeente Rotterdam (2008).

Conclusion

This chapter provides a concise overview of the current challenges to defining and measuring social sustainability in urban contexts. The overarching challenge for the topic of social sustainability is the current disconnect that exists between how social sustainability is defined within a wide and diverse multidisciplinary field and what indicators are then used to measure it. This chapter has suggested a taxonomical division between "hard" and "soft" themes and between traditional and emergent social sustainability indicators. The shift toward the analysis of more and arguably elusive "emerging" concepts in the social sustainability debate may continue for the foreseeable future. However, it is important that this new focus on emerging themes and indicators is not pursued at the expense of a more in-depth analysis of the traditional pillars of social sustainability, such as equity and poverty, which have received less attention in recent urban development works.

The Social Index is perhaps amongst the most developed and applicable social sustainability metric systems to date, and provides an encouraging starting point for the purposeful development of social sustainability measurement. Most specifically, the following elements would have to be developed in addition to those already outlined by the Social Index. Firstly, stakeholders' involvement in sustainability assessment is often deemed in practice more consultative rather than participative, due to the complexity of the overall assessment process and the availability of resources. Social sustainability indexes should thus involve more participation of area residents and stakeholders, incorporating them into the initial design of the index and allowing them to decide for themselves what themes are important in their local area.

Secondly, methodologically it is essential for aggregate indexes to (i) identify the sound balance between traditional and soft factors and apply them in ways that are reflective of local contexts, and (ii) find accurate methods of presenting indexes in ways that do not distort the nuances of specific areas or the severity of specific factors that may be offset or neutralized through composites and averages (e.g. gains in language skills may intact sense of attachment etc.).

Lastly, from a practical perspective, one of the major challenges of sustainability indicators will be to identify cost effective ways to generate and manage large quantities of data over regular intervals that are needed to monitor the progress towards more sustainable outcomes. This is especially important in the new economic landscape brought about by the 2008 global economic crisis in European countries in which the retreat of welfare policies, the reduction of urban regeneration funding at the national level and European, and the reduced possibilities of local economies and public finances is likely to impact how the "social dimension" in urban regeneration policies is addressed.

Indeed, the current economic and fiscal crises pose a threat to the future of urban development and regeneration programs and policies of many cities across the world, and their long-term sustainability. It is therefore crucial that future research will continue to highlight the importance of placing social sustainability at the heart of urban development.

References

Assefa, G. and Frostell, B. 2007. Social sustainability and social acceptance in technology assessment: A case study of energy technologies, *Technologies in Society* 29, 63–78.

Bacon, N., Cochrane, D. and Woodcraft, S. 2012. *Creating Strong Communities: How to Measure the Social Sustainability of New Housing Developments*. The Berkley Group.

Biart, M. 2002. Social sustainability as part of the social agenda of the European Community, in T. Ritt (ed.), *Soziale Nachhaltigkeit: Von der Umweltpolitik zur Nachhaltigkeit?* Informationen zur Umweltpolitik 149. Vienna: Arbeiterkammer Wien, 5–10.

Blom, D. 2009. Pact op Zuid—Pact of South. Presentation at Workshop on Social Sustainability and Urban Regeneration, Oxford Brookes University, Oxford, February 19–20, 2009.

Bramley, G. and Power, S. 2009. Urban form and social sustainability: The role of density and housing type, *Environment and Planning B: Planning and Design* 36(1), 30–48.

Bramley, G., Dempsey, N., Power, S. and Brown, C. 2006. What is "social sustainability" and how do our existing urban forms perform in nurturing it? Sustainable Communities and Green Futures Conference, University College London.

Brundtland Commission 1987. *Our Common Future*. New York: World Commission on Environment and Development.

Chiu R.L.H. 2004. Socio-cultural sustainability of housing: A conceptual exploration, *Housing, Theory and Society* 21(2), 65–76.

Colantonio, A. 2007. *Social Sustainability: An Exploratory Analysis of Its Definition, Assessment Methods, Metrics and Tools*, OISD (EIB) Working Paper 2007/01.

Dempsey, N., Bramely, G., Power, S. and Brown, C. 2011. The social dimension of sustainable development: Defining urban social sustainability, *Sustainable Development* 19(5), 289–300.

Egan, J. 2004. *The Egan Review: Skills for Sustainable Communities*. London: ODPM.

European Parliament (EP). 2007. *The Possibilities for Success of the Sustainable Communities Approach and Its Implementation*. European Parliament Study Directorate-General for Internal Policies of the Union Structural and Cohesion Policies Policy Department.

Gemeente Rotterdam. 2008. *Rotterdam sociaal gemeten.1e meting door de Sociale Index*. Rotterdam: City of Rotterdam Publishing.

Hardoy, J., Mitlin, D. and Satthertwaite, D. 1992. *Environmental Problems in Third World Cities*. London: Earthscan Publications.

Hens, L. and De Wit, J. 2003. The development of indicators for sustainable development: A state of the art review, *International Journal of Sustainable Development* 6, 436–59.

HM Treasury 2005. *The Green Book: Treasury Guidance*. TSO: London.

Keirstead, J. 2007. Selecting sustainability indicators for urban energy systems. International Conference on Whole Life Urban Sustainability and Its Assessment, SUE-MoT Conference Proceedings, Glasgow.

Koppelaar, P. 2009 Social index: A social monitor for the municipality of Rotterdam. Presentation at the Urban Regeneration and Social Sustainability Workshop, Oxford Institute for Sustainable Development, Oxford Brookes University.

Leidelmeijer, K., van Iersel, J. and den Herder, m.m.v. N. 2007. Sociale index RotterdamBijlagenrapport. Unpublished, RIGO Research en Advies BV, Amsterdam.

Littig, B. and Griessler, E. 2005. Social sustainability: A catchword between political pragmatism and social theory, *International Journal of Sustainable Development* 8(1–2), 65–79.

Manzi, T., Lucas, K., Lloyd-Jones, T. and Allen, J. 2010. Understanding social sustainability: Key concepts and developments in theory and practice. In T. Manzi, K. Lucas, T. Lloyd-Jones, and J. Allen (eds), *Social Sustainability in Urban Areas*. London and Washington, DC: Earthscan, 1–28.

Office of National Statistics (ONS) 2011. Measuring National Well-being: National Statistician's Reflections on the National Debate on Measuring National Well-being. Newport: ONS.

Office of National Statistics (ONS) and Department for Environment Food and Rural Affairs 2007. *Sustainable Development Indicators in Your Pocket*. London: DEFRA Publications.

Omann, I. and Spangenberg, J.H. 2002 Assessing social sustainability: The social dimension of sustainability in a socioeconomic scenario. Paper presented at the 7th Biennial Conference of the International Society for Ecological Economics in Sousse (Tunisia), March 6–9, 2002.

Polese, M. and Stren, R. (eds) 2000. *The Social Sustainability of Cities: Diversity and the Management of Change*. Toronto: University of Toronto Press.

Rees, W.E. and Wackernagel, M. 1996. *Our Ecological Footprints: Reducing Human Impact on the Earth*. Gabriola Island, BC, and Stony Creek, CT: New Society Publishers.

RIGO 2007. Sociale index Rotterdam Bijlagenrapport, RIGO Research en Advies BV, Amsterdam.

Sachs, I. 1999. Social sustainability and whole development: Exploring the dimensions of sustainable development. In B. Egon and J. Thomas (eds), *Sustainability and the Social Sciences: A Cross-Disciplinary Approach to Integrating Environmental Considerations into Theoretical Reorientation*. London: Zed Books.

Therivel, R. 2004. *Sustainable Urban Environment Metrics, Models and Toolkits: Analysis of Sustainability/ Social Tools*. Oxford: Levett-Therivel.

Townsend, I. and Kennedy, S. 2004. *Poverty: Measures and Targets*. Research Paper 04/23, Economic Policy and Statistics Section, House of Commons Library, London.

Weingaertner, C. and Moberg, Å. 2011. Exploring social sustainability: Learning from perspectives on urban development and companies and products, *Sustainable Development* 22(2), 122–33.

PART III
The Urban Product

Chapter 14

Emergent Urbanism as the Transformative Force in Saving the Planet

Peter Newman[1]

The most significant force in saving the planet is when cities begin to grow without using fossil fuels. The great urban revolution of the twentieth century was based around a continuing growth in the total and per capita consumption of fossil fuels leading to the problems of climate change, oil security, air pollution and urban sprawl.

The twenty-first century is beginning to show that this reversal may well be underway and that a new kind of city is emerging where economic growth is decoupling from fossil fuel growth and new greener, more competitive cities are emerging (Glaeser 2010). Some of this evidence will be presented before outlining how we can ensure the trends continue.

Peak Fossil Fuel Power Investment and Use

In 2008 the world began to invest more money in renewable energy than in fossil fuels to generate power (Wills and Newman 2012). Figure 14.1 shows the trend and the dotted lines shows the predicted levels that fossil fuel investment was going to reach through some global agencies. Since then we have been informed by the World Bank and the U.S. Government that they will no longer fund coal-fired power stations.

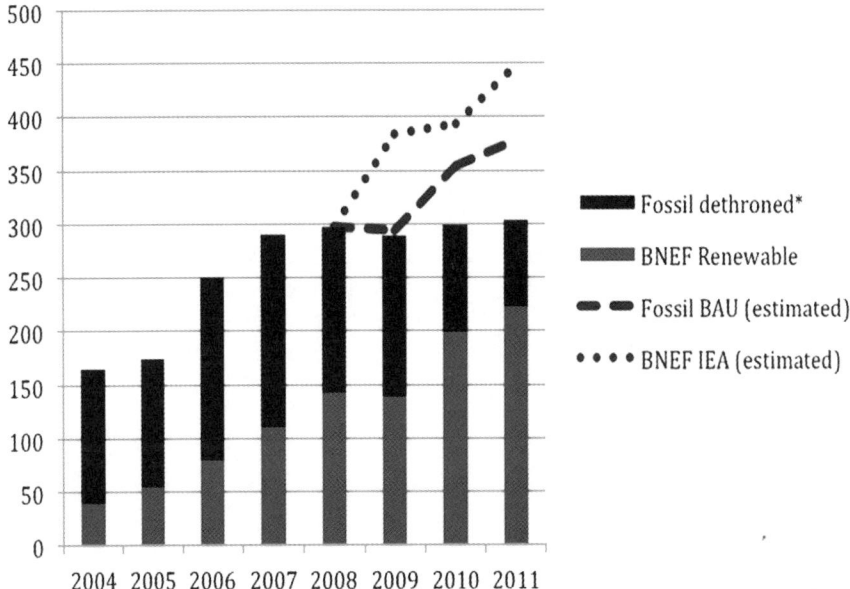

Figure 14.1   The peak of investment in power stations, fossil and renewable energy

---

1   Unless otherwise specified, all figures in this chapter are the author's own.

At the same time there is another emerging trend—decreased power consumption. In Figure 14.2 the decline in household power used in the UK is shown.

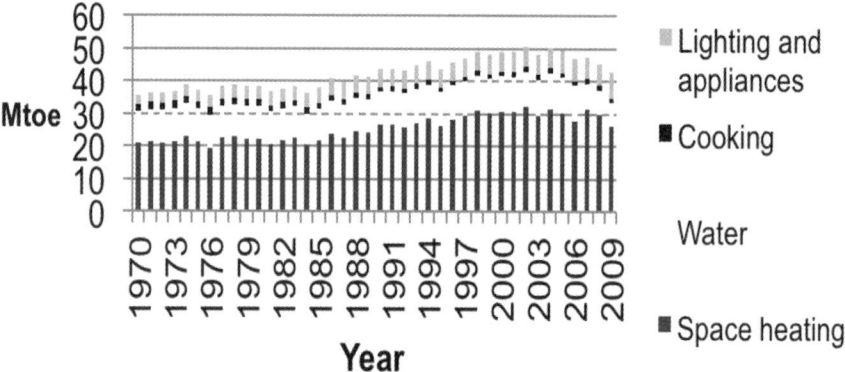

Figure 14.2   The peak in household power consumption, UK

The same has been found across the OECD nations including Australia where a new phenomenon is emerging of photovoltaic electricity as a major power part of urban power. Figure 14.3 shows how Perth has adopted PV on rooftops—mostly in the outer suburbs. The 140,000 homes that have adopted PV in the past three years are producing 310 MW of power—like a whole new centralized power plant.

The lack of space in the inner suburbs and the extra utility bills in large houses in the suburbs suggests an emerging Low Carbon Urban Transition Theory (Newton and Newman 2013). This suggests a model for the low carbon urban transition involving combinations of simple technological changes and harder structural changes, depending upon which parts of the urban fabric are in focus. In outer suburbs the PVs are easy but reducing oil in car use is hard and will require new infrastructure and urban centers (Dodson and Sipe 2008, and see below), whilst the inner suburbs have many more transport options that are relatively easy but power use will need new decentralized trigeneration systems at precinct scale.

In 2009 the Brookings Institution was the first to recognize a new phenomenon in the world's developed cities—declines in car use (Puentes and Tomer 2009). Peak car use suggests that we are witnessing the end of building cities around cars as the primary goal of planning—at least in the developed world—and probably the rediscovering of the compact city. Perhaps we are witnessing the demise of further automobile city building and the beginning of the end of automobility.

Peak Car Use

Puentes and Tomer (2009) first picked up the trend in per capita car use starting in 2004 in U.S. cities. They were able to show that this trend was occurring in most U.S. cities and by 2010 was evident in absolute declines in car use.

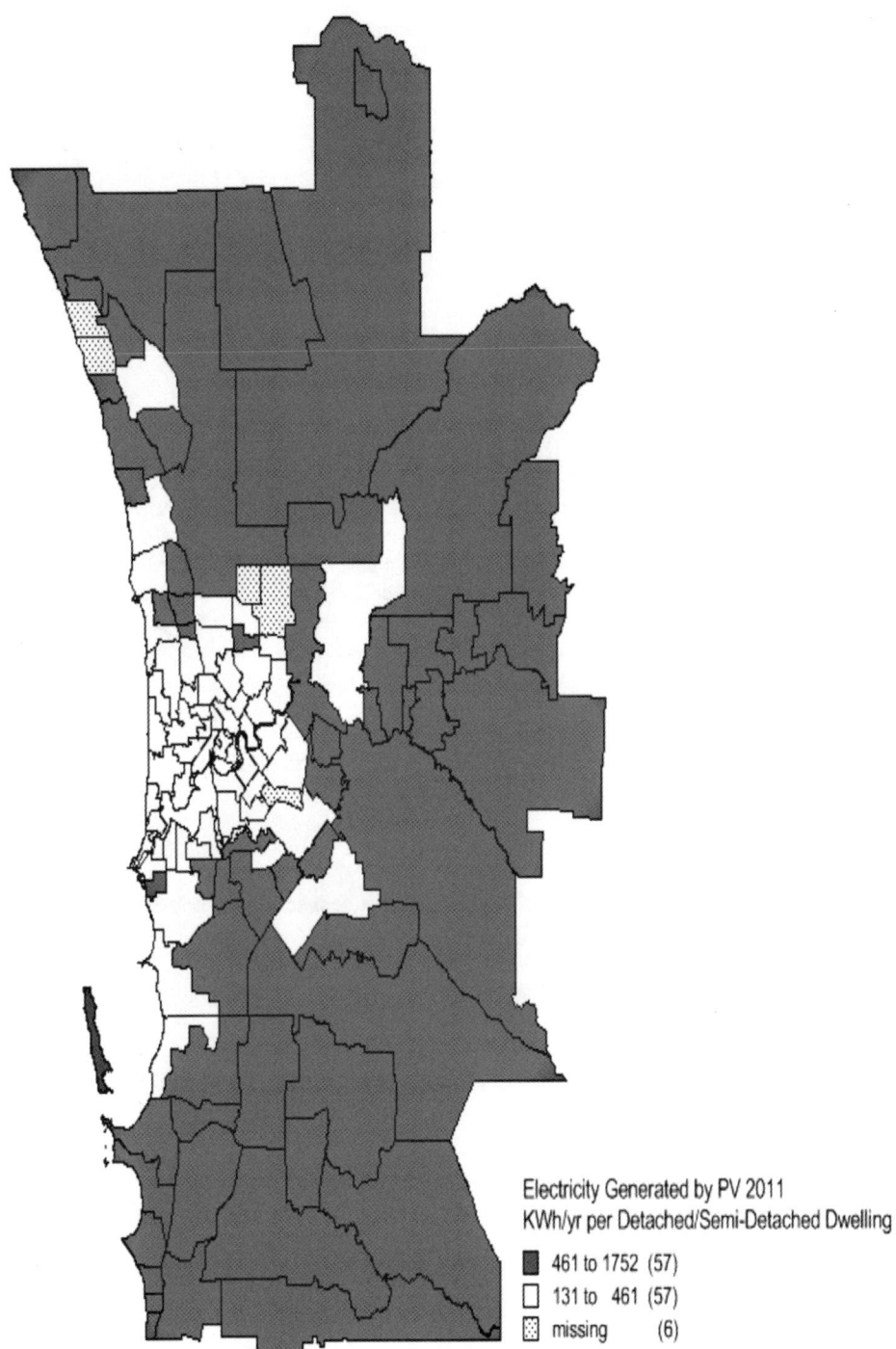

Figure 14.3   Spatial Distribution of PV Systems by Subrban Area in Perth, 2012

Stanley and Barrett (2010) found a similar trend was obvious in Australian cities and that the peak had come at a similar time—2004—and car use per capita at least seemed to be trending down ever since. We have since mapped this in all Australian cities, including small ones where congestion is no issue and relevant graphs and data can be found in Newman and Kenworthy (2011).

Millard-Ball and Schipper (2010) examined the trends in eight industrialized countries that demonstrate what they call "peak travel." They conclude that:

> Despite the substantial cross national differences, one striking commonality emerges: travel activity has reached a plateau in all eight countries in this analysis. The plateau is even more pronounced when considering only private vehicle use, which has declined in recent years in most of the eight countries … Most aggregate energy forecasts and many regional travel demand models are based on the core assumption that travel demand will continue to rise in line with income. As we have shown in the paper, this assumption is one that planners and policy makers should treat with extreme caution. (2010: 16–17)

The Global Cities Database (Kenworthy and Laube 2001, Kenworthy et al. 1999) has been expanding its global reach since the first data were collected in the 1970s. While the 2005/2010 data are yet to be completed the first signs of a decline in car use can be gleaned from previous data and were first recognized by us when it was seen that cities in the developed world grew in car use per capita in the 1960s by 42 percent, in the 1970s by 26 percent, and the 1980s by 23 percent. The new data now show that the period 1995–2005 had a growth in car use per capita of just 5.1 percent, which is consistent with the above data on peak car use (Newman and Kenworthy 2011). The reductions have started after this decade and appear to be continuing (Gargett 2012).

In the 26 cities that comprise the 1995–2005 percentage increase in car VKT per capita, some cities actually declined in this period. Some European cities show this pattern: London has declined 1.2 percent, Stockholm 3.7 percent, Vienna 7.6 percent, Zurich 4.7 percent. In the U.S., Atlanta went down 10.1 percent, Houston 15.2 percent (both from extraordinarily high levels of car use in 1995), Los Angeles declined 2.0 percent and San Francisco 4.8 percent. The acceleration in decline has mostly been since that time.

Peak car use appears to be happening. It is a major historical discontinuity that was largely unpredicted by most urban professionals and academics. So what is causing this to occur?

The Possible Causes of "Peak Car Use"

The following five factors are examined; they all suggest a less automobile-dependent city is emerging.

Hitting the Marchetti wall
As outlined above, the travel time budget matters. Freeways designed to get people quickly around cities have become car parks at peak hours. Travel times have grown to the point where cities based around cars are becoming dysfunctional. As cities have filled with cars the limit to the spread of the city has become more and more apparent with the politics of road rage becoming a bigger part of everyday life and many people just choosing to live closer in.

The trends in relative speeds are shown in Figure 14.4.

The ratio of overall public transit system speed compared to general road traffic has increased from 0.55 to 0.70 between 1960 and 2005, the ratio of rail system speed to general road traffic has gone from rail being slower than cars in 1960 (0.88) to a situation in 2005 where rail was on average faster (1.13). Thus rail has become increasingly more viable as an option in the world's cities. And with it will be a greater emphasis on rail-induced compact land use patterns and a growing move away from freeway-induced land use scatter. The remaining data presented in this chapter supports this.

The automobile city seems to have hit the Marchetti wall.

The growth of public transit
Globally there is a big increase in public transport (Newman et al. 2013). The extraordinary revival of public transit is especially evident in car-dependent Australian and American cities in terms of growth rates (see

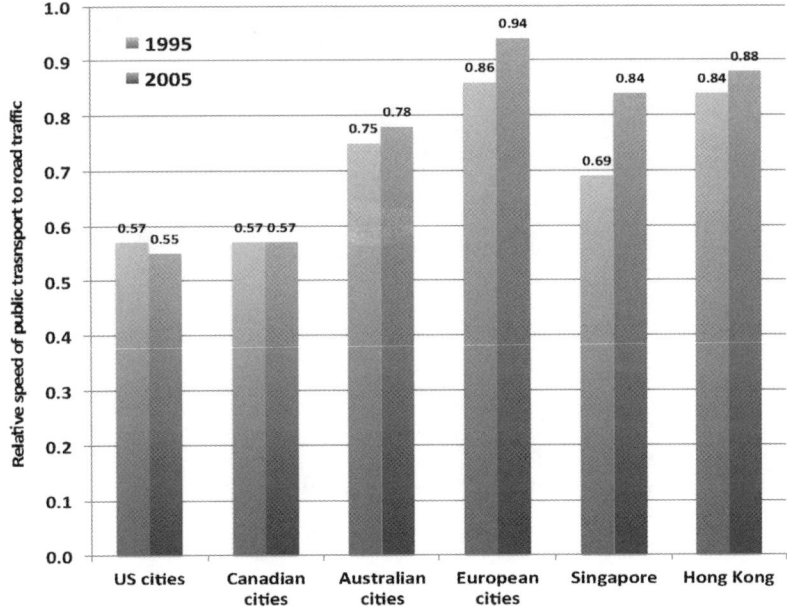

Figure 14.4   Relative speed of public transit to car traffic and rail to car traffic in global cities, 1960 to 2005

Source: Newman, Glazebrook and Kenworthy 2013.

Figure 14.6) but in terms of absolute numbers European and Asian cities continue to lead. This is demonstrated in Figure 14.5.

The growth in public transit was always seen by transport planners as a small part of the transport task and car use growth would continue unabated. However, there is an exponential relationship between car use and public transit use that indicates how significant the impact of public transit can be. By increasing public transit use per capita the use of cars per capita is predicted to go down exponentially. This is the so-called "transit leverage" effect (Neff 1996, Newman et al. 2008). Thus even small increases in public transit can begin to put a large dent in car use growth and eventually will cause it to peak and decline.

The reversal of urban sprawl

The turning back in of cities leads to increases in density rather than the continuing declines that have characterized the growth phase of automobile cities in the past 50 years. The data on density suggest that the peak in decline has occurred and cities are now densifying faster than they are spreading out. Table 14.1 contains data on a sample of cities in Australia, the USA, Canada and Europe showing urban densities from 1960 to 2005 that clearly demonstrate this turning point in the more highly automobile-dependent cities. In the small sample of European cities included in the table, densities are still declining due to *shrinkage* or absolute reductions in population, but the data clearly show the rate of decline in urban density slowing down and almost stabilizing as re-urbanization occurs.

The relationship between density and car use is also exponential as shown previously (Newman and Kenworthy 1989, 1999). If a city begins to slowly increase its density then the impact on car use can be more extensive than expected. The compact city is being rediscovered.

The growth of a culture of urbanism

Commentators are increasingly picking up a renewed interest in living a more urban and less suburban lifestyle (Leinberger 2007, Newman and Newman 2006). Puentes and Tomer (2009) suggest this is not a

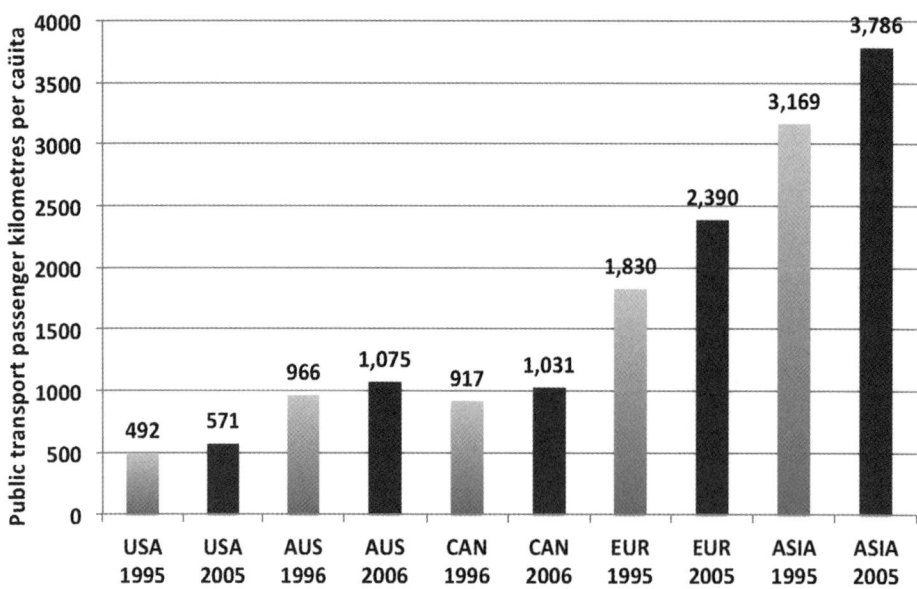

Figure 14.5   **Recent strong growth in U.S. public transit use, especially rail**
Source: American Public Transportation Association 2013.

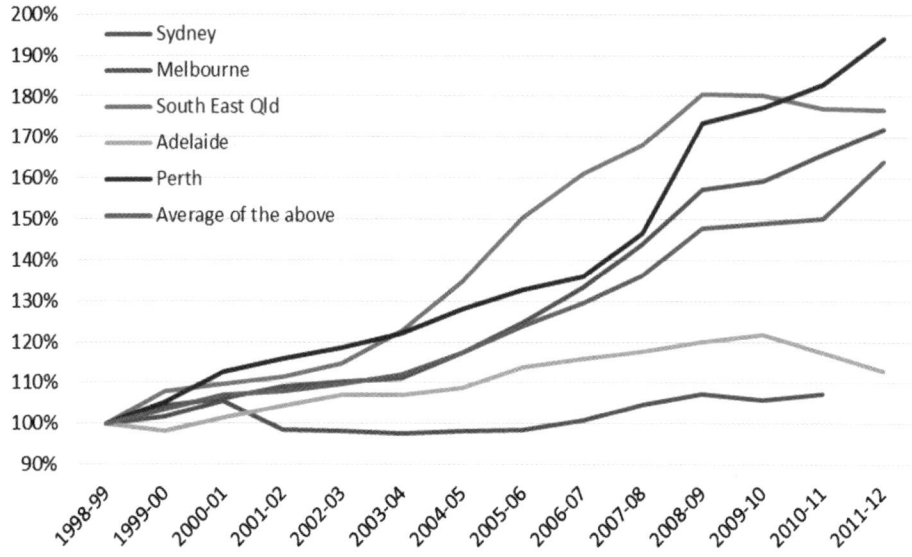

Figure 14.6   **Growth in public transit use in Australian cities since 1999**
Source: Authors' data compiled from Australian cities' public transit authorities.

Table 14.1   **Trends in urban density (persons per ha.) in a sample of U.S., Canadian, Australian and European cities, 1960–2005**

	1960	1970	1980	1990	1995	2005
Brisbane	21.0	11.3	10.2	9.8	9.6	9.7
Melbourne	20.3	18.1	16.4	14.9	13.7	15.6
Perth	15.6	12.2	10.8	10.6	10.9	11.3
Sydney	21.3	19.2	17.6	16.8	18.9	19.5
Chicago	24.0	20.3	17.5	16.6	16.8	16.9
Denver	18.6	13.8	11.9	12.8	15.1	14.7
Houston	10.2	12.0	8.9	9.5	8.8	9.6
Los Angeles	22.3	25.0	24.4	23.9	24.1	27.6
New York	22.5	22.6	19.8	19.2	18.0	19.2
Phoenix	8.6	8.6	8.5	10.5	10.4	10.9
San Diego	11.7	12.1	10.8	13.1	14.5	14.6
San Francisco	16.5	16.9	15.5	16.0	20.5	19.8
Vancouver	24.9	21.6	18.4	20.8	21.6	25.2
Frankfurt	87.2	74.6	54.0	47.6	47.6	45.9
Hamburg	68.3	57.5	41.7	39.8	38.4	38.0
Munich	56.6	68.2	56.9	53.6	55.7	55.0
Zürich	60.0	58.3	53.7	47.1	44.3	43.0

Source: Newman and Kenworthy 2011.

fashion but a structural change based on the opportunities that are provided by greater urbanism. The cultural change associated with this urbanism is reflected in many aspects of popular culture, especially the use of mobile digital devices which enables freedom and connection without a car (Florida 2010).

"Footloose jobs," particularly those related to the global economy, can theoretically go anywhere in a city and can make the difference between a viable center or not. However, there is considerable evidence that such jobs are locating in dense centers of activity due to the need for networking and quick "face-to-face" meetings between professionals. High amenity, walking-scale environments are better able to attract such jobs because they offer the kind of environmental quality, livability and diversity that these professionals are seeking.

As Florida (2012) says:

> Economic growth and development, according to several key measures, is higher in metros that are not just dense, but where density is more concentrated. This is true for productivity, measured as economic output per person, as well as both income and wages. (Florida 2012, November 12, 2012)

Other cultural factors seem to now be associating with higher density locations such as social integration, innovation and talent levels. This holds for both the share of college graduates and the share of knowledge, professional, and creative workers (Glaeser 2010). Most citizens who experience car dependence, and have long commutes stuck in traffic, can understand the need for more sustainable options, since they directly feel and bear the economic, social and environmental consequences of car dependence. They want other options provided for them. As cities continue to evolve, the politics of sustainable transport will demand both more livable and less car dependent options for the future.

The rise in fuel prices

The vulnerability of outer suburbs to increasing fuel prices was noted in the first fuel crisis in 1973–74 and in all subsequent fuel crisis periods when fuel price volatility was clearly reflected in real estate values (Fels and Munson 1974, Romanos 1978). The return to "normal" after each crisis led many commentators to believe that the link between fuel and urban form may not be as dramatic as first presented by people like us (Newman and Kenworthy 1989, 1999). However, many commentators now believe that rising oil prices, and the urban forms that compel demand for oil, are the source of financial crises.

Despite the global recession, the twenty-first century has been faced by a consolidation of fuel prices at the upper end of those experienced in the last 50 years of automobile city growth. Most oil commentators including oil companies now admit to the end of the era of cheap oil, even if not fully accepting the peak oil phenomenon (Newman et al. 2009). The compact city is being driven by transport factors outlined above but fuel price volatility and uncertainty will certainly have added to the value in living closer to urban activity.

The Future City

Will these trends continue? The economic drivers can be changed if priorities in infrastructure spending are artificially forced back into funding coal-fired power and freeways. However, this is unlikely as the world is now showing significant economic growth that is decoupling from fossil fuels (ADB 2012). For example Figure 14.7 shows there is now a clear trend emerging to decouple urban GDP from car use.

The future is likely to continue to emerge based around this decoupling process, though some cities are likely to emerge much quicker than others with new green economy systems (Newman et al. 2009, Gehl 2011).

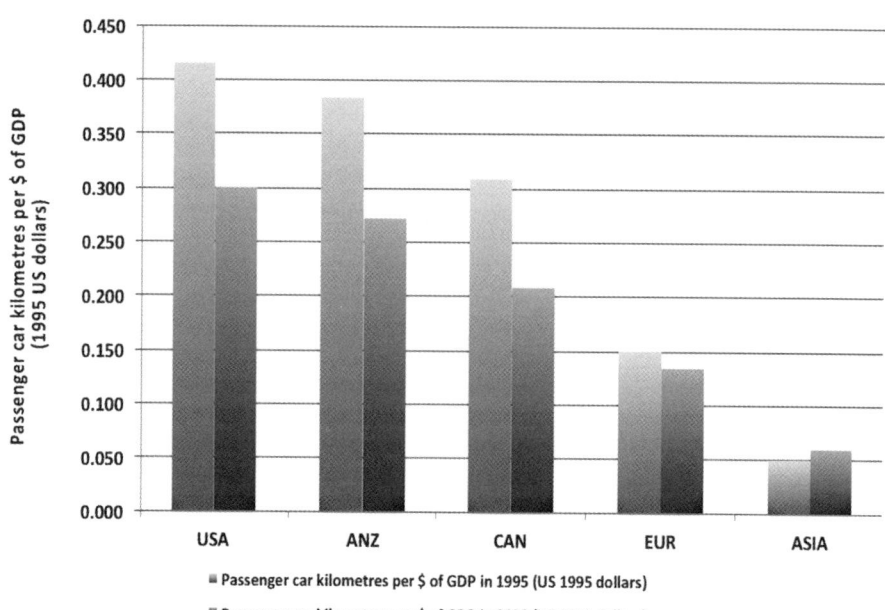

Figure 14.7   The decoupling of urban GDP per capita and car use per capita
Source: Kenworthy 2013.

Mechanisms for Facilitating the Emerging City

Facilitating the emerging renewably based city needs the easing of barriers to the rapid spread of PVs in outer suburbs and to the regulatory barriers preventing distributed power systems in inner areas (Bunning et al. 2013, Rauland and Newman 2011).

Facilitating the more resilient polycentric city with reduced car dependence needs a range of new and old planning tools. Old tools like strategic plans linked to infrastructure plans are essential. Building fast rail out into the automobile city's suburbs has been shown to work very successfully when the speed of public transit is better than the clogged freeways which the trains speed past (McIntosh, Newman and Glazebrook 2013). New tools, such as financing public transit through value capture builds the integration of dense centers into the building of public transit (McIntosh et al. 2013). New digital planning tools for assisting redevelopment, especially in the revitalization of middle suburbs can ensure that automobile city urban fabric is upgraded to provide more resilient outcomes (Glackin et al. 2013, Newton 2012). New forms of governance will be needed that can enable greater regional autonomy and more deliberative, participative processes (Briand and Hartz-Karp 2013, Bunning et al. 2013).

Some new approaches will benefit both the reduction in coal-fired power and the reduction in car dependence. The new techniques of biophilic urbanism with green walls and green roofs, which are appearing in the many compact cities of Asia, are also needed as more compact urban fabric demands new ways of bringing nature into the city (Beatley and Newman 2013, Newman 2013, Newman and Matan 2013). As well, for the car use that does remain, new vehicle technologies such as electric vehicles or plug-in hybrid electrics will provide additional environmental and livability benefits but can be very valuable in assuring a city has adequate storage for its renewable power.

Conclusions

A new kind of city is emerging that represents a combination of old techniques in creating walkable and transit-oriented urban fabric along with new green technologies. The first signs of reduced dependence on coal-fired power are emerging in the patterns of investment in power stations and also in power consumption. The first signs of movement away from car dependence are also now appearing. Only time will tell if these are a truly structural change or a small shift in a longer-term continuation of fossil fuel and automobile dependence over the past century or so. The evidence above suggests it may be a structural change, and that a more sustainable and resilient city may finally be appearing to reduce the impact of fossil fuels and automobile dependence. Tools to help accelerate this phenomenon are also emerging.

References

ADB 2012. *Toward Green Urbanization in Asia and the Pacific*. Manila: Asian Development Bank.

Beatley, T. and Newman, P. 2013. Biophilic Cities Are Sustainable, Resilient Cities, *Sustainability*, 5, 3328–45.

Briand, M. and Hartz-Karp, J. 2013. *From Surviving to Thriving: The Way of Participatory Sustainability*. Washington, DC: Island Press.

Bunning, J., Beattie, C., Rauland, V. and Newman, P. 2013. Low-Carbon Sustainable Precincts: An Australian Perspective. *Sustainability*, 5, 2305–26.

Dodson, J. and Sipe, N. 2008. *Unsettling Suburbia: The New Landscape of Oil and Mortgage Vulnerability in Australian Cities*. Queensland: Urban Research Program, Griffith University.

EIA 2013. *Annual Energy Outlook*. Washington, DC: Department of Energy.

Fels, M.F. and Munson, M.J. 1974. *Energy Thrift in Urban Transportation: Options for the Future*. Cambridge: Ford Foundation Energy Policy Project Report.

Florida, R. 2010. *The Great Reset: How New Ways of Living and Working Drive Post-Crash Prosperity*. New York: Harper Collins.

Florida R. 2012. Cities with Denser Cores Do Better, *The Atlantic*, United States. Available at: http://www. theatlanticcities.com/jobs-and-economy/2012/11/cities-denser-cores-do-better/3911/ [accessed June 15, 2013].

Gargett, D. 2012. Traffic Growth: Modeling a Global Phenomenon, *World Transport Policy and Practice*, 18(4), 27–45.

Gehl, J. 2011. *Cities for People*. Washington, DC: Island Press.

Glackin, S., Trubka, R., Newman, P., Newton, P. and Mouritz, M. 2013. Greening the Greyfields: Trials, tools and tribulations of redevelopment in the middle suburbs. Planning Institute of Australia National Conference, Canberra, April 2013.

Glaeser, E. 2010. *The Triumph of the City: How Our Greatest Invention Makes Us Richer, Smarter, Greener, Healthier and Happier*. London: Macmillan.

Kenworthy, J. 2013. Decoupling Urban Car Use and Metropolitan GDP Growth, *World Transport Policy and Practice*, 19(4), 8–21.

Kenworthy, J. and Laube, F. 2001. The *Millennium Cities Database for Sustainable Transport*. Perth/Brussels: ISTP Murdoch University and UITP Brussels.

Kenworthy, J. and Newman, P. 2001. *Melbourne in an International Comparison of Urban Transport Systems: A Report to the Department of Infrastructure, Melbourne as Part of the Melbourne Strategy*. Perth: Institute for Sustainability and Technology Policy.

Kenworthy, J., Laube, F., Newman, P., et al. 1999. *An International Sourcebook of Automobile Dependence in Cities, 1960–1990*. Boulder, CO: University Press of Colorado.

Leinberger, C. 2007. *The Option of Urbanism: Investing in a New American Dream*. Washington, DC: Island Press.

McIntosh, J., Newman, P. and Glazebrook, G. 2013. Why Fast Trains Work: An Assessment of a Fast Regional Rail System in Perth, Australia, *Journal of Transportation Technologies*, 3, 37–47.

McIntosh, J., Newman, P., Trubka, R. and Kenworthy, J. 2013. Framework for Land Value Capture from Transit in Car Dependent Cities, *Journal of Land Use and Transport Planning*, forthcoming.

Millard-Ball, A. and Schipper, L. 2010. Are We Reaching Peak Travel? Trends in Passenger Transport in Eight Industrialized Countries, *Transport Reviews*, 31(3), 1–22.

Neff, J.W. 1996. Substitution Rates between Transit and Automobile Travel. Association of American Geographers' Annual Meeting, April, Charlotte, North Carolina.

Newman, C.E. and Newman, P.W.G. 2006. The Car and Culture, in Beilhartz, P. and Hogan, T. (eds), *Sociology: Place, Time and Division*. Oxford: Oxford University Press.

Newman, P. 1995. The End of the Urban Freeway, *World Transport Policy and Practice*, 1(1), 12–19.

Newman, P., Glazebrook, G. and Kenworthy, J. 2013. Peak Car and the Rise of Global Rail, *Journal of Transportation Technologies*, 3(4), 37–47.

Newman, P. and Kenworthy, J. 1989. *Cities and Automobile Dependence: An International Sourcebook*. Aldershot: Gower Publishing.

Newman, P. and Kenworthy, J. 1999. *Sustainability and Cities: Overcoming Automobile Dependence*. Washington, DC: Island Press.

Newman, P. and Kenworthy, J. 2011. Peak Car Use: Understanding the Demise of Automobile Dependence, *World Transport Policy and Practice*, 17(2), 31–42.

Newman, P. and Matan, A. 2013. *Green Urbanism in Asia*. Singapore: World Scientific Publications.

Newman, P., Beatley, T. and Boyer, H. 2009. *Resilient Cities: Responding to Peak Oil and Climate Change*. Washington, DC: Island Press.

Newman, P., Kenworthy, J. and Glazebrook, G. 2008. How to Create Exponential Decline in Car Use in Australian Cities, *Australian Planner*, 45(3), 17–19.

Newton, P. and Newman, P. 2013. The Geography of Solar PV and a New Low Carbon Urban Transition Theory, *Sustainability* 5(6), 2537–56;

Newton, P., Newman, P., Glackin, S. and Trubka, R. 2012. Greening the Greyfields: Unlocking the Development Potential of Middle Suburbs in Australian Cities, *World Academy of Science, Engineering and Technology*, 71, 138–57.

Puentes, R. and Tomer, A. 2009. The Road Less Travelled: An Analysis of Vehicle Miles Traveled Trends in the U.S. Brookings Metropolitan Infrastructure Initiatives Series, United States, December 16.

Rauland, V. and Newman, P. 2011. Decarbonising Australian cities: A New Model for Creating Low Carbon, Resilient Cities. 19th International Congress on Modelling and Simulation (MODSIM) Conference, Perth, December 12–16, 2011.

Romanos, M.C. 1978. Energy Price Effects on Metropolitan Spatial Structure and Form, *Environment and Planning A*, 10(1), 93–104.

Stanley, J. and Barrett, S. 2010. *Moving People: Solutions for a Growing Australia*, Australia: Australasian Railway Association, Bus Industry Confederation and UITP. Available at: https://www.google.com.au/we bhp?hl=en&tab=ww#hl=en&q=Stanley%2C+J.+and+Barrett%2C+S.+2.+Moving+People%3A+Solutions +for+a+Growing+Australia%2C+Australia%3A+Australasian+Railway+Association%2C+Bus+Industry+ Confederation+and+UITP.

Wills, R. and Newman, P. 2012. King Coal Dethroned, *The Conversation*, May 14 and June 16.

World Bank. 2013. *Turn Down the Heat: Climate Extremes, Regional Impacts and the Case for Resilience.* Washington, DC: World Bank.

Chapter 15
Does the City Have Speech?

Saskia Sassen

Speech is a foundational element in theories about democracy and the political. As a concept it has seen both expansions and contractions of its meaning. But it has not yet been expanded to include the concept that the city might have speech, as far as I can tell and others tell me. Arguing, as I do in this chapter, that cities have speech, albeit of a very different sort from that of citizens and corporations, is in many ways a question transversal to both the law and urbanism. It is not present in either one of these bodies of scholarship; this is particularly so since I do not confine the notion of speech to that of urban government, nor do I construct the content of the city's speech in the terms provided by the law. Thus this inquiry requires expanding the analytic terrain for examining the concept of each, speech and the city.

Cities are complex systems. But they are incomplete systems. In this incompleteness lies the possibility of making—making the urban, the political, the civic. The city is not alone in having these characteristics, but these characteristics are a necessary part of the DNA of the urban—cityness. Every city is distinct and so is each discipline that studies it. And yet, if it is to be a study of the urban, it will have to deal with these key features: incompleteness, complexity, and the possibility of making. These take on urbanized formats that can vary enormously across time and place.

Given such diversity, urban research need not recognize the distilled, abstract versions of these three core concepts—complexity, incompleteness, and making. Mostly, researchers and interpreters of the urban use or invoke the concepts of their disciplines or their imaginations and the concrete features of the cities they observe. But those three abstract features are present if it is indeed the urban and not simply dense built-up terrain of a single sort—endless rows of housing, or of offices, or of factories. Thus a vast stretch of suburban housing is not a city; it is built-up terrain and so are office parks. If we want to make the concept of the city work analytically, we will have to be conceptually discriminating.

Here I use these features of cities to engage in an experimental search. I will argue that there are events and conditions that tell us something about the capacity of cities to respond systemically—to talk back. Let me offer an initial sketch of what I mean by way of a simple example: a car, built for speed, exits the highway and enters the city. It hits a traffic jam, composed not just of cars but of people bustling around. Suddenly, this car is crippled. Built for speed, its mobility is arrested. The city has spoken.

A first approximation is to think of such speech as an urban capability. The term capability is by now well established. But adding urban to this term is unusual. I introduce it to capture an elusive mix of space, people, and particular activities, especially commerce and the civic. This term captures the social and material physics of the city. Understood this way, the notion of urban capability functions as an analytic borderland—neither simply urban space nor simply people (see Sassen 2008, Ch. 8). It is their combination under specific conditions, in thick settings, confronting particular potentials and particular assaults that can generate speech. These urban capabilities become visible in a range of situations and forms. In this becoming visible they become a form of speech.

It is impossible to do full justice to all the aspects of this process in such a short chapter; here I limit myself to the basic building blocks of the argument. One is the city as a complex and incomplete system that enables making and has given cities their long life; the combination of these two features has allowed cities to outlive systems that are more powerful but also more formal and closed—national states, kingdoms, financial firms. The other is the mix of diverse urban capabilities that can be conceived of as speech acts and in turn signal the larger notion that cities have speech, albeit informal and mostly unrecognized as such.

The substantive rationality underlying this inquiry about the city and speech rests on two matters. One is the fact that the city is still a key space for the material practices of freedom, including its anarchies and contradictions, and a space where the powerless can make speech, presence, a politics. The other is that these features of cities are under threat by a range of acute processes that deurbanize cities, no matter how dense and urban they may look; these threats include extreme forms of inequality and privatization, new types of urban violence, asymmetric war, and massive surveillance systems.

But to see this takes time listening to, and perhaps understanding, the speech of the city, and we may well have forgotten how to listen, let alone understand. In what follows I explore some of the speech acts of the city.[1]

Analytic Tactics

When doing this type of experimental rumination, I find myself needing the freedom to engage in what I think of as analytic tactics. Method is too confining. One of these tactics is to operate in the shadow of powerful explanations. Powerful explanations are to be taken seriously, but they are dangerous. My first move is to ask what such an explanation obscures precisely, because it sheds such a powerful light on some aspects of a question. In exploring the notion that cities have speech, I cannot stay with the powerful explanations that tell us what a city is. The city's speech happens in an in-between zone: it is not quite simply the city as material and social order. It is an elusive urban capability—not fully material, not fully visible.

A second analytic tactic, partly arising from the first, is the need actively to destabilize stabilized meanings. Such destabilizing allows me to see or understand that which is not contained in the main narratives that explain an epoch or organize a field of scholarship, and we need to do this especially at a time of rapid transformations.

Thus the notion itself that the city has speech entails destabilizing the notion that the city is a self-evident condition marked by density, materiality, and crowds and their multiple interactions. The overwhelming facticity of the city needs to be destabilized. I am interested in recovering the possibility that the interactive deployment of people, firms, infrastructures, buildings, projects, imaginaries, and more, over a confined terrain, produces something akin to speech: resistances, enhanced potentials, in short, that the city talks back.

Complexity and Incompleteness: The Possibility of Making

Cities are one of the key sites where new norms and identities are made. They have been such sites at various times and in various places and under very diverse conditions. Thus even as cities have long been home to racisms, religious hatreds, expulsions of the poor; they have historically evinced a capacity to triage conflict through commerce and civic activity. This contrasts with the history of the modern national state, which historically has tended to militarize conflict.

The conditions that enable cities to make norms and identities and to transform conflicts into a strengthened civicness vary across time and place. Epochal change, as in our shift to the global, is often a source of new types of urban capabilities. Today, given globalization and digitization—and all the specific elements they entail—many of these conditions have once again undergone change. Globalization and digitization produce dislocations and destabilizations of existing institutional orders that go well beyond cities. But the disproportionate concentration and acuteness of these new dynamics in cities, especially in global cities, forces the need to craft new types of responses and innovations, especially on the part of both the most powerful and the most disadvantaged, albeit for very different reasons.

Some of these norms and identities justify extreme power and inequality. Some reflect innovation under duress: notably much of what happens in immigrant neighborhoods or in the slums of megacities. While the strategic transformations assume sharp forms and are concentrated in global cities, many are also enacted (besides being diffused) in cities that are not centers of power and extreme inequalities.

---

1   I use speech in the abstract sense of the law, as in, for instance, the way corporations have speech as articulated by the Supreme Court in 2010 in *Citizens United v. Federal Election Commission*, which upheld the rights of corporations to make political expenditures under the First Amendment right of free speech. Cities, like corporations, do not speak in the human voice; they speak in their voice.

Cities are not always the key sites for the making of new norms and identities or institutional innovations generally. For example, in Europe and much of the Western hemisphere, from the 1930s up until the 1970s, the factory and the government were the strategic sites for innovation through the social contract and the enablement of a prosperous working and middle class based on mass manufacturing and mass consumption. My own reading of the Fordist city corresponds in many ways to Max Weber's notion that the modern city is not a space of innovation, unlike the medieval cities of Europe. The strategic scale under Fordism is the national scale, in which cities lose significance. But I part company from Weber in that historically the large Fordist factory and the mines were sites of innovation: the making of a modern working class and a syndicalist project. In short, it is not always the city that is the site for making norms and identities.

In our global era, cities have emerged once again as strategic sites for cultural and institutional change. The conditions that today make some cities strategic sites are basically two, and both capture major transformations that destabilize older systems organizing territory and politics. One of these is the rescaling of the strategic territories that articulate the new politico-economic system and hence at least some features of power. The other is the weakening of the national as container of social process due to the variety of dynamics encompassed by globalization and digitization. The consequences for cities of these two conditions are many; what matters here is that cities emerge as strategic sites for major economic processes and for new types of political actors, including nonurban processes and actors.

A distinction that matters for my examination is between ritualized spaces we recognize as such and spaces either that are not ritualized or that we fail to recognize as such. Much of what we experience as urbanity in our Western European tradition is a set of practices and conditions that have gone through a refining and a ritualizing over time and across space. Thus, in our partly imagined European tradition, the passeggiata is not just any walk, and the piazza is not just any square. Both have embedded genealogies of meaning and ritual, and both contribute to the constituting of a public domain via ritualization.

Across time and space also, history has given us glimpses of a very different type of space, one that is less ritualized and with few, if any, embedded codes. It is a space for making by those who lack access to established instrumentalities. I have been working at a conceptual recovery of this type of space and have called it the "global street" (Sassen 2011). This is a space with few, if any, of the ritualized practices or codes that the larger society might recognize. It is rough, easily seen as "uncivilized."

The city, and especially the street, is a space where the powerless can make history, in ways they cannot in rural areas. That is not to say that it is the only space, but it is certainly a critical one. Becoming present, visible, to each other can alter the character of powerlessness. This allows me to make a distinction between different types of powerlessness (Sassen 2008, chs 6, 8). Powerlessness is not simply an absolute status that can be flattened into the absence of power.

Under certain conditions, powerlessness can become complex, by which I mean that it contains the possibility of making the political, the civic, a history. This brings to the fore the fact of a difference between powerlessness and invisibility/impotence. Many of the protest movements we have seen in the Middle East and North Africa, Europe, the United States, and elsewhere are a case in point: these protesters may not have gained power; they are still powerless, but they are making a history and a politics.

This leads me to a second distinction, which contains a critique of the common notion that if something good happens to the powerless, it signals empowerment. Recognizing that powerlessness can become complex makes conceptual room for the proposition that the powerless can make history, even if they do not become empowered, and that thereby their work is consequential even if it does not become visible promptly and can indeed take generations. Elsewhere (Sassen 2008, chs 2, 3, 6) I have interpreted several historiographies as indicating that the temporal frame of the histories made by the powerless tends to be much longer than the histories made by those with power.

Urban Capabilities: They Precede Speech and Make It Legible

If the city has speech, what might it look or sound like? What language does it speak? How does it become legible to us who speak another language and whose voice is at best a cacophony?

A first, little step is to posit that the city's speech is a capability to alter, to shape, to provoke, to invite, all following a logic that aims at enhancing or protecting the city's complexity and its incompleteness. Let me elaborate on this in a somewhat exaggerated way for the sake of clarity and argue that focusing only on the facticity of the city is not enough to understand the question of whether the city has speech.

The question of speech cannot be reduced to that facticity even as it requires recognition and an analytic awakening of that facticity. That is to say, we have flattened the facticity of the city, when we should make visible its differentiations so that it can work analytically. Such flattening does not help us see how this facticity interacts with people's actions or that there is a making here, a collective making between urban space and people. For instance, rush hour in the city is a process where we bump into one another, rip off a button here and there, step on one another's feet. Yet we know none of these actions are personal in the city's center at rush hour, unlike the neighborhood, where they would all be provocations.

What makes this possible is a tacit code embedded in this type of time/space—not place per se, but the space that is constituted by people in the city center during rush hour. We need to name this capability that is a collective production emerging out of an intersection of time/space/people/routinized practices.

I think of this as an urban capability—urban centrality is made through built environments, people's routinized practices, and an embedded and shared code. It enables a series of complex interactions and sequences and, in so doing, mobilizes a specific meaning.

Not just the outcome but the work itself of making the public and making the political in urban space is constitutive of cityness. In cities we can see the making of new subjects and identities that would not be possible in, for example, rural areas or a country at large. There is a kind of public-making work that can disrupt established narratives and thereby make legible the local and the silenced even in visual orders that seek to cleanse urban space. One example is the early high-end gentrification in Manhattan—a whole new visual order that could not, for a while, render invisible the homeless it had produced. A second example is the immigrant street vendor on Wall Street catering to the high-level financier in a rush, altering the visual corporate landscape with the robust smell of roasted sausages. I see in these examples the city talking back, altering the outcome sought with elegant visual orders. At the other extreme, a city's sociality can bring out and underline the urbanity of subject and setting and dilute more local or more essentialist signifiers; the need for new solidarities when cities confront major challenges can bring this shift about.

In my research, I find that key components of cityness have been crafted out of the hard work of going beyond the conflicts and racisms that might mark an epoch (Sassen 2008, Ch. 6). It is out of this type of dialectic that came the open urbanity that historically made European cities spaces for expanded citizenship. More generally, movements that comprise disparate groups with a variety of grievances can coalesce no matter how diverse their politics. The actual lived interdependence of daily life in a city enables such coalescing—if water, electricity, or transport fails in a city, it affects all regardless of their social or political differences. Such a coalescing would be unlikely and unnecessary in national political space given less mutual interdependence/ dependence and generally in a more abstract space. These partial orderings we see in cities can add to the DNA of the city's civicness: they feed the making of an urban subject, rather than a religious or ethnic or class-based subject. These are among the features that make cities a space of great complexity and diversity.

Large cities at the intersection of vast migrations and expulsions often were and are spaces with the capacity to accommodate enormous diversity of groups. And such accommodating is often the work of further developing cityness—either this or spatial segregations that deurbanize a city. It is worth noting that when it all succeeds, such cities actually enable a kind of peaceful coexistence for long stretches of time. Coexistence does not mean equality and mutual respect: my concern here is with built-in features and constraints in cities that produce such a capacity for interdependence even if there are major differences in religion, politics, class, and more. I am thinking here of urban capabilities more akin to infrastructural or subterranean capacities whose outcomes are partly shaped by the necessity of maintaining a complex system marked by enormous diversities and by incompleteness. This gives cities speech.

Perhaps the most familiar and clearest instances are periods of peaceful coexistence in cities with sharp religious differences; these make visible that conflict does not necessarily inhere in such differences. And it is not only the famous cases of Augsburg and Moorish Spain, with their much-admired coexistence of very diverse religions, collective prosperity, and enlightened leaderships. It is also Old Jerusalem's bazaar as a space of commercial and religious coexistence across centuries. Baghdad was a flourishing polyreligious

Figure 15.1   Hilary Koob-Sassen, "Speech Acts of a Different Sort"
Source: Still from Transcalar Investment Vehicles, a film produced by FLAMIN, Film London.

city under the Abbasid caliphs, around the year 800, and even under Saddam Hussein's extremely brutal leadership was a city where religious minorities, such as Christian and Jewish communities, often centuries old, lived in relative peace.

But history also shows us that this is a capability that can be destroyed and has often been destroyed. The destruction has inevitably brought with it a deurbanizing and ghettoizing of urban space. Thus, in sharp contrast with that older period, Baghdad is today a city where ethnic cleansing and intolerance are the de facto "regime," one catapulted by the disastrous and unwarranted U.S. invasion.

These and so many other historical cases show that a particular exogenous, indeed a deurbanizing, event can suddenly reposition religious or ethnic difference as agents for conflict. The same individuals can experience and enact that switch. The systemic logic in Hussein's Baghdad was of indifference to minorities like Christians and Jews; it was not a question of tolerance by residents or an enlightened leadership.

Systemic indifference, I would argue, can in many cases function as a kind of subterranean urban capability at work: a civicness that does not depend on tolerant citizens and enlightened leaders but is an outcome of interdependencies and interactions in the physical and economic life of the city. Conversely, its breakdown becomes visible as collapse into lethal conflicts and ethnic cleansings that deurbanize the city and savage that urban capability.

Versions of urban capabilities can be found in a series of cases, some more elusive than others. One of these concerns the question of repetition, a basic feature of the built environment of cities and generally of our economic and technical worlds. Yet, in the city, repetition becomes the active making of multiplication and iteration. Further, urban settings actually unsettle the meaning of repetition.

There is plenty of repetition in any city, but it keeps being captured by the specifics, the conditionalities, across different urban spaces. A bus, a telephone booth, an apartment or office building, even if standardized throughout much of a city, will take on diverse meanings and utilities across the diverse types of spaces of a city. It makes visible how the diversity of urban environments re-marks even the most standardized item and makes it part of that neighborhood, that public space, that city center. On a more complex level, neighborhoods in the same city can exude very different auras, sounds, smells, choreographies of how people move through that neighborhood, and who is welcome and who is not. In short, repetition in a city can be quite different from mechanical repetition as in an assembly line or the reproduction of a graphic. I want to take it a step further and posit that we see in these instances a capacity that I would like to see as speech.

A more elusive form of speech is the making of presence. In my own work I have developed notions of "making presence" to rescue an actor, an event, from the silence of absence, invisibility, the virtual/representational eviction from membership in the city. I am especially interested in understanding how groups and "projects" at risk of invisibility due to societal prejudices and fears become present to themselves, to others like themselves, and to others unlike themselves. What I seek to capture is a very specific feature. It is the possibility of making presence where there is silence and absence. A variant of such making of presence is the terrain vague, an underutilized or abandoned space that lies forgotten among massive structures and construction projects. It is not unique to today's period—under other arrangements, and with variable particularities, it also existed in the past. I think that this elusive in-between space is essential to the experience of urban living and that it lends legibility to transitions and the uneasiness of specific spatial configurations. We can find the terrain vague in even the densest city. With its visual marking as underutilized space, these spaces are often charged with memories of other visual orders, with presences of the past, thereby unsettling their current meaning as underutilized space. They are thus charged precisely because they are underutilized. As memories, these spaces become part of the "interiority" of the city, the city's present, but it is the making of an interiority that is outside the dominant profit-driven utility logics and their spatial framings. They are the vacant grounds that enable residents who feel bypassed by their city to connect with it via memory at a time of rapid changes—an empty space that can be filled with memories. And it is where activists and artists find a space for their projects. This is a making of presence that is an act of speech.

Deurbanizing Forces

Given their complexity and incompleteness, cities have historically evinced a capacity to survive upheavals, in part by talking back and constraining deurbanizing tendencies. But they never succeed fully. Power, whether in the form of elites, government policies, or innovations in built environments, can override the speech of the city. We see this in the development of megabuildings, highways running through the city, extreme high-income gentrification that privatizes urban space, the proliferation of vast concentrations of poor-quality high-rise residential buildings without commercial centers and workplaces, and more. All of these are among current deurbanizing trends.

Ours is a time when stabilized meanings have become unstable. The large complex city with all its diversities is a new frontier zone. This is especially true if it is a global city, defined by its partial shaping within a network of other cities across borders. Actors from different worlds meet there, but without clear rules of engagement. Where the historic frontier was in the far stretches of colonial empires, today it lies in our large complex cities. For instance, much of the work by global firms to push for deregulation, privatization, and new fiscal and monetary policies took shape and has become concrete in global cities. It is how global firms construct their equivalent of the old military fort of the historic frontier: their network of forts is the regulatory environment they need in city after city worldwide to ensure a global space of operations (Sassen 2008, Ch. 5). This is a formidable onslaught on the city and its capabilities to ensure cityness.

In my research on our current period (Sassen, forthcoming), I have examined especially three types of developments that can deurbanize the city. One is the sharp growth in inequalities of diverse sorts that can lead to radical expulsions—from homes and neighborhoods, from middle-class lifestyles. These trends take particularly acute and visible shapes in cities, with their expanded luxury spaces and poverty spaces. A second is the building of whole new cities, including intelligent cities often built as a business for profit; there are well over 600 cities either under construction or in the planning stage. A particular concern is the extreme use of closed intelligent systems to control whole buildings. Given the accelerated rate of obsolescence of technologies, this may well shorten the life of vast stretches of such new cities. One challenge, in my view,

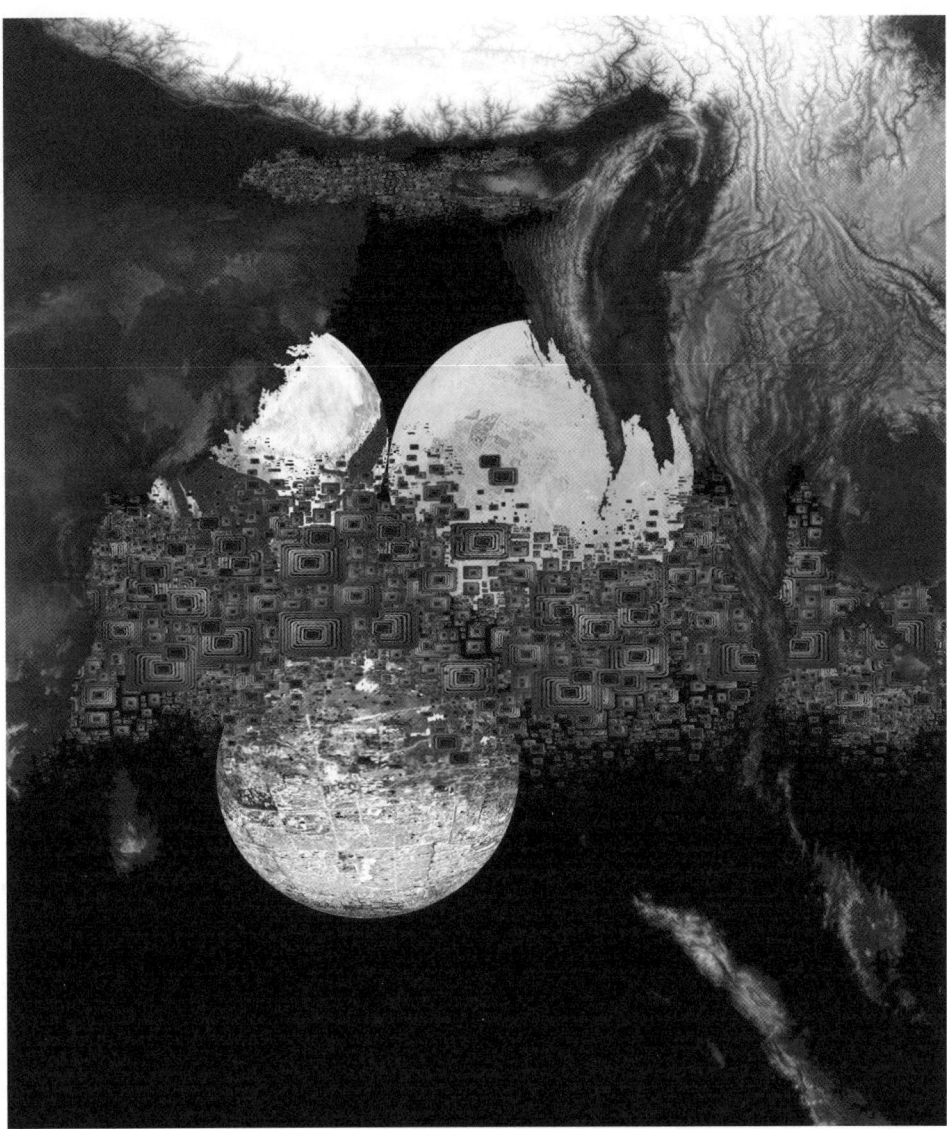

Figure 15.2   Hilary Koob-Sassen, "Subterranean Shapes"
Source: Still from Transcalar Investment Vehicles, a film produced by FLAMIN, Film London.

is the need to urbanize these technologies so that they might contribute to the urbanity of those areas. The third project concerns the large-scale surveillance system now being developed cooperatively by several countries, notably the United States, Germany, and the United Kingdom. I turn to this third aspect with some detail below. In July 2010, the Washington Post published the findings of a two-year investigation, "Top Secret America," in three parts (Priest and Arkin 2010a, 2010b, 2010c). Constituting this "top secret America" are 1,271 government organizations and 1,931 private companies, collectively employing an estimated 854,000 people with top secret security clearance—nearly 1.5 times as many people as live in Washington, DC—including 265,000 private contractors (Priest and Arkin 2010a). They work on programs related to counterterrorism, homeland security, and intelligence. There are about 10,000 locations where this work is conducted across the United States. Of these buildings, 4,000 are in the Washington, DC, area, occupying 17 million square feet—the equivalent of almost 3 Pentagons or 22 U.S. Capitol buildings (Priest and Arkin 2010a).

Housed in these buildings are powerful computers that collect vast amounts of information from wiretaps, satellites, and other surveillance equipment monitoring people and places both within and outside of U.S. national territory. Each day the National Security Agency alone intercepts and stores 1.7 billion e-mails, instant messages, IP addresses, telephone calls, and other bits of communications, a small proportion of which is sorted and stored on 70 different databases (Priest and Arkin 2010a, 2010c). Some of this information will make it into the tens of thousands of top secret reports produced by analysts each year, but only a handful of individuals have access to all of them, and the volume is so great that many go unread (Priest and Arkin 2010a, 2010c).

This surveillance apparatus is there for our "security." For our security we are all under surveillance; that is to say, we are all constructed as suspects, for our security. It does lead me to ask: under these conditions, who are we, the citizens—the new colonials?

Cities, with their diversities and anarchies, with their built-in capabilities to contest deurbanizing trends, become a strategic space to contest reducing us all to suspects. The city is one place where a kind of structural convergence could develop beneath visible familiar separateness and racisms and work itself into the social level and bring together people from very different communities to contest overwhelming surveillance. This potential does not fall ready-made from the sky—it needs to be made with hard work. But diverse complex cities are one key site for such making.

Conclusion

Why does it matter that we recognize the fact of urban capabilities and the possibility that this might be a mode of speech, with all the weight this concept evokes? It matters because these capabilities are systemic properties that aim at securing cityness, that is to say a complex space that thrives on diversities and tends to triage conflict into a strengthened civicness. Further, such capabilities get constituted as hybrids—mixes of the material and social physics of a city. This interdependence entails a continuous transformation of both the material and the social, with periods of stability and continuity and periods of upheaval, as is the current one that took off in the 1980s. The project is not about anthropomorphizing the city. It is about understanding a systemic dynamic that has the capacity to contest what is destructive to its DNA—to repeat, a DNA that is conducive to cityness and its diversities. At the limit, the city allows the powerless to make a history, thereby producing a critical difference—between mere powerlessness and complex powerlessness where the making of presence and of a history come into play. But there are limits to the city's capabilities, and historically we see both the capacity of cities to outlive other more formal closed and rigid systems and powerful forces that deurbanize cities. Among these deurbanizing forces in the current period are extreme forms of inequality, the privatizing of urban space with its diverse expulsions, and the rapid expansion of massive surveillance of citizens in the most "advanced" democracies across the world. These forces silence the speech of the city and destroy urban capabilities.

References

Priest, Dana, and Arkin, William M. 2010a. A Hidden World, Growing beyond Control. *Washington Post*, July 19.

Priest, Dana, and Arkin, William M. 2010b. National Security Inc. *Washington Post*, July 20.

Priest, Dana, and Arkin, William M. 2010c. The Secrets Next Door. *Washington Post*, July 21.

Sassen, Saskia. 2008. *Territory, Authority, Rights: From Medieval to Global Assemblages*. 2nd edn. Princeton, NJ: Princeton University Press.

Sassen, Saskia. 2011. The global street: Making the political. *Globalizations* 5 (8): 565–71.

Sassen, Saskia. Forthcoming. *Expulsions: When Complexity Produces Elementary Brutalities*. Cambridge, MA: Harvard University Press.

Chapter 16

Planning the Emergent and Dealing with Uncertainty: Regulations and Urban Form

Emily Talen

A significant and intractable problem in urban planning in Western capitalist democracies—virtually unchanged since the birth of the profession a century ago—is the following: how is it possible to implement visions of a desired future outcome for cities while at the same time (a) remaining flexible and open to refinement; and (b) grappling with the larger structural—e.g., economic—forces that transform cities. The first problem concerns planning's inability to express changing preferences and needs; the second problem concerns planning's futility. In both senses, the potential for negative and unintended effects is substantial.

The attempt to regulate cities via codes—like zoning—illustrates how this tension plays out. A century ago, the vision of a desired future city was to be implemented via zoning. It was a regulatory system that started with much fanfare and then devolved into something almost universally despised for both its lack of flexibility and its inability to adjust to larger structural forces. Given this history, it is understandable that new regulatory schemes—form-based codes in particular—would be viewed skeptically as yet another city planning approach that will fail either through its inflexibility or its irrelevance.

This chapter provides a historical overview of the problem and attempts to sort out the various issues involved. Given the historical record, is there reason to believe that regulations in an uncertain, emergent world are viable, or even desirable? I focus on the American case to highlight the enduring tensions involved in the attempt to reconcile vision, regulation, flexibility, and structural condition. I will argue that the ability of codes to be responsive and flexible—within limits—is the key to resolving the inherent intractability of visionary, normative planning in Western capitalist democracies.

Background

By the end of the nineteenth century, those involved in city building began to embrace the concept of zoning, which was an idea imported from Germany. The embrace was buoyed by new kinds of powerful political and social institutions. To some, this regulatory turn meant that cities could no longer adapt to change (Konvitz 1985), and the individual would be rendered helpless. But to others, rules represented a powerful form of collective protection (Whitnall 1931). At least in principle, for the new profession called "city planning," rules represented the triumph of community needs over market capitalism.

Zoning regulations had a powerful impact on the American landscape. The ostensible goal of zoning was to remedy the negative externalities of the industrial city, stabilizing residential property values, maximizing profit for commercial areas, and keeping industrial areas efficient and functional. Practically speaking, however, zoning was really nothing more than building codes adapted to location. At the time, many believed that building codes that were not place-based were a serious problem: "building laws, apart from those applying to fire limits, treated all parts of the city alike whether inside or suburban, whether business centers or residential outskirts" (Bassett 1920: 315). Thus zoning was defined as "planning in recognition of the differences in different parts of the city," whereby regulation would "adapt itself to these differences." Under zoning, one area of the city was allowed to be denser, taller and more diverse, while another area was required to be sparsely populated and more homogeneous.

This idea, where rules would vary by district, was an 1870s invention of a German engineer, Richard Baumeister. Germans called it "zoning" (or the zone system) because of the way cities were so clearly differentiated into zones of land value and intensity. Baumeister spelled everything out in a book titled *Town*

Expansions Considered with Respect to Technology, Building Code and Economy. He traced the origins of zoning back to an 1810 decree of Napoleon I, which divided industry into three classes, and established the boundaries of a "protected district." The creation of zones for different kinds of uses, therefore, was an essential aspect of this early approach. Next came bulk zoning, which laid out two sets of regulations, one for the city and one for the suburbs, and specified things like building height, setbacks, and the amount of lot area that could be built on. German cities adopted use and bulk zoning throughout the 1880s and 1890s.

By 1916, when comprehensive zoning was officially implemented in the U.S. (in New York City), Germany had more than 30 years' experience with the regulatory tool. But unlike the more nuanced zoning regulations of Europe, what unfolded after the 1916 adoption of the New York City zoning law was "the great American zoning parade" (Peets 1931: 225), or as it was also described, a "storm" (Kimball 1923). New York's code seemed to be a "reasonable plan for preventing over intensive development," containing only, proponents said, "a limited degree of segregation" (New York City Board of Estimate and Apportionment 1916: 144–5). In fact it is sometimes difficult to view the numerous, impassioned writings justifying zoning in the early 1900s as anything other than reasonable. Proponents lamented the way cities were developing: "a landowner could put up a building to any height, in any place, of any size, and use it to any purpose, regardless of how much it hurt his neighbors" (Bassett 1920: 315). According to Alfred Bettman, a leading zoning advocate, order was intended to prevent "a premature and avoidable spread-out of the city," and simultaneously help the business district develop "compactly and promptly" (Bettman 1925: 90). Zoning was the best tool, planners believed, to overcome the problem that Americans were "esthetically defective" and "blindly devoted to obsolete ideas" about property rights (Hall 1917: 1). They looked to zoning to create an urban form that could provide "visual assurances of maturity and success" (Scott 1969: 33) and overcome the dog-eat-dog world of development that "stimulated each owner to build in the most hurtful manner" (Bassett 1920: 315).

There was a populist aspect to zoning, a sense that neighborhoods should have the right to protect themselves against greed, pollution, and speculation, and that rules like zoning would provide those protections. Rules attended to the needs of the "community as a whole," and were even described in the early 1920s as "sustainable" (Baker 1927: 148). Zoning was thought to "stir the imagination of the community" and "invoke the public spirit" (Bartholomew cited in Davies 1958: 146). People believed it would alleviate poverty, increase productivity, wages, and profits, and "improve" architecture (Hason 1977, Adams 1935: 96). It would stop the "indiscriminate scattering" of industry and business, and put a stop to "unthinking or selfish individuals" (Illinois Chapter of the AIA 1919: 118). Zoning, in short, was a progressive cause. Its purpose was, according to Alfred Bettman, "always positive and constructive and not merely negative and preventive" (cited in Hubbard and Hubbard 1929: 164). It was to bring "order out of chaos" (Cheney 1920: 276) and would be capable of fostering "urban co-operation" (Baker 1927: 35). An editorial in 1912 in The American City magazine proclaimed: "wise regulations do not hamper civic activities; but, on the contrary, stimulate and encourage them" (American City 1912: 6).

In short, in the latter part of the Progressive Era, around 1920, rules seemed an embodiment of a united civic interest, and this helped zoning expand rapidly. In just two years, from 1924 to 1926, the number of zoned cities in the U.S. increased from 62 to 456 (Baker 1927). By 1927, half of the urban population in the U.S. was living in zoned cities. Herbert Hoover, as Secretary of Commerce, crafted enabling legislation that pushed zoning even further, and by 1929 nearly 800 cities in the United States had zoning ordinances (Hubbard and Hubbard 1929).

Critiques

After the brief period in which regulations were ascribed civic-minded ideals, zoning devolved into a regulatory machine devoted to narrow economic purpose. There was a reliance on individuals as opposed to codes to accomplish an urban form that was flexible and responsive, but individuals tended to act singularly rather than collectively. Visionary plans lacked the force of regulation, which created a vacuum in which codes were left to dictate intrinsically sterile and even destructive city arrangement.

Thus despite the appeal to progressive reform, the popularity of zoning declined rapidly. A major criticism was that zoning lacked flexibility and adaptability. Professional planners had been aware of this problem from the outset. At the Second National Conference on City Planning and Congestion of Population, held in 1910, Frederick Law Olmsted Jr. said that regulation should always be in a state of "flux and adjustment—on the one hand, with a view to preventing newly discovered abuses, and, on the other hand, with a view to opening a wider opportunity of individual discretion at points where the law is found to be unwisely restrictive" (1910: 14). Lewis Mumford, writing in 1923, described the application of zoning as "narrow." Clarence Perry lambasted the inflexibility and weakness of zoning and its ability to invest a residential district with "attractiveness" (Perry 1939: 114).

The response was to introduce more flexibility by prioritizing procedure. An array of techniques and legal mechanisms were developed. First there was the "special use" or "conditional use" permit, introduced just after World War II. Special exceptions might be granted to allow, for example, hospitals and public garages in a neighborhood if a voting board could be convinced that it was in the public's (or their) best interest. Next came "performance standards" in zoning, first introduced in Chicago for manufacturing districts in 1957, in which development was regulated through the measurement of its impacts on adjoining properties. In the 1960s, performance standards were famously adopted in Petaluma, CA and Ramapo, NY. Other attempts to increase flexibility included the planned unit development (PUD) and related variants (PAD, PD, PCD, etc.), overlay zoning, floating zones, and the floor area ratio (FAR). Complicated overlay zones, planned unit ordinances, and other installations of discretionary review—even as part of a legal code—meant that there was plenty of room for interpretation. Additional calls for flexibility in regulation continued through the 1960s, '70s and '80s—for example in Kevin Lynch's *The Image of the City* (1960), and Babcock and Weaver's *City Zoning* (1979).

Ironically, increased flexibility did not simplify zoning. Discretion triggered additional layers of review, creating "a costly and time-consuming negative synergism" disliked by planners, architects and others for its tendency to open the door to manipulation, favoritism, and unfairness (Salins 1993: 167). Thus, in the attempt to make rules more flexible, they became more unwieldy. New York's 1961 zoning document ballooned from 261 to 835 pages by adding more precise rules designed to tweak the right effect, in the process trading taller buildings for plazas and other "amenities."

But the more fundamental problem with so-called flexible approaches—at least as they've been implemented so far—is their track record: they have often resulted in sprawl disguised as "planned unit development," or "innovative" arrangements that are really nothing more than lifeless open spaces, insular and disconnected superblocks, or anti-pedestrian thoroughfares. In effect, the negotiated, flexible approach to regulation can easily result in bad form and bad politics. In the Chicago Tribune's investigation of zoning reforms that were supposed to take place after a sweeping overhaul in the late 1990s—in a series aptly entitled "Neighborhoods For Sale" (Chicago Tribune 2008)—reporters uncovered a world of corruption, political pay-backs, and a complete disregard for community input.

A related issue concerns the degree to which zoning is detached from the underlying structural forces at play in city development. This renders them unresponsive and extraneous—a band-aid solution to urban problems. Since regulations like zoning are divorced from underlying economic forces, the critique goes, they are unable to achieve positive social purpose. Zoning in particular seems incapable of doing anything other than stimulating land development that maximizes private gain. As a practical matter, in the largely uncritical world of zoning regulation, there is no connection between the form of the city and the source and method of production, nor with how the distribution of goods and services should be carried out.

It is worth reviewing the history of this critique, as it is not new. It was first articulated in the early twentieth century by members of the Regional Planning Association of America (the RPAA). Lewis Mumford and other influential members promoted the idea that regionally decentralized governance and cultural life was entirely possible, and that it would happen through localization of production supported by transportation and social service planning (Lubove 1963). RPAA members believe that advancing plans and regulations independent of the means of production and consumption exposed city planning to the critique of being "inauthentic." Benton MacKaye's early twentieth-century critique of the system was that ends were being distorted to fit predetermined means; that instead of industry being called upon to help achieve culture, culture was being made to "echo the intonations of industry"; oil paints were not being made to produce art, but art was being made to advertise oil paints. It all amounted to the "unnatural tendency of the metropolitan process" (MacKaye 1928: 71).

Decades later, a similar critique was leveled at New Urbanism. The book *How Cities Work* (Marshall 2000) criticized New Urbanism for failing to understand how cities work and attempting to proscribe a form at odds with the underlying processes of urbanism. The author does not leverage the earlier critiques of the RPAA in this account, because, while both are using the authenticity argument, they are working from opposite directions. One authenticity critique is about form needing to follow function; the RPAA authenticity critique was about the need to adapt means in order to achieve particular ends. The difference has to do with whether economies and transportation systems are viewed as givens or adaptable means. If they are givens, then the notion that city planning should be more realistic about following the structural forces of capitalism renders city planning an uncritical enabler of it, as is the case with current zoning regulations. This has not had the effect of producing good places, as any observer of American suburban sprawl knows.

Modernist urbanism provides an example of what happens when there is an attempt to match form to process. The idea that urban form must intrinsically match the underlying processes that generate it is a mindset that was translated by the modernists to mean that "antiquated" urban places with small streets should be wiped clean in order to make way for large-scale housing projects and high-speed expressways. The obsession with corresponding to the needs "of our time" and to "new rates of speed" was used to rationalize destruction. In the rush to be modern (and therefore, presumably, more in line with the underlying processes of capitalism), pedestrian routes in the form of streets were the "heritage of past eras" that could "no longer fulfill the requirements of modern types of vehicles (automobiles, buses, trucks) or modern traffic volume" (Sert 1944: 74, 162).

The question for city planning and its regulations boils down to this: can the reproduction of certain urban qualities irrespective of the processes that generated them in the past be validated by other means? Peter Hall asked a similar question when he wondered, "in the new urban landscape of technology-led deconcentration, what exactly is the role of the traditional city?" Some will see it as a matter of wanting to save appearances, "Disney-style parodies of the places they once were" (Hall 1989). Some will see it as a matter of compromise. Others will see it as wanting to retain workable urban forms and patterns that can be validated by other means.

Reform

Where do these critiques—lack of flexibility and lack of connection to larger structural forces—leave the current movement to reform failed regulations? Form-based codes, which describe the most popular current effort at regulatory reform, succumb to both types of critiques. In addition to the easy critique that they are too constraining and too disconnected from the structural forces at play, critics view them as promoting hegemonies devoted to corporate capitalism, or worse, conservative ideologies about traditional family type.

Regulations like zoning will never address the structural flaws of capitalism. But what if regulations were flexible enough to be responsive to local consumption patterns, which translated to the need to make the grain of consumption and production integrated, small-scale, and localized?

Perhaps flexibility is the key to a regulatory approach capable of responding to this need. In the process, rather than streamlining conventional capitalist land development practices, regulations could make a structural connection by streamlining localized patterns of production and consumption. Flexibility of a certain kind would be required: to ensure that services are well-distributed to reach a broad geographic range, and to encourage the accommodation of small operations, family-run businesses, and multi-use properties—allowing homes that can function as workplaces for, e.g., making clothing, operating a repair shop, or engaging in other types of non-noxious, light industries. In American cities, the network of alleys in many places makes it possible to accommodate this level of smallness and integration: small businesses within the residential fabric that do not disrupt a socially functioning street. Codes could streamline—by allowing as of right—the building of resilient, small, flexible units to accommodate small entrepreneurs of all kinds. In short, codes could be relaxed to develop the kinds of enterprises that combine, and are essential to, localized production and consumption.

Somewhat ironically, this kind of flexibility requires *some* controls over form. The loosening up of use controls and the enabling of form controls are just what form-based codes are trying to achieve. Jane Jacobs made a similar argument more than 50 years ago: "Streets need controls ... but the controls needed are not controls on kinds of uses. The controls needed are controls on the scale of the street frontage permitted to a use" (Jacobs 1961). Form-based codes are needed to ensure compatibility and minimize friction.

This strategy does not equate to the manipulation of an underlying process in order to generate an emergent urban form—the RPAA approach. But it is an approach that, at least, encourages and enables localized production and consumption. This may seem like a straightforward task, but planners—at least in the U.S. context—have not had much experience with applying such principles to regulation. Planners were initially focused on getting the profession to be taken seriously, not on luxuries like adaptation and structural responsiveness. In the quest for legitimacy, there was plenty of rhetoric about the organic nature of cities, the relation between the formal and informal, proportion and scales in plan-making, and other signals of flexibility and adaptation. But there was a failure to translate the holistic, complex understanding of cities into a regulatory system.

A flexible regulatory approach capable of fostering local consumption and production requires that only the most essential elements of urbanism be subjected to rules. The idea would be to permit a culturally distinctive response within a coding framework, a paring down of rules to just the essentials. Such codes might stipulate a few key principles that, from there, "let it go" (Jacobs 2002: 139; see also Ben-Joseph 2009). It is an approach whereby codes regulate "the essentials of urbanism," while at the same time help to "mediate the tyrannies of practice" (Carmona 2009: 2643). The idea would be to regulate typological pattern, not style or details about materials, colors and window sizes. A focus on a few simple rules, like how a building sits on the lot, frontage type, and whether to allow attached or freestanding buildings would avoid irritating levels of control that ultimately create bland buildings and prevent "the happy accidents and individual quirks" that not only create a more vibrant street and a more vital place (Scheer and Scheer 1998: 153), but respond to the needs of an emerging, local economy.

The idea is not new. The planner Tracy Augur called for this approach in the 1920s, arguing that planners should "designate a few things which cannot be done and leave the rest to individual initiative" (Augur 1923: 17). In Europe, Unwin had earlier proposed an approach allowing "something of that elastic character which belongs to natural restraints" (1909: 387), and "a little give and take, a little averaging of one part with another" (1909: 393). Some FBCs like the SmartCode attempt this balance by being parametric, defining minimum and maximum ranges rather than absolutes, in the hopes of leading to greater visual variety and an opening up of use.

In short, regulations can, if framed right, be helpful in the quest to produce good urban places—in a way that goes beyond window dressing to instead engage with generative process. This outlook requires an acceptance of the validity of normative goals and the ability of regulations to implement them. But it also requires much more flexibility in the system than is currently allowed, and relatedly, more responsiveness to the needs of local communities fighting against the fallout of globalized economics.

The call for flexible and responsive regulations represents something far less than overhauling the destructive forces of capitalism. But neither does it suggest accepting the status quo of land development as currently dictated by globalized forces. The flexibility of codes represents, perhaps, a middle ground between needing to either radically change, or uncritically accept, the emergent, structural forces of city-making.

References

Adams, T. 1935. *Outline of Town and City Planning: A Review of Past Efforts and Modern Aims*. New York: Russell Sage Foundation.

American City Magazine 1912. Editorial comment: The Housing Problem. *The American City* 7, 1, July, 1–8.

Augur, T.B. 1923. The laws and regulations relating to platting of land in the United States as affecting the desirability of lows for dwelling purposes. *Landscape Architecture* 15–26.

Baker, N.F. 1927. *Legal Aspects of Zoning*. Chicago, IL: University of Chicago Press.

Bassett, E.M. 1920. Zoning. *Supplement to the National Municipal Review* 9, 5, 315–41.

Ben-Joseph, E. 2009. Commentary: Designing codes: Trends in cities, planning and development. *Urban Studies* 46, 12, 2691–702.

Bettman, A. 1925. The fact bases of zoning. *City Planning* 1, 2, 86–95.

Carmona, M. 2009. Design coding and the creative, market and regulatory tyrannies of practice. *Urban Studies* 46, 12, 2643–67.

Cheney, C.H. 1920. Removing Social Barriers by Zoning. *The Survey*, May 22, 275–8.

Chicago Tribune 2008. Neighborhoods for Sale: Zoning Reality, Reform Divide. *The Chicago Tribune*, August 20, 2008.

Davies, P.J. 1958. *Real Estate in American History*. New York: Public Affairs Press.

Hall, P. 1989. The turbulent eighth decade: Challenges to American city planning. *Journal of the American Planning Association* 55, 3, 275–82.

Hall, P.F. 1917. *The Menace of the Three-Decker*. New York: National Association of Housing, 1–10.

Hason, N. 1977. *The Emergence and Development of Zoning Controls in North American Municipalities: A Critical Analysis*. Toronto, ON: Department of Urban and Regional Planning, University of Toronto.

Hubbard, T.K. and Hubbard, H.V. 1929. *Our Cities, Today and Tomorrow: A Study of Planning and Zoning Progress in the United States*. Cambridge, MA: Harvard University Press.

Illinois Chapter of the American Institute of Architects 1919. A wise zoning plan for Chicago. *The Western Architect* 28, 118–19.

Jacobs, A. 2002. General Commentary. In Todd W. Bressi (ed.), *The Seaside Debates: A Critique of the New Urbanism*. New York: Rizzoli International, 136–52.

Jacobs, J. 1961. *The Death and Life of Great American Cities*. New York: Vintage Books.

Kimball, T. 1923. *Manual of Information on City Planning and Zoning*. Cambridge, MA: Harvard University Press.

Konvitz, J.W. 1985. *The Urban Millennium: The City-Building Process from the Early Middle Ages to the Present*. Carbondale, IL: Southern Illinois University Press.

Lubove, R. 1962. *The Progressives and the Slums: Tenement House Reform in New York City, 1890–1917*. Pittsburgh, PA: University of Pittsburgh Press.

MacKaye, B. 1928. *The New Exploration: A Philosophy of Regional Planning*. New York: Harcourt, Brace and Co.

Marshall, A. 2000. *How Cities Work: Suburbs, Sprawl, and the Roads Not Taken*. Austin, TX: University of Texas Press.

New York City Board of Estimate and Apportionment 1916. *Final Report of the Commission on Building Districts and Restrictions*. New York: Board of Estimate and Apportionment, Committee on the City Plan.

Olmsted, F.L. Jr. 1910. *City Planning*. An Introductory Address at the Second National Conference on City Planning and Congestion of Population, at Rochester, New York, May 2, 1910. American Civic Association Series 11, no. 4.

Peets, E. 1931. *Current Town Planning in Washington*. Liverpool: Liverpool University Press.

Perry, C. 1939. *Housing for the Machine Age*. New York: Russell Sage Foundation.

Salins, P.D. 1993. *Zoning for Growth and Change*. In Todd W. Bressi (ed.), *Planning and Zoning New York City: Yesterday, Today and Tomorrow*. New Brunswick, NJ: Center for Urban Policy Research, 165–84.

Scheer, B. and Scheer, D. 1998. *Typology and Urban Design Guidelines: Preserving the City without Dictating Design*. In Attilio Petruciolli (ed.), *Nineteenth Century Urban Morphology*, Aga Khan Series. Cambridge, MA: Harvard University Press.

Scott, M. 1969. *American City Planning since 1890*. Berkeley, CA: University of California Press.

Sert, J.L. 1944. The Human Scale in City Planning. In Paul Zucker (ed.), *New Architecture and City Planning*. New York: Philosophical Library.

Unwin, R. 1909. *Town Planning in Practice: An Introduction to the Art of Designing Cities and Suburbs*. London: T. Fisher Unwin.

Whitnall, G. 1931. History of Zoning. *The Annals of the American Academy of Political and Social Science* 155, 2, 1–14.

Chapter 17

The Responsive City:
The City of the Future Re-Imagined from the Bottom Up

Sarah Williams[1]

Our fascination with how technologies can improve cities is timeless. Take the last hundred years: there was the Efficient City movement of the 1930s, the Modernist city of the 1950s and 1960s, and more recently Bill Mitchell's "City of Bits" (1995) where technology became the thing underneath it all. We are now in an age of mobile technologies where our interaction with the city is in fact "beneath it all" but also literally in our finger tips. In this new era, which I call the Responsive City, local governments and private institutions meet the needs of visitors and inhabitants by providing information almost anywhere. This new Techno-Utopia involves embedded sensors, command centers, mobile and web-based service applications, and analysis of Big Data. With all its possibilities, a city embedded with sensors navigates a thin line between providing citizens with a "public good" and creating a surveillance system that puts its citizens under watch, there is a fine balance between total digital control and open information systems. For good or for bad, in the Responsive City data is king, and the analytics are heralded as transformative for urban policy and strategy. Data analytics can be transformative—it can both obscure the needs of marginalized communities as well as elevate them. Like no other era before it, today's techno-city can be top-down or bottom-up and the popularization of a "Do it Yourself" (DIY) culture, Civic Hacking and Open Government has created a space for this bottom-up innovation. The ease in which cities and their citizens can make mobile applications has generated partnerships between the city and its civic minded technology community. This collaboration allows governments to be more facile in the way they develop infrastructure to meet the needs of its citizens, by removing barriers to innovation. The Bottom-up Technology City is highly mobile, adaptive, analytical, and reacts to the needs of the citizens by forming alliances that allow for innovation outside formal governmental channels.

Smart Cities can be defined in many ways, but overall the term usually refers to the idea of embedding technology within normal city infrastructure, whether it be adding sensors in roads to route traffic or creating applications that allow people to find parking spaces (Hollands 2008). Smart Cities also use technology to help navigate and manage the complexity of the urban landscape. They are therefore synonymous with Big Data analytics. As with anything in life, the motivation for Smart City development reflects the values and interests of those implementing them. This leaves us with technology-enabled cities that help facilitate total governmental control, others which allow the city to use their resources more efficiently, and others that are shared and open to the public.

Technotopia: Technology and Control

IBM has promoted itself as having the solution for smarter cities as early as 2008, but it wasn't until 2010 that they had a city they could use as an example of what they meant. The mayor Eduardo Paes of Rio de Janeiro hired IBM to help him create a Smart City infrastructure that would help him meet the complex needs of his city, which was to be host to the FIFA World Cup 2014 and the Olympics in 2016. Rio de Janeiro quickly became the poster child for the IBM's Smarter Cities Marketing campaign. IBM had worked on data analytics for the police department in cities including New York City and Madrid; this was the first city which took on their ad campaign and set out to integrate their diverse infrastructure and service systems (Singer 2012, Wakefield 2013). The Rio project integrates the needs of over 30 agencies and city organizations into one

---

1   Unless otherwise specified, all figures in this chapter are the author's own.

system that is managed and operated in a control room at the city's center. The result is a command center that many have describes as looking like NASA headquarters (Singer 2012). In interviews with the mayor, he points to the many benefits of his operation room. He discusses how the new system allowed him to better manage and provide safety to residents during a building collapse. He mentioned having a better reaction time to crime, and a system that will alert him to the threat of natural disasters, including floods, with a precision that is better than the natural weather service (Garcia-Navarro 2013). For the mayor of Rio, technology is allowing him to take better care of his city in a way that integrates his resources and allows him to be more responsive to the needs of the city and the citizens. For good or for bad Rio's version of the Intelligent City is top-down. The government controls the feeds of the video cameras, the data, and what is looked at and when it is looked at. The command center analyzes the data feeds and makes decision for the public at large (Sennett 2012). The result seems to benefit the city's ever-expanding population and certainly illustrates

Figure 17.1   Picture of Rio de Janeiro, center of operations
Source: http://blogs.sap.com/innovation/mobile-applications/smart-cities-is-your-city-as-intelligent-as-rio-032184.

Smart City ideals. However, the Smart City in Rio is not a city that advocates for open government and shared control of data and analytics.

The innovations in Rio are exciting because it doesn't fit the normal paradigm of a Smart City. The idea of a technology-enabled city has a long history of being a utopia built from scratch where all the systems work together to make a more efficient way of the life—a kind of technotopia—where technology saves the problems of the environment and transport, and citizens can enjoy a "green" lifestyle. This Smart City type still exists and two recent examples are Songdo, Korea and Masdar, Saudi Arabia. These cities have grown almost overnight. They are designed to showcase how technology can help control the environment and create a more "sustainable" way of life (Sennett 2012, Jaffe 2013). In many ways they are meant to fulfill the environmental utopia and the technotopia all in one. Heavily funded with streams of money pouring in from governments, major industries, and real estate developers who want to demonstrate their prowess these top-down technotopias often appear to be more for show.

DIY Cities: The Bottom-Up Technology City

The new technology city might be more bottom-up than what we see in places like Rio, Songdo, and Masdar as many cities across the country are taking cues from the popularization of "Do it Yourself" movement and are encouraging their tech community to use their programming prowess to help develop new technological innovation. The result might be called Civic Hacking, and just this past summer "Code for America" among other civically minded coding organization co-sponsored the National Day of Civic Hacking, where coders partnered with governments, citizens and private organizations from all over the nation to "create, build, and invent new solutions using publicly-released data, code and technology to solve challenges relevant to our neighborhoods, our cities, our states and our country" (National Day of Civic Hacking Website 2013). These new community of Civic Hackers are advocating for cities to open up their data and are developing a space for them to create technologies for the city where government cannot, the result has inspired some innovative new applications that might not have come out of the traditional government processes. The result may be exactly what the government needs and influx of fast innovation and prototypes for civic technology, creating a more Responsive City.

So what exactly is the "Do it Yourself" (DIY) community? The term "Do It Yourself" generally implies a self-reliant attitude; it also implies a need to develop a technology, tool or innovation where the formal marketplace is lacking the ability to do so, or the costs are too high. DIY implies a kind of counter culture where those participating in it are doing something outside the formal channels of innovation allowing for independence and empowerment (Wolf and McQuitty 2011). In the case of the city, the establishment is the government and the idea is to develop innovation that can empower communities where the formal channels of the government are unable to do so. DIY as it applies to the city has manifested itself in a number of ways. There is "Do it Yourself Urbanism," which is largely based on the idea of making incremental changes to a city's urban design that is flexible and almost anyone can implement (Iveson 2013). While DIY can often mean doing something outside government channels, the government themselves often participate in these efforts. The pop-up parks developed by New York City's Department of Transportation are an example of just that.

DIY Tech City has also come to mean the development of prototype technologies that can make the city more open and accessible. This association is best described on the DIYCity website (diycity. org), developed by John Geraci, a New York technology activist during the early days of the open source technology movement. Started in 2008 the site advocated and promoted open source data and applications that addressed civic issues. According to its website it "DIYcity is a site where people from all over the world think about, talk about, and ultimately build tools for making their cities work better with web technologies." The site goes on to say that the collective desire to improve city living is channeled into three areas on DIYCity: (1) discussions, where people exchange thoughts and come up with ideas for products; (2) design, where people boil these discussions down into actual products; and (3) development, where teams of programmers build and launch DIYcity products. The site has helped to advocate for technological change in cities, but has largely disbanded since its originator went on to work for the private sector. While DIYCity.org is no longer active, it helped to give life to a fledgling Civic Hacking community.

Among the first tools advocated on the DIYCity site was "SeeClickFix" an early version of online 311 (NYC 311—The Official Website of the City of New York) which became extremely popular and was adapted and included into formal city infrastructure across the country including, Chicago, San Francisco, and Baltimore among others. SeeClickFix became to the poster child for the possibilities of leveraging private sector "can do" and applying it to governmental responsibilities and empowering citizens by creating a community along the way. SeeclickFix is a web-based 311 hotline, and people use the site to complain about everything from a pothole to missed trash pick-ups. But unlike the one-to-one audio interface of the phone, which often gets archived in a closed institutional database, SeeClickFix itself creates a space in which people with similar neighborhood concerns can learn about them and about each other. Users in New Haven, Connecticut, for instance, created a community advocacy group called the Downtown-Wooster Square Management Team after reading each other's messages on the SeeClickFix website and realizing that they had common problems and interests. Now the group campaigns for community issues such as bringing back a full-service grocery store and installing solar lights in their neighborhood.[2] Publicizing and visualizing the data about the community, rather than entrusting it to the vault of 311 complaints, has allowed the community to organize itself rather than wait for the city to respond. Taking control over the data that they themselves generated, they have been able collectively to make a difference using it.

Figure 17.2   Downtown-Wooster Square Community Management Team page, SeeClickFix
Source: http://seeclickfix.com/watch_area/1044-downtown-wooster-square-community-management-team Participatory City: Making Technology to Inform Communities and Empower Citizens, www.seeclickfix.com.

In 2012 New York City Makers Faire, which according to their website is a festival that "Celebrate arts, crafts, engineering, science projects and the 'Do it Yourself' mindset," featured several civically minded technologies including a KickStarter campaign called the "Air Quality Egg" which is a popular "Do it Yourself" kit for measuring indoor air quality.[3] The Air Quality Eggs are a great example of how DIY culture can influence the city as they use the power of the device to educate, inform and communicate environmental issues about the city. Focused on sensing pollutants in the air, these eggs which are often mobilized for educational rather than scientific data collection, teach people about environmental conditions through the act of making them, using the devices, and ultimately interpreting the results. The Air Quality Eggs themselves are part of a DIY movement called "Citizen Sensing" or "Participatory Sensing," which seeks to enable citizens to collect, own, and visualize data themselves. Citizen Sensing devices, which are often homegrown, are designed to collect data and empower communities by allowing the public to characterize their environment. The devices allow citizens to check formal governmental data or provide data where the government has not created a way to measure it.

Public Labs, a non-profit that holds workshops on using the Air Quality Egg, is an example of an organization that believes that they can transform the places we live through a "Do it Yourself attitude," a non-profit collective that "grew out of a project that used balloon-borne cameras to map the effect of the 2010 Deepwater Horizon oil leak on the Gulf Coast" (Scola 2013). The resulting images of the project allowed the local community to gain a better understanding of the extent of the oil spill through aerial pictures they took

---

2   Ben Berkowitz, founder of SeeClickFix, interview with authors, 2010.
3   Maker Fair Website, http://makerfaire.com/.

and therefore trusted. The local community who developed these images presented them to the government creating a way to verify governmental reports on the extent of the oils spill on the Gulf coast. The mapping project created an instant community—filling balloons with helium and sending in the sky affixed with cameras takes a team of people and so too does interpreting the results that are seen. According to their website, Public Labs creates "a community where you can learn how to investigate environmental concerns." They believe using inexpensive DIY techniques can "change how people see the world in environmental, social, and political terms." Public Labs believes that citizens should be involved with framing questions, interpreting results and drawing conclusions. The Balloon Mapping Project illustrates how a low-tech solution to measuring critical environmental issues that can also bring people together to change their community. Public Lab's literature emphasizes using citizen science for community-building (Dosemagen 2011, Dosemagen et al. 2012).

Participatory Sensing such as that advocated by Public Labs has been defined as "a citizen-powered approach to illuminating the patterns that shape our world" (Goldman et al. 2008). Those who advocate for Participatory Sensing or Citizens Sensing believe that the technique can provide new mechanisms of accountability, enabling independent monitors to explore—and in principle, challenge—the accuracy of government reporting (Goldman et al. 2008). For example, private individuals can take their own personal air quality measurements, and when they aggregated with data from others, groups can create alternative datasets and use them to understand environmental conditions where government records are flimsy, corrupt, or simply don't exist. Participatory sensing can also put new issues on the map, identify otherwise

Figure 17.3   Balloon mapping project in process
Source: http://store.publiclab.org/products/balloon-mapping-kit.

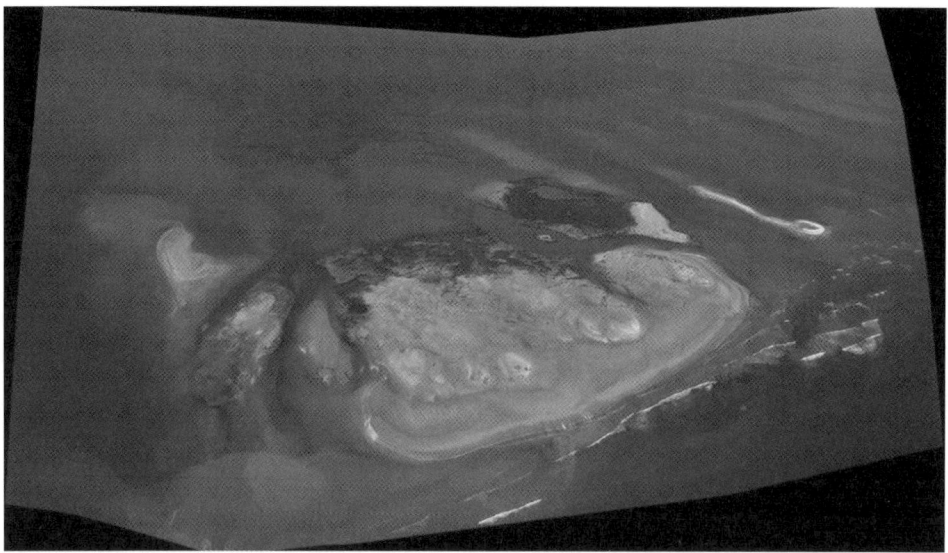

Figure 17.4   An image developed from Balloon mapping during the Oil Spill in the Gulf coast
Source: https://informationactivism.org/en/balloon-mapping-documenting-gulf-coast-oil-spill-and-student-protests-chile.

unmeasured or uncollected data, challenge the criteria by which existing data has been collected or the modes in which it's been visualized, correct misleading or inadequate information from other interested parties in a debate.

Citizen Sensing devices developed by the Spatial Information Design Lab and the Associated Press provided a check on government air quality data or lack of government data at the Beijing Olympics in 2008. In this project Columbia University's Spatial Information Design Lab created air quality sensors that were attached to the Associated Press reporters' cell phones and reported in real time at the events the current air quality conditions in Beijing. The results showed levels of particulate matter, the fine particles in the air that cause asthma and other respiratory problems were often significantly higher than world health standard in developing countries (Williams 2013). The data collected by the sensors provided the only air quality figures available during the Olympics. The government did release an "Air Quality Index"; however, the index was largely un-interpretable because little information was provided on how the numbers were developed. Someone reading the index would have to rely on the government interpretation of a "good" or "bad" air quality day and the numbers themselves could not be traced back to real air pollutants (Williams 2013). Beijing Air Tracks, as the project came to be known in the press, showed how DIY technologies, such as the sensors built for the Associated Press during the Olympics, can be used to provide data where the government is not cooperative in releasing the information. "The lessons learned from this experiment go beyond exposing air quality conditions in China as the devices developed showed that ubiquitous computing, such as mobile phones, can allow us to take control of information and use it to advocate for change" (Williams 2013).

Leveraging mobile phones to take control of data can work at multiple scales. They can measure discrete conditions throughout the city, such as was done in Beijing, or record information about city-wide infrastructure systems. Digital Matatus, a project that uses cell phones to map Nairobi's informal bus system is an example of how a small group can collect data for an essential infrastructure, give it out freely, and in the process encourage the government to develop channels to provide better access to information. Informal buses, called matatus, make up the Nairobi transit landscape. They range from 32-seat vehicles to small vans that can hold up to 9–14 passengers. Almost everyone in Nairobi uses matatus as they are the main form of transit, yet a map of the system had not been developed. The lack of data made it hard for residents to know how to navigate their city, but more importantly created limitations for urban planners involved in

Figure 17.5   Above shows a montage of photos taken of Associated Press reporters while they were measuring particulate matter and carbon monoxide during the Olympics in Beijing 2008
Source: Photos credited to Sarah Williams and Cressica Brazier.

modeling traffic flows. Matatus often clog the already overstrained roadways and lead to accidents, lose time for passengers, create poor air quality and an overall unpleasant urban experience for the majority. Knowledge of matatu routes is therefore essential for developing informed transport plans for the city.

Digital Matatus collected data on the routes and stops of the informal transit system by deploying University of Nairobi students to travel on matatus and use cell phones to collect GPS data traces of the routes. Once captured the students created an application to transfer the data into a standardize transit data format known as GTFS. The data was collected and stored in this way so it would be easy for private developers to make web or mobile applications that could be used wherever GTFS data was collected. The GTFS standardization would also make it easier to incorporate into Google Maps as Google uses this format for their map-based routing program. Since its beta release in the summer of 2013 several private sector companies in Nairobi have begun to develop matatu routing applications that can be used by anyone. Google and other map companies have expressed interest in acquiring the data to include in transit applications. KIPRRA, an NGO working on urban policy in Nairobi, is interested in housing and maintaining the data.

The project leverages the ubiquitous nature of cell phone use in the developing world to collect, map and provide user friendly *open access* to data on these dynamic systems. This project explicitly aims to empower citizens, app developers, operators and city planners in their quest for improved mobility—and hence urban living—for the majority. It was conceived out of a partnership between the Civic Data Design Lab at MIT, the Center for Sustainable Urban Development at Columbia University, the University of Nairobi, and Groupshop to think about how technology could be more equitable in developing countries. The project shows how

Figure 17.6   A University of Nairobi student collecting data on a matatu route
Source: Photo by Adam White.

citizens themselves can provide examples to the government how to collect data sets that they formally thought were impossible. More importantly it shows how those outside the government can create innovation that can change governmental processes. Since the launch of the project several cities in the developing world have expressed interest in using the application and methods developed as part of this project to map their informal transit systems.

Civic Hacking: Advocating to Create Technological Innovation

Projects like Digital Matatus are powerful examples of the Bottom-up Technology City because they happen outside the formal channels of government. The role of non-profit organizations has been essential for the kind of structural change. The popularization of the DIY movement has created organizations that are leaders for using technology for an open city. These include Code for America, Code for Good, Random Hack of Kindness, GeekswithoutBounds, Data Kind, New Urban Mechanics and DIYCITY, among many others. Code for America, one of the earliest non-profits advocating for technology change in government, best illustrates the mission of using Civic Hacking to transform the modern city. According to their website:

> Code for America helps city governments become more transparent, connected and efficient by connecting the talents of cutting-edge web developers with people who deliver city services and want to embrace the transformative power of the web to achieve more impact with less money. Inspired in part by Teach for America, CfA works with city officials and leading web development talent to identify and then develop web solutions that can then be shared and rolled out more broadly to cities across America.

Code for America is about developing civic technology where government politics or resources create barriers to innovation.

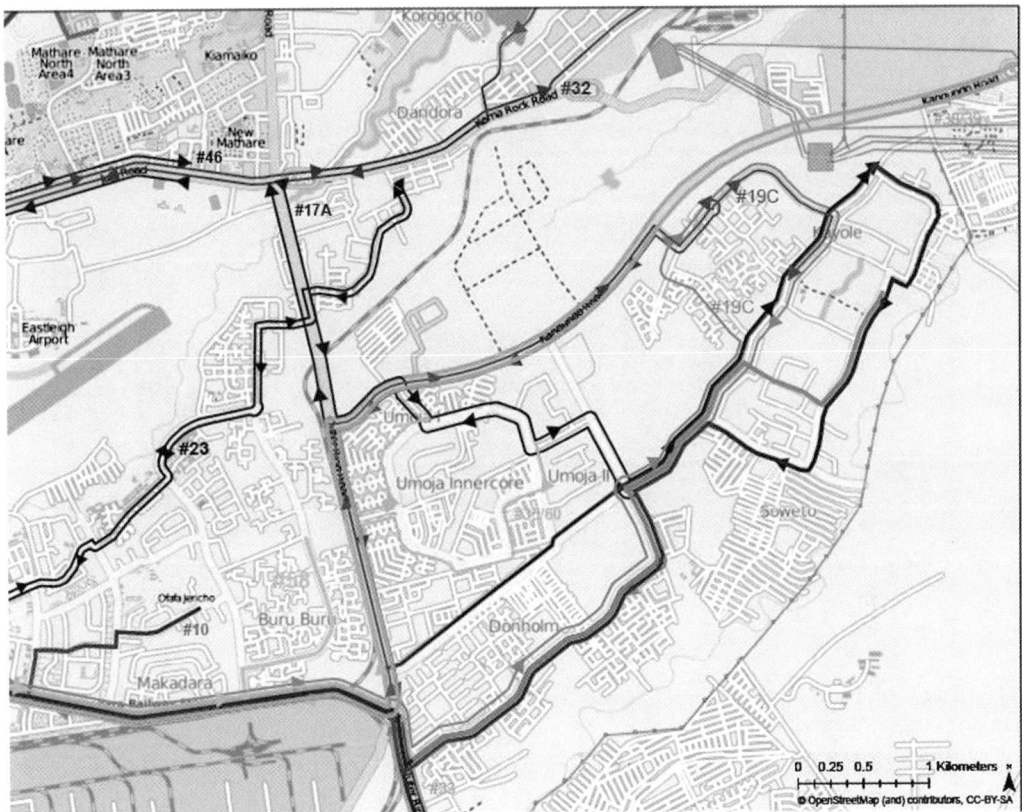

Figure 17.7   **Raw data of matatu routes generated for Nairobi, Kenya. At the time of this article in 2013 we were 70 percent complete**

Source: Sarah Williams, Civic Data Design Lab MIT.

Code for America was conceived in 2009 at the Gov. 2.0 Summit in Washington, DC where Jen Pahlka, Code for America's Founder, was talking with Andrew Greenhill, the City of Tucson's Chief of Staff who said, "You need to pay attention to the local level because cities are in major crisis. Revenues are down, costs are up—if we don't change how cities work, they're going to fail" (Kamenetz 2010). The conversation helped to shape the idea of leveraging people from the civically minded technology community and apply their skills to solve complex governance problems. The first fellow program was launched in 2011 and quickly showed the success of the program. Joel Mahonney, a Boston fellow, who was taking a break from a tech career as a chief technology officer, created a website for the city of Boston that helped parents navigate the exceedingly complex requirements for choosing a public school in the city of Boston. According to a *Washington Post* article:

> as soon as the office of Mayor Thomas M. Menino (D) explained the problem to Mahoney, he could get to work, talking to parents and building a prototype. The Boston city government saved tens, if not hundreds, of thousands of dollars in costs for private contractors or man-hours for their own software developers. Most important, the problem was quickly solved to the satisfaction of all parties. (Wadhwa 2011)

Another Boston fellow made an application, Adopt-a-Hydrant, that allowed Bostonians help out with the huge task of digging out the city's fire hydrants during snow storms. Both projects show how technology

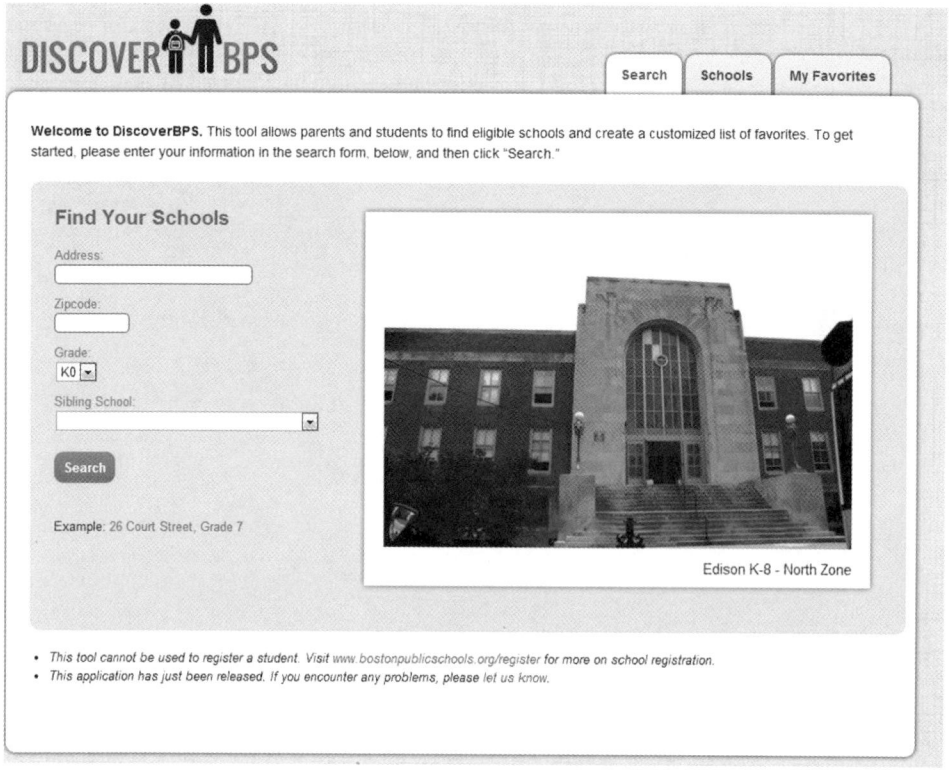

Figure 17.8   Discover BPS

can improve the public's interactions with the city and the city's ability to leverage its public. This increased awareness created through these civic-based technologies exemplifies the Civic Hacking movement.

The success of Code for America's program in Boston helped to start the Boston's Department of New Urban Mechanics, which is a department in the Mayor's Office which is meant to encourage and foster relationships between the private sector community and academics interested in making civic tools. Run by Chris Osgood and Nigel Jacobs the department has several successful innovations under its belt. One of the most talked about applications is "Street Bump" where users collectively crowd source the smoothness of the roads simply by having the application running on their phone (New Urban Mechanics Website 2013). The data is sent back to the city to help them identify areas critical for repair. The app itself is innovative as it takes advantage of the phone's accelerometer to find the bumps and links that with the phone's internal GPS to determine location. The success of the program has led New Urban Mechanics to create a partner city in Philadelphia and both cities have a long list of innovative technologies that they have helped to support. New Urban Mechanics shows how the DIY culture has been integrated in the formal governance structure by creating a space where the government can partner with anyone interested in developing technological change.

Today's technology city is unlike those of the past which were often characterized by top-down strategies for creating more efficient city infrastructure. While this type of Smart City still exists the Bottom-up Technology City shows how cities can empower citizens to create more efficient, adaptable and responsive communities. Inherent in the current manifestation of this responsive technology city is the idea of self-reliance and community-building through technological innovation, a motto of the DIY movement which has been guiding the methods for technological change. The prevalence of technology in our daily lives has created a community of people interested in leveraging the ubiquitous nature of mobile devices and web-based technology to change how we interact with the places we live. This is not only true for cities in the developing world, as cities in many developing countries are leap-frogging technology, and smart phones are often their main source of information. The ability to connect through these devices almost anywhere has created the potential for collecting and disseminating information about cities anywhere, anytime. City inhabitants can make their own city through the civic applications they download and advocate for and this city can be adaptive and responsive to their needs. More importantly cities are learning how to free their dependence on large corporations for the development of innovations in civic technology. Organizations like Code for American and New Urban Mechanics are giving these cities a space to quickly prototype ideas and develop new technologies for city infrastructure, with limited barrier to innovation. Most importantly the bottom-up city helps us to steer away from government control and surveillance and create a partnership for analyzing the prodigious amounts of information we now collect about almost everything. While the bottom-up city has been effective for creating new technologies in cities, the question we should ask is, "Can it persist?" as it is highly dependent the good will those citizens involved.

References

Dosemagen, S. 2011. Public Laboratory: Don't Just Report Science, Do It!, *Media Shift*, 2011–11–07.

Dosemegen, S., Warren, J. and Wylie, S. 2012. Grassroots mapping: Creating a participatory map-making process centered on discourse, *The Journal of Aesthetics & Protest*, Issue 8, Winter 2011/12.

Garcia-Navarro, L. 2013. Rio goes High-Tech, with an Eye toward Olympics, World Cup, *NPR*, 2013–05–03.

Goldman, J., Shilton, K., Burke, J., et al. 2008. Participatory sensing: A citizen-powered approach to illuminating the patterns that shape our world. Washington, DC: Woodrow Wilson International Center for Scholars, The Foresight and Governance Project.

Hollands, R.G. 2008. Will the real smart city please stand up? Intelligent, progressive or entrepreneurial?, *City* 12(3), 303–20.

Iveson, K. 2013. Cities within the city: Do-it-yourself urbanism and the right to the city. *International Journal of Urban and Regional Research*, 37(3), 941–56.

Jaffe, E. 2013. How are those cities of the future coming along?, *The Atlantic Cities*, 2013–09–11.

Kamenetz, A. 2010. How an Army of Techies Is Taking On City Hall. *Fast Company Magazine*, December 2010 – January 2011.

Mitchell, W.J. 1995. *City of Bits*. Cambridge, MA: MIT Press.

National Day of Civic Hacking website, http://hackforchange.org/.

New Urban Mechanics website, http://www.newurbanmechanics.org/.

Sennett, R. 2012. No one likes a city that's too smart, *Guardian*, 2012–12–04.

Singer, N. 2012. Mission control, built for cities: IBM takes "smarter cities concept to Rio de Janeiro," *New York Times*, 2012–03–03.

Scola, N. 2013. DIY science for civic good, *Next City*, 2013–04–16.

Wadhwa, V. 2011. Code for America: An elegant solutions for government IT problems, *Washington Post*, 2011–12–18.

Wakefield, J. 2013. Tomorrow's cities: Rio de Janeiro's bid to become a smart city, BBC, 2013–09–08.

Williams, S. 2013. Bejing air tracks: Tracking data for good, in Dietmar Offenhuber and Katja Schechtner (eds), *Accountability Technologies: Tools for Asking Hard Questions*. Vienna and New York: Springer.

Wolf, M. and McQuitty, S. 2011. Understanding the do-it-yourself consumer: DIY motivation and outcomes. *AMS Review*, 1(3–4), 154–70.

Chapter 18

The Environmental Paradox of the City, Landscape Urbanism and New Urbanism

Douglas Kelbaugh[1]

> The City Council, as you can well imagine, swallowed this line whole. Who wouldn't? Landscape is good; building is landscape; therefore building is good. One hears this three-car train of logic constantly in architectural discourse today ... Nothing sells like landscape. It's our sex.
>
> David Heymann, 2011

> If you love nature, live in the city.
>
> Edward Glaeser, 2011

As the first quote above suggests, the proponents of Landscape Urbanism have been winning design competitions and commissions, as well as gaining professional and academic acclaim. Closely associated with hallowed ecological values, it has been given a wide berth in the media and public process. However, it has received limited analysis and criticism in the professional and academic worlds. New Urbanism, on the other hand, is an older and more organized movement whose agenda has been repeatedly dissected and critiqued. A critical comparison of the two is illuminating and timely in an era of increasing ecological degradation and climate disruption, as well as of rapid urbanization. Before comparing the two, the *environmental* merits and demerits of urbanism in general will be discussed.

I. The Environmental Paradox of Urbanism

It's obvious that cities consume enormous amounts of resources and produce prodigious amounts of pollution and waste—far more per acre than suburban sprawl. Yet, cities are surprisingly greener in environmental ways than their more verdant suburbs. This paradox can be explained in a number of ways for different audiences:

For the *average citizen*: The average urbanite's carbon and other eco-footprints are smaller than the average suburbanite's. Leafy suburbs may *look* greener, but on a *per capita* basis they produce more pollution and waste than cities, and consume more energy, water and natural resources.

For the *economist*: Measuring carbon and other footprints on a per capita basis is the equitable way to measure environmental costs and level the playing field in a world of wildly uneven wealth. (For instance, a large LEED Gold house isn't very sustainable if only two people live there.) Cities are also more efficient in terms of land consumption, infrastructure, and the mechanical heating and cooling of buildings, as well as transportation. Placing people in the denominator of the metric is the key that unlocks this paradox, however narrowly or widely it is applied.

For the *climate scientist*, the environmental paradox is more complex: On top of producing a higher amount of Greenhouse gas (GHG) per acre, the city also tends to warm the *local* climate. Its extensive dark rooftops and pavements absorb solar radiation and release heat into the atmosphere. There are fewer trees than in suburbia to provide shade and evaporative cooling; there is more waste heat, i.e., hot gases spewing from tailpipes and chimneys that heat the air. This "anthropogenic heat" raises the temperature of the climate in the city higher than in its suburbs and countryside, producing the "Urban Heat Island Effect" (UHIE or UHI). GHGs produced in the city contribute to *global* Climate Change (CC) as opposed to *local* warming. However,

---

1   Unless otherwise specified, all figures in this chapter are the author's own.

the city's GHG production is smaller *per capita* than its suburbs, paradoxically making urbanization an environmentally beneficial trend.

For the *local government official:* Urbanism is a powerful and under-utilized strategy to mitigate global CC. And because mitigation strategies for global CC are complementary to UHI mitigation strategies, the more immediate impacts of local climate change can be used in already-hot cities to motivate people to simultaneously address both problems. Urban deforestation is a major contributor to local warming. For instance, metro Atlanta lost almost half its trees in the last quarter century; replanting these trees would cut its UHI in half, dropping average summer temperature about 3 degrees F and shaving up to 12 degrees F off the daily highs (Stone 2012).

Last, for the *urban planner* it would be no surprise that residents in a dense city have less impact on global climate change than automobile-dependent sprawl. What might surprise her is that a city of *the same*

Figure 18.1   **Cities like Dubai with a superhighway/superblock/supergrid can be "highrise sprawl," a compromise that provides neither the space and privacy of suburbia nor the walkable and transit benefits of urbanity. This relentless overlay of the Emirate-wide grid of superhighways encourages making every trip by car. It is indifferent to natural topography and ecology, while encouraging the continuous, undifferentiated sprawl and monoculture of Modernist development**

statistical density that does not have a wide mix of uses, a well-connected road grid, walkable streets, and good transit produces a per capita impact on CC much like suburbia.

In short, the ecological footprint and environmental impacts of cities are larger per acre but smaller per capita than suburban sprawl; and the footprint with a mixed use network of small blocks is even smaller than fragmented cities with cul-de-sacs, superblocks and limited access highways.

II. Three Relevant Benefits of Urbanization

The environmental paradox is central to this comparative study, as well as a very timely benefit to a rapidly urbanizing planet. The paradox is elucidated by scientific research at the Santa Fe Institute (West 2011). Its findings, which are based on big data, indicate that the *metabolism* of cities increases in a sub-linear manner—that is, their metabolic rate, due to the inherent efficiencies, grows at a slower rate than their increase in size and density. Similar to Kleiber's Law for animal metabolism, doubling the size of a city with a commensurate increase in density, has been shown to increase energy consumption by about 70%—not 100% as might be expected. Bigger cities are more efficient at using and conserving energy—like the elephant, which has a slower heartbeat and metabolism than the beaver, whose heart in turn beats slower than a hummingbird.

The increasing energy efficiency arises from higher rates of walking, biking and transit ridership, as well as fewer and shorter automobile trips. Larger buildings are typically more efficient per SF to mechanically heat and cool (although more difficult to *naturally* light and ventilate). To solarize, whiten or vegetate their roofs and walls has lower initial and operating costs less per occupant, as does urban infrastructure—from streets, bridges, tunnels, utilities and transit to sanitary and solid waste systems. The metabolic benefits are less in new or rapidly expanding cities, where the energy and material flows resulting from construction are much higher than in mature cities.

As aggressive interventions in the landscape, cities could be called ecological sacrifice zones. This may be inflammatory terminology, but even the greenest of cities inflict local environmental wounds that nature must heal; they leave scar tissue that must be compensated or justified with other trade-offs and benefits that outweigh the ecological costs. This compromise is illustrated in countless cities, vividly so in cities like Venice, Italy and Charleston, SC. These virtuoso examples of compact, traditional urbanism were built on landfill in sensitive environments—ones where development would be highly regulated if not prohibited today.

Any visitor to or resident of these cities can attest to the many ways that the merits of these and other cities compensate for their intrusion into local ecological systems. This is not to say that *new* cities should be built in sensitive areas. We should select development sites as mindful of ecological constraints as possible, while also recognizing that humans need and want to be in proximate contact with "nature." On the other hand, physical distance is no guarantee of protection; indeed humans can disrupt ecologies without living in or near them.

Cities are better understood in a broader meta-ecological way, and seen not as *metaphors* for ecological systems but as *actual* ecological systems. They can be as or more negentropic than forests and estuaries. And as seats of human ecology—from Muppets to Mozart to Metaphysics—their culture can be profound, even operatic in its complexity and intelligence.

Although not central to this study, the following two important benefits of cities are also relevant:

1. *Cities are on average more productive and creative per capita than suburban and rural communities.* Kleiber's Law is inverted—doubling the density increases creativity roughly 2.8 times, as measured in metrics like patents and publications per capita (West 2011). Per capita productivity and income also enjoy a better-than-linear rise. Jacobs (1961) has written about this phenomenon, as have Florida (2004) and Glaeser (2011).
2. *Cities sponsor a positive social paradox: they can maintain socio-cultural diversity within a large population while simultaneously providing a sense of identity for neighborhoods, social groups and individuals.* They can promote tolerance and absorb the social chafing and competition of everyday urban life without homogenizing the variety of a city or bleaching out difference. Their public realms bring people closer together—while keeping them apart—much like a dining or conference table

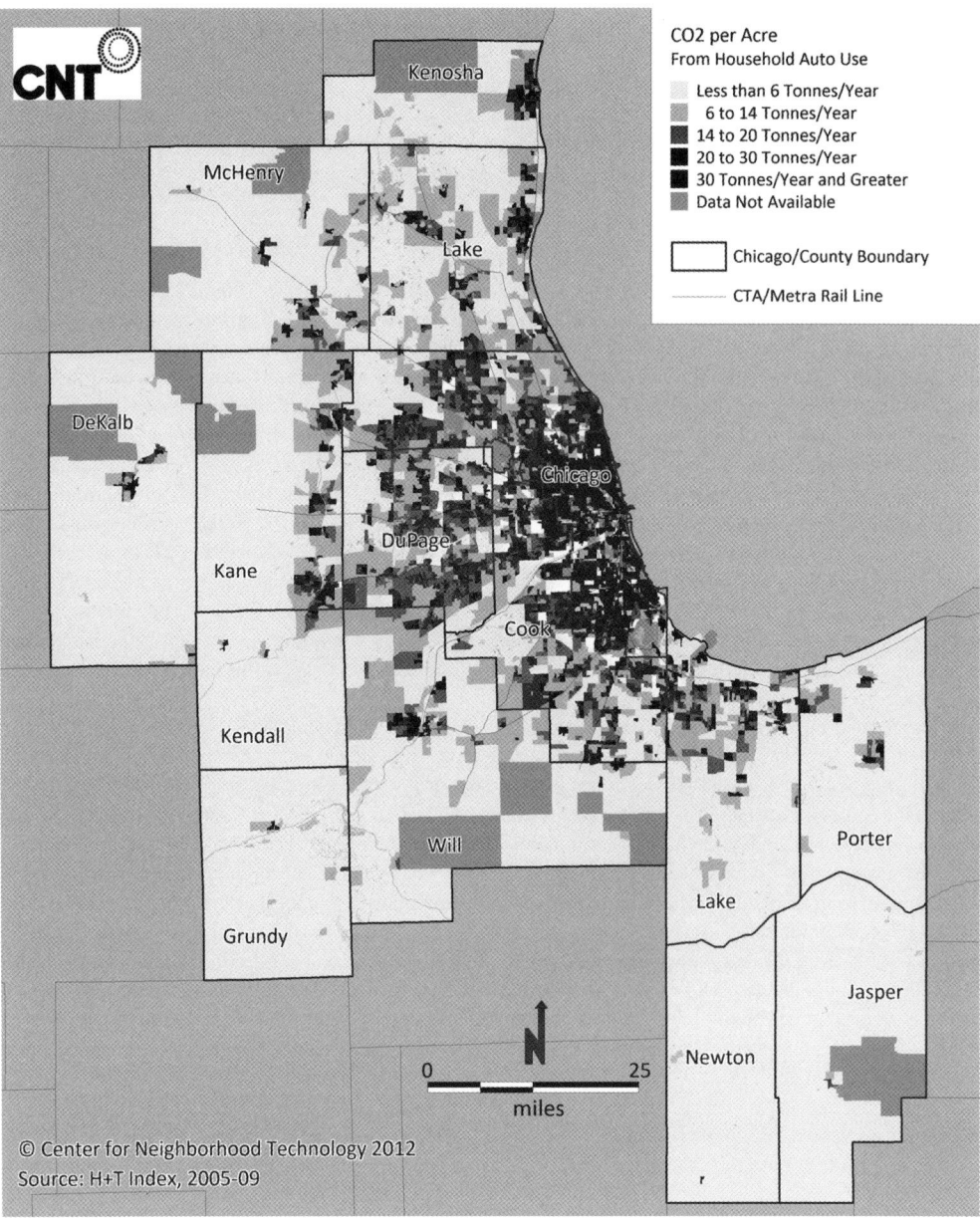

Figure 18.2 This map of metro Chicago's GHG production illustrates the environmental paradox of cities. While vehicular travel in the center city produces more emissions per acre, it produces less per capita or, in this case, per household. The paradox would be even greater if the per household heating and cooling of buildings were also included, not to mention water consumption as well as the GHG production from building and maintaining the buildings and infrastructure

Source: Center for Neighborhood Technology.

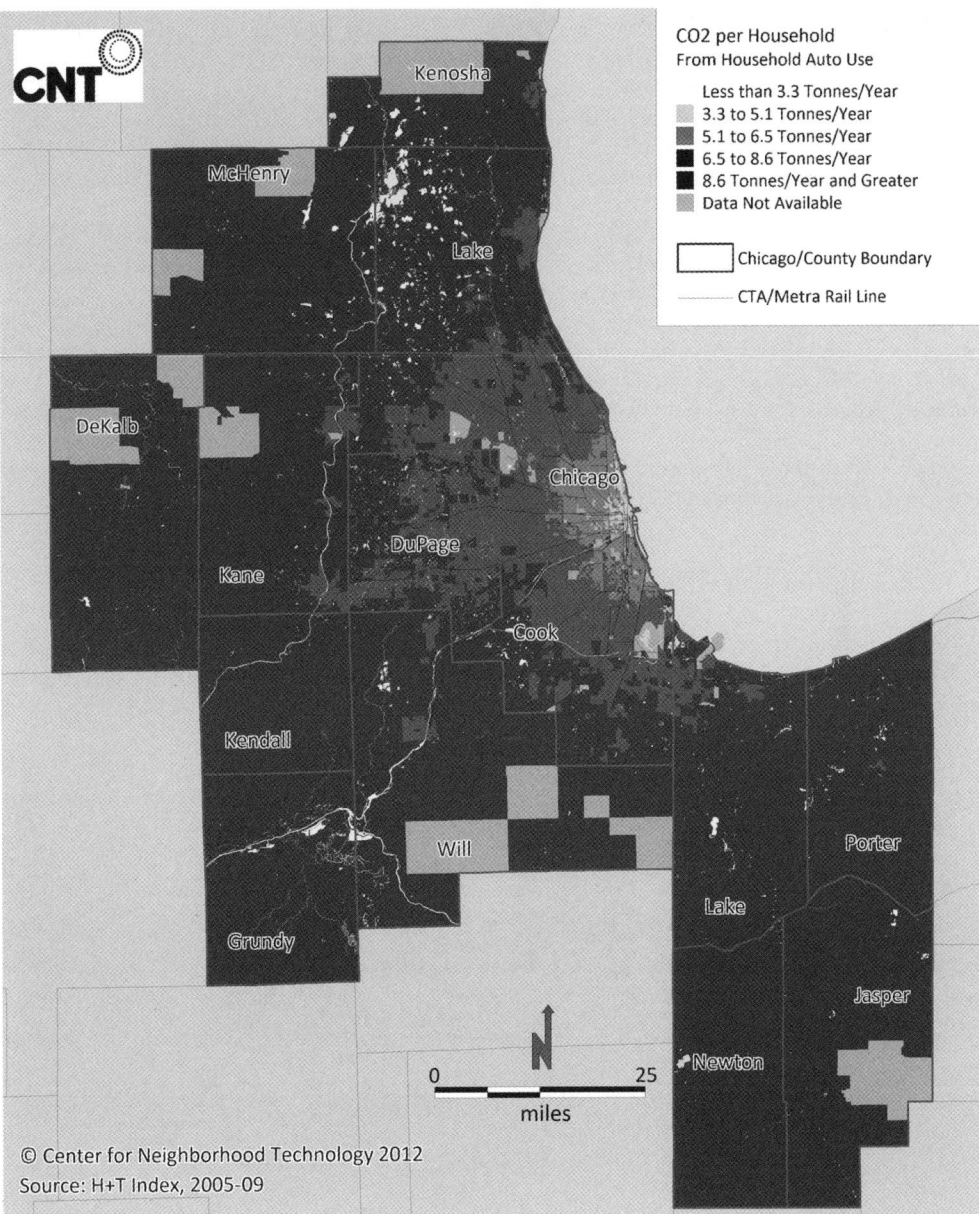

Figure 18.2 continued

simultaneously connects and separates people (Arendt 1958). Social and demographic inclusiveness is essential to sustainability; without it civilization will not endure.

Before discussing Landscape Urbanism (LU) and New Urbanism (NU), some of the environmental *downsides* of cities should be be mentioned. As suggested above, "cities are acts of violence" (Krier 2011). They are getting bigger and more environmentally disruptive, requiring more resources and land to support their appetites and absorb their voluminous wastes. Cities are typically not as resilient or self-reliant in times of environmental crisis as more self-sufficient rural communities. Urban living can disconnect our species from the wild nature that runs deep in our genes, and it can be stressful with more concentrated crime, disease, pollution, noise and social friction, as well as impersonal and alienating to newcomers.

Despite these and other downsides, cities have become the primary habitat of, by, and for the human species—soon to surpass 60% of the world's population and rising rapidly. Can growing cities contribute to the ongoing success and happiness of our species, without compromising thousands of other species and fouling the ecological systems that we share with them and mutually depend on? If, as climatologists claim, the ten thousand years of near-perfect climatic conditions for humans to flourish are now giving way to a less stable and less hospitable climate, how can cities help our species continue to thrive? LU and NU offer answers that both coincide and differ.

III. Landscape Urbanism and New Urbanism, their Similarities and Differences

These two primarily American movements of academicians and professionals have a number of values and aspirations in common. In the broadest sense both LU and NU are reactions to Modernism and the impacts

Figure 18.3   **Charleston as built (left), and as a hypothetical non-urban/anti-urban configuration that contemporary regulations might require it to be built today (right). Cities unavoidably entail environmental trade-offs and sacrifices, but the myriad benefits of good cities seem well worth the deficits**

Source: DPZ.

of its static, mechanistic view of the natural world. Each purports to be empirical and pragmatic, claiming to be evidence-based and outcome-based, which is why there is the potential for rational discourse between them. Each considers environmental sustainability and resilience to be a very consequential *design* issue, and cares fervently about *form*—believing design has a basic agency in life and an indispensable role to play in addressing society's problems. They feel that sustainability as an ongoing ethic and practice isn't sustainable if it doesn't result in aesthetically pleasing places, ones that are expressive of community sensibilities and tastes. A designed environment that is ugly and unpleasant isn't beloved, and if people don't *love* it, they aren't motivated to care for and sustain it.

To a varying degree, each rejects Post-Structuralism and the academy's endless critiques of society's flaws in favor of more "projective," proactive theory and performative practice. Both eschew the nihilism, subjective relativism and "critical project" of the late twentieth century, but in different ways—with LU deploying more *imaginative* solutions to problems and NU more *proven* solutions. LU has raised the ecological bar, or at least the conversation, on urban infrastructure, just as NU has on suburban retrofit, TOD, and more recently urban infill.

Each rejects the rational reductionism and the one-variable-at-a-time, one-size-fits-all, engineering syndrome common to Modernism. Both seem to repudiate the human-nature dichotomy—whether the Cartesian duality of mind and body, or the Emersonian distinction of "rural strength and religion" vs. "city facility and polish." Essentially, they both believe cities are as "natural" as beehives, anthills and coral reefs, albeit with more elaborate gizmos and props. Both would no doubt agree with Jane Jacobs that *people watching* in cities is as much about "nature" as bird-watching in the wilderness, or, for that matter, *birds* watching *people* in cities.

Both movements focus on public space and infrastructure, LU almost exclusively. LU seems to embrace the walkable neighborhood that is bedrock to NU, although LU's ideal neighborhood is typically more campus-like, with their pedestrian routes through the park rather than along the street. NU rejects the Modernist dendritic, tree-like network of streets, and unabashedly promotes the connected grid/network. However, LU leader Charles Waldheim champions Detroit's Lafayette Park, a superblock urban renewal project by Mies van der Rohe and Ludwig Hilberseimer. It's campus-like setting of townhouses and a few high-rises may be a lush green sanctuary in a distressed city, but its suburban-like density, freestanding towers and cul de sacs do not make for a scalable building block of urbanism.

Each movement embraces a more *regional* approach to urban planning, preferring to coherently address the entire metropolitan area and bioregion. Both claim to be *regionalist* in design. For instance LU believes in native plants and permaculture, just like NU aspires, if not always successfully, to traditional and passive solar architecture rooted in local climate and local building materials and practices. Despite celebrating regionalist design, NU also advocates underlying if not universal patterns and typologies in design, aiming to reject local design that is arbitrary or capricious.

Here the similarities between the two movements end and the differences begin. LU is professionally and academically more fashionable, if beginning to fade within its strongholds in several Ivy League design schools, which avoid NU as nostalgic, retrogressive, and dismissive of their avant-garde tendencies.[2] Waldheim (2012) claims to disassociate the movement from most of the rarefied, relativistic literary and art theory that dominated the architectural academy for a generation and that openly criticized normative practice. This high theory has given way in the last decade to "a shift toward collaborative, practice-based research," often focused on the environment and urbanism (Allen 2012). But LU seems to be still enthralled with forms that look Post-Structuralist. The fractal geometries, in particular the flowing, interweaving stream forms may be hydrologically-driven and ecologically-inspired, but this large scale landscapes seem to be as much about style. When formal audacity is obligatory in every project—as is usually the case with starchitecture—inventiveness has become more slavish than liberating.

LU has direct roots in Ian McHarg, downplayed as it has been since his view of nature has been shown to be too static. LU touts the fluidity and indeterminacy of natural systems more than their stability. Because its

---

2   Architecture programs at Notre Dame, University of Miami, Andrews University, and University of Maryland, have included NU to varying degrees in their pedagogy, and the Urban Design program at University of Michigan embraced its urban principles if not the neo-traditional architecture for the decade that the author was dean there.

focus is typically on hydrology, LU privileges linear, flowing form. It has embraced ecological theories and practices that emphasize more dynamic ecosystems with the rapid changes and oscillations that rattle longer periods of equilibrium (most significantly the increasing climate wobble that has not been seen for over ten thousand years). NU has also become very concerned about climate flux and disruption, but is much less fluid and continuous in its formal vocabulary, with its roots more in traditional urban syntax and architecture.

The original East Coast contingent of NU grew out of a European formalism and has consistently promoted traditional architecture, Traditional Neighborhood Development (TND) and the Transect. The original West Coast contingent (including the author) arose from the environmental/passive solar movement and regionalism, and has been less interested in traditional architecture. It has focused more on the regional scale and on Transit-Oriented Development (TOD), and has tended to be more accepting of high-rise buildings.

Although NU has refrained from inventive or flamboyant form, it has been urbanistically skillful, even bold. George Baird suggests that Peter Calthorpe's regionalism is arguably more radical and critical (in a positive sense) than the work of Peter Eisenman, the arch-champion of discomforting "critical design" that challenges convention and leaves issues like sustainability to others (Fishman 2005). Despite its too-frequent architectural mediocrity and pasty historicist tectonics, NU *is* in some senses more radical than cutting edge, avant-garde design, in which audacious urban form often cloaks the socio-economic status quo and even complicity with entrenched power and privilege. As Princeton's Stan Allen writes, LU stars—and their clients—are well "aware of the branding and marketing potential of the avant-garde mood that adheres to the work" (Allen 2012).

There is a basic difference in the way that the two movements think about urbanism and nature. Not surprisingly, landscape design comes first in LU and urban design comes first in NU. The latter doesn't believe in *maximizing* the amount of "nature" per se in the city, but in *balancing* it with human priorities. It opts for less open space, streams, forest or grasslands than LU, which has criticized NU for promoting a "parks desert." NU would rather concentrate development *within* the city than spread or dilute it with conventional suburbs. Neither is LU in favor of conventional sprawl, but it prioritizes open space and parkland deep in the city.

Since the Great Recession, NU has dramatically shifted its focus from large greenfield projects to smaller, greener and leaner urban infill (and to reform of policy and standards). Although it has come to fully embrace environmental sustainability later in its trajectory than LU, it believes the first obligation and role of towns and cities is to provide livable, resilient human habitat that is compact enough to reap the inherent benefits of urbanism and *leave intact as much of a region's wilderness and natural habitat for other animal and plant species.*

This host-guest distinction can be seen as an ironic return to the compartmentalization of Euclidean land-use zoning that NU has so roundly rejected—this time separating the built habitat of humans from the wild one of animals. The separation varies in intensity across the urban gradient of the Transect, as explained below. Nor is it exclusive: the more street trees, the better; there is room for urban food growing, and a place for domesticated animals and wild species, some of which thrive better than in the wild (e.g., the Peregrine Falcon and the Red-tailed Hawk, and the more ubiquitous squirrel, rat and pigeon). Habitat separation is like zoning land by *species* rather than by *function*—as an act of community building and of respect for other species. This interpretation may be stretching the zoning analogy, but compact human habitat intensifies the environmental paradox of cities: density not only shrinks per capita eco-footprints but also human intrusion into animal and plant habitat.

Perhaps *the* most salient design difference between these schools of thought is the attitude toward the *street*, which NU sees as the most important public infrastructure—the city's vascular system, commercial locus and social stage—"the river of life for the city" (Whyte, 1980). As one NUist says about this debate: "It is more than being about 'two movements'. It is about the primacy of the 'street' as opposed to the primacy of the 'park' as the primary setting for a civil society. The distinction is stark and nothing is more fundamental in urbanism." [3]

LU takes us back to the tower-in-the-park urbanism and CIAM's early death warrant on "the street" written several generations ago. It is the apex of a long list of differing design tendencies: dendritic street

---

3   Email from Paul Murrain, January 9, 2011.

Figure 18.4   James Corner's firm Field Operations designed these parks in Santa Monica, CA, and Seoul, South Korea. The smooth, curvilinear mounds of land (left) and the sculpted towers in a park/superblock (right) are more elegant than NU, but will they be as empty of pedestrians and denuded of trees as depicted? Despite rhetoric to the contrary, is LU still in the thrall of Post-Structuralist formalism? For formal clarity and contrast must it be embedded in the ordinary urban fabric that LU seems unable to deliver? LU is often accomplished, exquisite landscape architecture, but is it urban enough to be landscape urbanism?

Figure 18.5   Two well-known LU projects are the redevelopment and restoration of the Lower Don River in Toronto (left), and the highly popular High Line in New York City (right)—in two of North America's densest cities, despite LU's alleged focus on decentralized cities. In the Toronto, the high-rise towers are set amidst parks more than streets. In Manhattan, the elevated park cuts through the traditional, dense, street-based urbanism that LU dismisses in theory but needs in practice for counterpoint

hierarchy vs. highly connected networks; freestanding, object buildings vs. background, fabric buildings; high-rise vs. low-rise density; artistic license vs. norms and codes; artist vs. artisan; void-dominated vs. solid-dominated urban fabric; fragmented urban patterns vs. the Transect; surface vs. mass; and abstract vs. figural form and composition—all of which reveals that LU has not left Modernist urbanism or Post-Structuralist architecture as far behind as claimed.

On the other hand, NU should incorporate more contemporary geometries, such as fractal and parametric form, on top of the Euclidean/Platonic circle, square, and ellipse. Nor should it ignore technological breakthroughs such as digital fabrication; or the contemporary tectonics of glazed transparency that seamlessly connects interior and exterior space; or the apparent weightlessness of contemporary structures that visually defy gravity, an effect that can uplift the human spirit. Each movement should embrace the full range of local/low/vernacular design to high design, remembering that an urban fabric of many modest background buildings is needed to set off the few iconic ones. Indeed, what seems most promising going forward is street-oriented, walkable, mixed use, socially diverse fabric *that is realized with contemporary architecture* and *punctuated with a modicum of iconic buildings that are of contemporary, sometimes avant-garde design.* It's the best of what the design professions have to offer. Even new urban fabric realized in *traditional* architecture with contemporary/avant-garde foreground buildings—the original premise of Seaside—is a fuller, more culturally and tectonically authentic urbanism. But formal audacity shouldn't be obligatory in every major building—as is usually the case with starchitecture—or inventiveness and originality will be more slavish than liberating.

It is easy for the neo-traditional New Urbanists to blame their often mediocre, even banal architecture on middle class taste and the market economics that dominate speculative development (where, admittedly, one failed project can bankrupt a developer). However, they *could* fight for better design with the same fervor with which they've battled for mixed use, walkability and transit. A loyal minority of NUists has been pushing since the movement's birth over two decades ago for more contemporary architecture.[4] A standard response has been that NU is beyond style, but relatively few CNU Charter Awards have been given to contemporary buildings. A more convincing response has been that you can move public taste and the market only so far so fast, and that *urban reform* is more important and impactful than *architectural style*—a tactical argument to use familiar styles as a Trojan horse in which to hide less acceptable social and environmental programs. This argument is less and less compelling with the wider public acceptance of NU principles.

These aesthetic comparisons focus on more emotive, subjective and less discursive preferences that tend to run deeper and change slower than more rational positions and constructs. Formal sensibilities are no doubt at the crux of the friction between LU and NU; they often speak louder than words. The difficulty of verbally unpacking aesthetics notwithstanding: LU is more enthralled with surface and "thick," continuous horizontal form, especially folded, abstracted ground planes or interweaving, curvilinear landscapes and feathery wetlands. The geometries are neither finite nor finitely composed—they refrain from formal borders or frames and are more inspired by parametric forms and fractals than, say, the proportions of the human body. However voluptuous and biomorphic, the palette can be as formulaic as NU's formalistic master plans of grids, radials and terminated axes (another criticism that can be true). Nor do LU building designs define the outdoor rooms of plazas and streets, which people from all cultures seem to find spatially comfortable and pleasantly sociable. And like suburbs, there tends to be too much open space devoted to grass and not enough to trees, with the universal sense of refuge and prospect that tree canopies provide. This lack of enclosure brings into question Waldheim's assertion that LU has "the ability to produce urban effects traditionally achieved through the construction of buildings simply through the organization of horizontal surfaces" (2006). Will the vast, open green spaces actually attract the many pedestrians photo-shopped into the exquisite renderings, or will they become empty "border vacuums" (Jacobs 1961)?

---

4 A number of inhouse NU activists, most notably CNU founder Dan Solomon, current CNU Board Chair Ellen Dunham-Jones and the author, have long argued for both higher quality and more contemporary architectural design.

IV. Learning From and Moving Beyond the Differences

Built habitat needs to function in a way that is beneficial to its host species. Curvy *biomorphic* shapes and patterns may *appear* to be more natural than rectilinear ones, but they are not necessarily more bio*philic*, which is design that makes humans innately feel alive, comfortable, and secure. Biophilic environments need not be biomorphic in shape or literally full of greenery (e.g., the Alhambra in Granada, which primarily consists of rectilinear forms and patterns). They are sustainable because they *resonate* with humans. Both movements need biophilic more than biomorphic design to achieve lasting cultural relevance.

LU's focus has been more on *water* in the city, whereas NU has paid more attention to *fire*, i.e., the inherent energy conservation of cities. NU can learn more about hydrology, as well as ecological infrastructure, habitat, and horticulture, from LU, which in turn could profit from NU's detailed knowledge of the Transect, street networks, TOD, its higher Walkscores, form-based codes, and the public/private declension of urban space. NUist principles, carefully compiled in its Charter are based on millennia of city design, updated and methodically refined over 25 years of numerous congresses, councils, writings, listservs and built projects. It's inspired by enduring precedents like Nolli's Rome, which is held up as a quintessential setting for human ecology.

Like TOD, the *Transect* is basic to NU, with its gradient of density, use, and height that builds from wilderness to rural to suburban zones to three zones of urbanism, plus a special District zone for uses that don't fit in neighborhoods easily (warehouse districts, industry, airports, etc.). This six-zone gradient works across both the metropolis and the individual neighborhood, which typically consists of 2 or 3 T-zones. It includes a sliding repertoire of habitat for plant and animal species, as noted earlier. The urban end of the Transect promotes social diversity, in keeping with NU's increased focus on urban redevelopment. LU's large open spaces promote ecological diversity, but its less granular urbanism is not as likely to induce socio-economic mixing.

If sociocultural diversity increases with density while natural/ecological diversity decreases, a more sustainable urbanism would keep sociocultural diversity AND natural/ecological diversity as high as possible in all zones. Illustrated in the chart, this balance would take fuller advantage of both the environmental and the social paradox of cities.

In short, there's not enough urbanism in LU, and not enough ecology in NU. To be more specific, at the urban end of the Transect there's not enough human habitat, figural outdoor space, socio-economic diversity and street life in LU, and not enough natural diversity, vegetation and hydrology in NU. Because both social diversity and natural diversity are weak in suburban sprawl, both movements should minimize its spread and aggressively retrofit it with urban interventions.

Even with these changes, both movements are *transitional* steps to a world that needs to be far less carbon-based and consumptive than current versions of LU and NU, as well as much denser and leaner, more democratic and inclusive, more racially and ethnically equitable. Reducing carbon and consumption needs to be particularly dramatic in North America, where voracious consumption and rapacious lifestyles typically yield ecological footprints that exceed their planetary fair share by a factor greater than three, and where inequalities are expanding. LU and NU may both represent advances, but ultimately they are not transformative enough to mitigate and adapt to the ongoing, compounding impacts of CC, resource depletion, and world-wide cultural, economic and socio-political stresses. The deeper and more immediate the mitigation, adaptation and cultural transformation, the less costly and disruptive they will be.

V. The Global Challenge

The world can no longer afford the time or the resources to endlessly produce and insatiably consume novelty and needless change, for which industry needs ongoing avant-garde design. The need for variety and change, as well as for some fantasy and spectacle, may be in our DNA, but frenetic, unquenchable love of

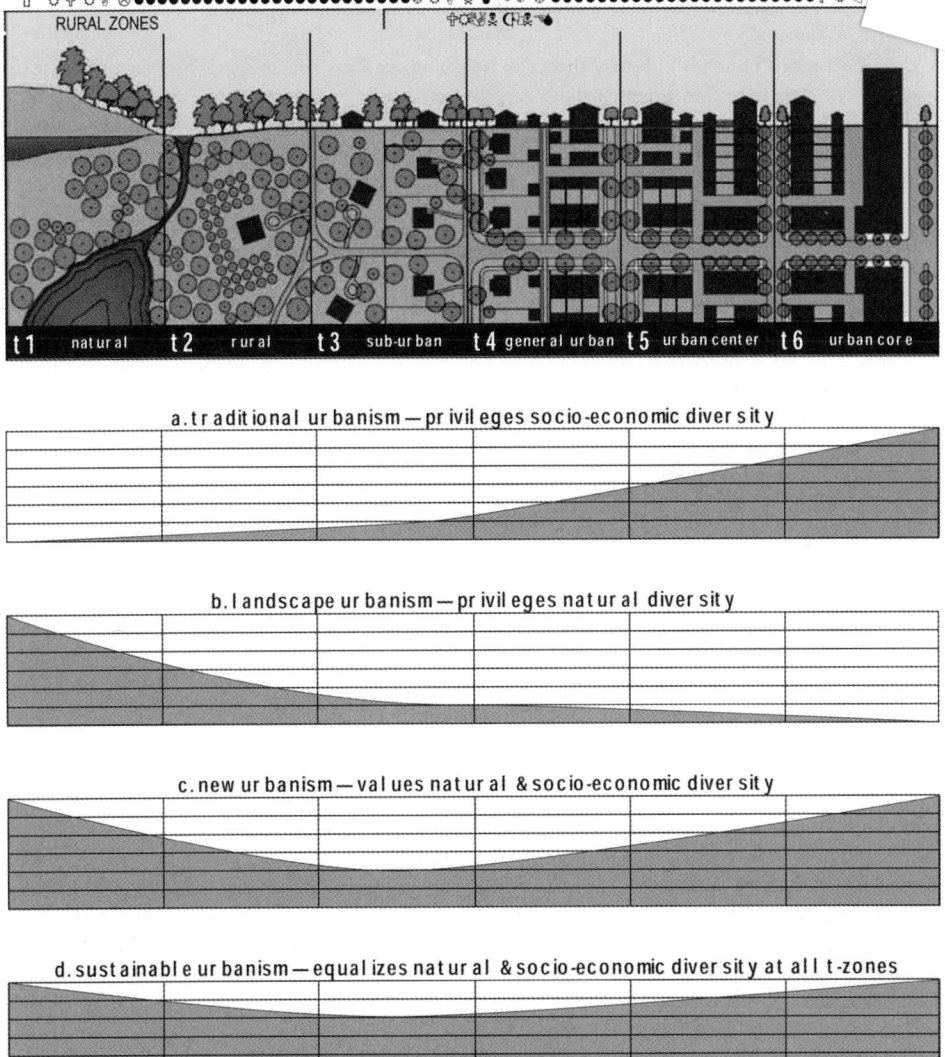

Figure 18.6   **The natural and socio-economic transects of the city. If NU learned more from LU about the ecology of the low-density Transect zones, and vice versa at the urban end of the Transect, it would produce a more ecologically and socially diverse city, as shown in chart D**

Source: DPZ.

the new—neophilia if not neomania—is unsustainable.[5] We don't have enough time or wealth to address all our problems one at a time; we need to deal synergistically and mindfully with multiple problems at the same

---

5   I admit to becoming addicted to following the world news and some shows on TV, often for its sheer entertainment value; indeed, electronic media have never been more titillating and habit-forming.

time. Designers are especially adept at elegantly integrated solutions, and can help show the way toward a more holistic urbanism.

We are hardwired by evolution to respond to more immediate problems and less abstract threats than CC, as well as driven by our desire for immediate pleasures and attachments. It is genetically easier to focus on short term gratification and on closer, more tangible crises, such as poverty, corruption, terrorism, extreme weather events, unemployment, pollution or diminishing resources.[6] It's socially and psychologically challenging to deal with the slow tragedy of the global environmental commons—the biosphere's atmospheric blanket that now traps too much of the sun's otherwise beneficent energy. Market economies and electoral politics have trouble rallying to long-term problems. This is where UHI can help motivate behavior change. As a city's hot season becomes more uncomfortable and unhealthy, there are ways to mitigate and adapt to local climate change more quickly than global CC. Residents can focus on a 5 to 10 year local challenge with more direct, measurable feedback, rather than dither on a 50 to 100 year global challenge that offers vague, indirect feedback. Because the local adaptation and global mitigation strategies are almost always complementary, these cities can focus on UHI, while tackling global CC at the same time. Although urbanites in cool climates may *welcome* warmer weather; so residents of Stockholm and Seattle will need to find other ways and reasons to motivate themselves to deal with CC and do their share of stewarding the global commons. In all cases, a sense of planetary citizenship, fair play and altruism are needed to help those unlucky areas of the planet most devastated by CC, especially in the poor countries that have contributed least to the problem.

The built environment is *the largest* single contributor to both local and global climate change. Billions of lights—powered by primeval hydrocarbons taken from the Earth's crust—keep the planet glowing in the night sky. This gossamer veil of urban lights visible from outer space is perhaps the grandest testimony to what glorious marvels and desperate challenges humans have wrought.

New green technologies and helpful scientific breakthroughs are sure to emerge, thanks to the intelligence and resourcefulness of our ingenious, adaptive species. They will bring benefits that hopefully will exceed their unintended but unavoidable negative consequences. Our planet, which has been through far bigger changes. And its hardiest, most adaptive species will survive if not thrive. The big question is whether the most advanced and powerful of its species will survive CC and live fulfilling lives in numbers anything like today's seven+ billion human inhabitants.

Paul Hawken lost count when the tally approached a million organizations devoted to the environment and social justice—from tree planters to micro-loan programs to 350.org to the United Farm Workers. He describes their loose agglomeration as the *largest social movement ever.* (Hawken 2007) The sooner LU, NU, and the multitude of other movements get their acts together—both within and between themselves—the better they can act together. It will take every bit of collaboration we can muster to sustain humankind and human civilization.

References

Allen, S. 2012. *Architecture School.* Cambridge, MA: MIT Press (with ACSA Press).

Arendt, H. 1958. *The Human Condition.* Chicago: University of Chicago Press.

Fishman, R. 2005. *New Urbanism & ReUrbanism.* Ann Arbor, MI: Taubman College of Architecture and Urban Planning, University of Michigan.

Florida, R. 2004. *Cities and the Creative Class.* New York: Routledge.

Glaeser, E. 2011. *Triumph of the City.* New York: Penguin Press.

Hawken, P. 2007. *Blessed Unrest.* New York: Penguin Press.

---

6   It is also more politically effective. For instance, the ozone hole and selected species decline and loss have been sufficiently mitigated or reversed in less than a lifetime through government intervention and behavior change. Problems as big as global poverty, many diseases, and the universal provision of clean water could be solved in a lifetime with sufficient political will. (A popular example is universal clean water might cost less than the money spent globally on bottled water every year.)

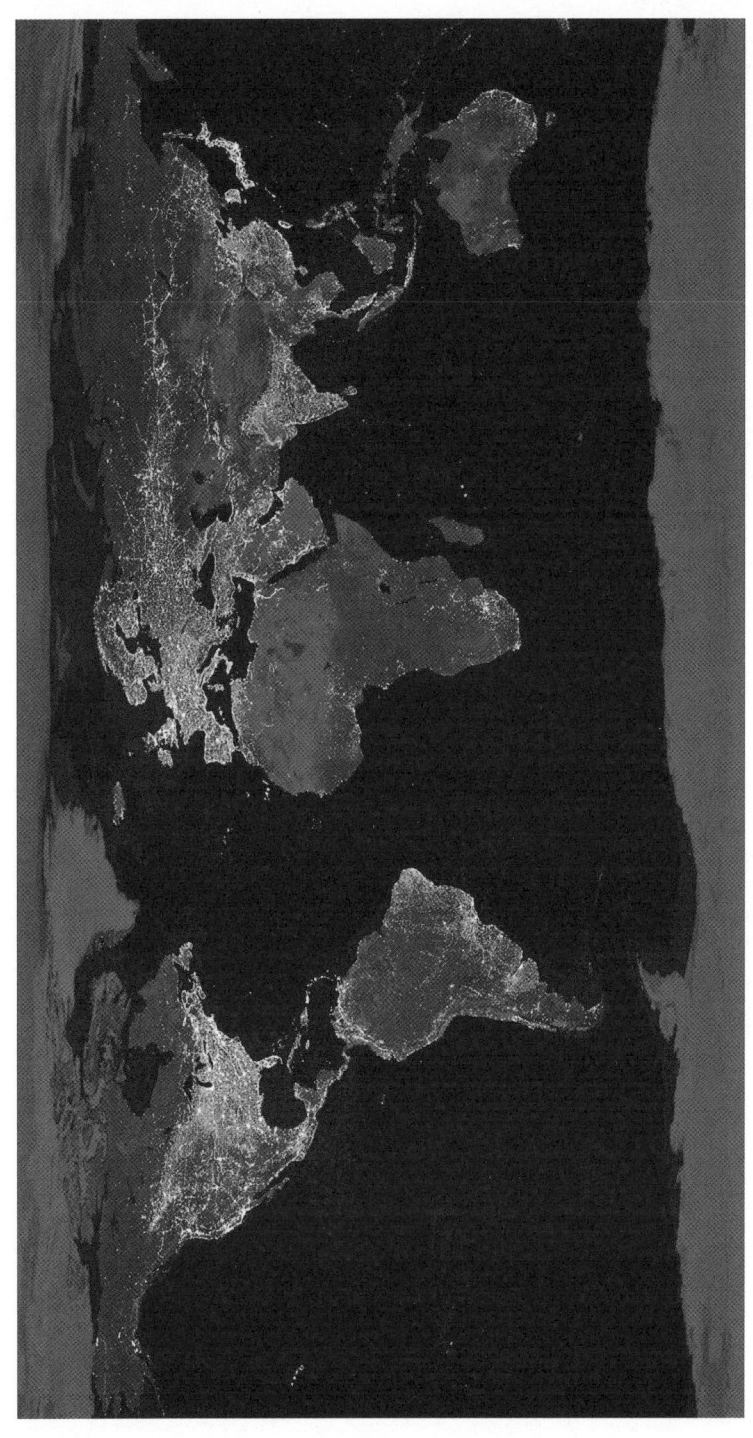

Figure 18.7   The diaphanous twinkling of our earth aglow at night —the picture of a planet intentionally on fire—closely maps cities that consume immense resources but paradoxically reduce per capita GHG production for half of its human inhabitants

Heymann, D. 2011. Landscape is Our Sex. *Places.* Available at: places.designobserver.com/feature/landscape-is-our-sex/31228/ [accessed 9 October 2013].

Jacobs, J. 1961. *The Death and Life of Great American Cities.* New York: Random House.

Krier, L. 2011. *Seaside at 30.* South Bend, IN: University of Notre Dame.

Stone, B. 2012. *Cities and the Coming Climate.* Cambridge: Cambridge University Press.

Waldheim, C. 2006. *The Landscape Urbanism Reader*. New York: Princeton Architectural Press.

West, G. 2011. The Suprising Math of Cities and Corporations. Available at: www.ted.com/talks/geoffrey_west_the_surprising_math_of_cities_and_corporations.html.

Whyte, W. 1980. *The Social Life of Small Urban Spaces*. Washington, DC: The Conservation Foundation.

Index